DISASTER MANAGEMENT IN THE HILLS

About the Author

Dr. Satendra is an Indian Forest Service officer of 1986 batch. He holds a doctorate in Himalayan Geo-tectonics from Delhi University. A gold medalist of the University, he completed Masters Degree in Geology and holds Post Graduate Diploma in Forestry (equivalent to M.Sc. Forestry) from Indira Gandhi National Forest Academy, Dehradun. He passed Master of Business Administration (MBA) from University of Hull, U.K. and as part fulfilment of the degree he did his project work on Disaster Management in Garhwal region of Uttranchal. He also holds a Post Graduate Diploma in Ecology and Environment.

Having knowledge of seven languages, Dr. Satendra is basically a Himalayan Geologist by background and a Forester by profession with analytical capacity to understand ecology, environment, natural resource management and forestry. Experience of working as in-charge of "Forest Fire Division", Ministry of Environment and Forest, Government of India helped him in better understanding of the forest fire problem in the country, specially in the Himalayan states.

The stint with Ministry of Rural Development, Government of India further strengthened his skills to use the gained knowledge and experience for sustainable and eco-friendly rural development and poverty alleviation. Being an active member of Central Teams to disaster affected areas in Himalayas and Gujarat and his association with National Centre for Disaster Management, IIPA, New Delhi enabled him to understand the problem of Disaster management in the country and suggest a more appropriate and innovative approach of linking rural development with disaster mitigation.

Dr. Satendra has published many research papers and articles and written three books. One of his books published by National Book Trust of India has been awarded by Department of Science and Technology, Government of India.

Currently Dr. Satendra is on deputation to Ministry of Rural Development, Government of India and also carrying out post-doctoral research in the field of Disaster Management at National Centre for Disaster Management, Indian Institute of Public Administration, New Delhi.

DISASTER MANAGEMENT IN THE HILLS

Dr. SATENDRA (I.F.S.)

CONCEPT PUBLISHING COMPANY, NEW DELHI-110059

The views and opinions expressed in this book are those of the authors and do not necessarily reflect the views of the organizations to which they belong.

ISBN-81-8069-014-8

First Published 2003

Published and Printed by
Ashok Kumar Mittal
Concept Publishing Company
A/15-16, Commercial Block, Mohan Garden,
NEW DELHI-110059 (India)

Phones : 5351460, 5351794
Fax : 0091-11-5357103
E-mail : publishing@conceptpub.com

DEDICATED
TO
LATE SHRI SANJAY KUMAR, I.F.S.
(D.F.O. SAHABAD)
WHO SACRIFICED HIS LIFE
FOR
THE FOREST PROTECTION.

"Oh, Mother Earth!
Your hills, snow clad mountains, forests,
In all shapes and formations,
Bring happiness to us.
I bow to you
With all my might, I shall save
Your cultivable, fertile and nourishing
black and red
Soils which are strong and resistant,
And protected by our ancestors,
From getting weak by destruction and
degradation !!"

— Atharva Veda

अजित सिंह
AJIT SINGH

कृषि मंत्री
भारत सरकार
कृषि भवन, नई दिल्ली–110001
MINISTER FOR AGRICULTURE
GOVERNMENT OF INDIA

FOREWORD

Indian subcontinent with its typical geographical position; climate and geological settings is prone to natural disasters like cyclone along the coastal lines of the country, seismic movements in the plateau region and hilly region etc. on the one hand and droughts and floods in the plains on the other hand. In nutshell, we can say that this subcontinent is among he world's most disaster prone area.

Though each and every part of the country is prone to the natural disaster but Uttranchal, due to its geological position, is more susceptible to seismic movements. The human interference in the name of development has made this area more precarious due to ecological imbalances. In the past hundred years, four earthquakes with intensity of 8 or more have hit this area. The landslides due to deforestation have further intensified the problems in hilly regions resulting in extensive loss of life and property besides various infrastructures roads, bridges and means of communication.

Though India has been marred by unfortunate disasters and natural calamities but still the disaster management of the country has not been fully evolved to cater to the people in distress. Various reasons can be assigned to it. Poor rehabilitation efforts, delay in relief and rescue, unscientific assessment survey, ignorance of local needs, poor monitoring and evaluation, lack of coordination among the departments, poor training and technology of rescue workers add to the miseries of affected people.

The Natural disasters have multi-dimensional impacts, personal, socio-cultural and economic. Though disasters are inevitable, their adverse impacts can be reduced by better management practices. It involves forecasting, operating of warning systems, maintenance of communication, mobilization of finance, transportation, availability of essential commodities, relief, rehabilitation and restoration work.

The present book is a good attempt to critically analyse the situation prevailing in the State. To know the factual position, the author has carried out an extensive survey in some disaster affected parts of the State and views of various stakeholders have been collected to arrive at an appropriate and more effective solution to the problem. The author has also critically examined the present strategies and approaches for disaster mitigation and has suggested a model for disaster management by adopting innovative ways of linking disasters with development plans and policies.

I hope the book will help in understanding the problem of the disaster management in Uttranchal and encourage various sections of the society to think over the issue with a different perspective. The book will be of immense use for policy makers and planners in carving out specific need based plans for the region, taking into consideration the various aspects elaborated by the author. This will certainly help in reducing the adverse impact of disaster and mitigating the woes of the people of the State.

Ajit Singh

अनिल सिन्हा भाप्रसे
Anil Sinha IAS
Head, National Centre for Disaster Management and
Member Secretary, High Powered Committee on
Disaster Management

Tel. : 91-11-3702445
Fax : 91-11-3702446, 3702442
E-Mail : anilsinha@nic.in
National Centre for Disaster Management
Indian Institute of Public Administration
Indraprastha Estate, Ring Road,
New Delhi-110 002 (India)

August 9, 2002

MESSAGE

The Great Himalayas have been the center of attraction for pilgrims, saints, poets and artists since time immemorial. Explorers, mountaineers, scientists and philosophers have extensively traversed different pockets of the gigantic Himalayan ranges. Dwarfing all other mountains of the world in sheer height, this mighty mountain is the youngest mountain system, which is still undergoing tectonic movement due to prevailing geological conditions. The very structural constitution coupled with other extraneous factors exposed this mountain to natural hazards. The ruthless exploitation of natural resources through human induced activities such as deforestation, mining, dam, building and road construction; unscientific agricultural practices; grazing and ever increasing need and greed due to demographic pressure have adversely affected the natural environment of the fragile Himalayan eco-system. The environmental degradation along with increasing human vulnerability has also exponentially increased the intensity and magnitude of natural disasters and thus has been the major factor for transforming natural hazard or a climatic extreme into a disaster in fragile domain like Himalayas.

The present book "Disaster Management in the Hills" after describing the hill regions of the country in general and Uttranchal in specific has discussed their vulnerability to natural disasters. Reference is drawn to the detailed analytical description of the deteriorating environmental conditions in these regions and its adverse impact on the frequency and intensity of natural disasters. This book is an outcome of an intensive research work carried out to understand and analyse the prevailing conditions, which affect disaster management in these areas. The book emphasizes the need for linking development with disaster management as an alternative, suggesting practical solutions for effective disaster management in hills. The approach of developmental programmes in hilly regions must be on a positive note and with emphasis on building a strong socio-economic and physical infrastructure, which is resilient to the adverse impact of natural hazards.

More than 90 per cent of Uttranchal is rural based, hence the suggestions is to link rural development schemes/programmes for achieving the dual objectives of Disaster Mitigation and Poverty Alleviation. This in turn, will reduce the vulnerability of the region to natural hazards. By adjusting or suitably modifying these programmes, Disaster Management can be carried at a minimal cost for appropriate results leading to sustainable development. Modelling as an innovating technique has been suggested for evolving effective Disaster Management Plans at state, district and Gram Panchayat levels, which would be comprehensive to include effective implementation and monitoring.

I am confident that the book will prove to be an asset for planners, practitioners of development and researchers, working in hilly regions of the country.

Anil Sinha

PREFACE

Man has been striving hard since the time immemorial for his survival. He has been constantly struggling with nature for his mere existence and fighting against the odds and vagaries of nature. The ancient historical evidences are indicative of traditions and cultures adopted by man to survive through variable climatic, ecological and hydrological situations in resonance to the natural system. Fortunately or unfortunately, the present scientific wisdom and advancement in the technology has opened up many avenues and possibilities to explore and exploit Nature to man's advantage even at the cost of its protection and preservation. The ruthless exploitation of nature in the recent past has increased the incidences of natural calamities resulting in real catastrophes. The international community has realised the dual linkage between environmental degradation, disaster and development. The decade 1990-2000 was declared as "International Decade of Natural Disaster Reduction." The strategy has shifted towards preventing natural calamities and the world has now realised and recognised that *"Prevention Pays"*.

Though each and every part of Indian subcontinent is more or less susceptible to natural disasters, the hill regions due to their topographic, geological and climatic conditions experience natural calamities very frequently. Uttranchal State, carved out of Uttar Pradesh on November 9, 2000 has suffered a lot due to its physiographic, climatic and geological features which lead to various natural disasters. The unplanned and unscientific development process, ignoring environmental aspects has further accelerated the intensity, frequency and magnitude of these natural catastrophes.

The present book has made a conscious attempt to delineate the various disasters to which the hill regions of the country, specially the State of Uttranchal are prone, namely, landslides and soil erosion, earthquakes, forest fires, floods and avalanches.

The book is an outcome of an exhaustive study undertaken in Uttranchal for assessing the impact of /most recent disasters. Taking clue from the strategies adopted for disaster mitigation, a new management policy and approach has been evolved. The suggested emphasis is on preventing disasters by dovetailing the various developmental schemes already being implemented under various programmes. A comprehensive and sustainable rural development strategy and approach can reduce the frequency, intensity and adverse impacts of natural disasters. The role and responsibilities of various organisations have been elaborated which can be instrumental in reducing the impact of these disasters. Modelling as an approach has also been suggested to formulate appropriate disaster management plans and their proper implementation to get maximum output in the field.

It is visualised that the book will be of immense use in understanding the natural disasters, their impact and management in hill regions of the country. The book will also be of help to researchers, policy makers/planners and last but not the least to the general public of the area in many ways.

15th August 2002 SATENDRA
New Delhi

ACKNOWLEDGEMENTS

The present work is an outcome of extensive study followed by intensive meetings, discussions, interviews and consultations held with various stakeholders like the people affected by disasters particularly in Uttranchal, the administrators, professionals and experts (including academicians), institutions, Central and State Government officials dealing in the field, panchayat representatives, NGOs etc. The list is very long and it is not only difficult but almost impossible to thank each and every individual who spared their valuable time and suggestions for completing the work.

First of all I would like to thank Shri Arun Bhatnagar, Secretary, Shri Satish Chandra, Joint Secretary and Shri A.K. Singh, Director, Ministry of Rural Development, Government of India, who sanctioned my study leave and provided me the opportunity to know more about the subject of disaster management.

My sincere gratitude are due to Prof. V.K. Sharma, (my supervisor) and Shri Anil Sinha, Head NCDM for their personal interest and guidance from time to time. I am extremely thankful to Dr. P.L. Sanjeeva Reddy, Director, IIPA and Shri M.C. Gupta, former Director of IIPA for their valuable suggestions and discussions on various aspects of disaster management and allied issues.

I also feel immense pleasure in offering my sincere thanks to Prof. Brian Levitt, Prof. Bruce Partridge and Prof. Ian Mill of Hull University, U.K. for their sincere suggestions and guidance during my MBA course at the University. Thanks are due to Prof. P.S. Saklani, former Vice Chancellor, H.N.B. University, Sri Nagar for his guidance for my Ph.D. work at the University of Delhi, which helped me a lot in completing the book.

I extend my sincere thanks to my friends and other senior officers of various ministeries and departments for their sincere help and cooperation. Thanks are due to Dr. V.K. Bahuguna, Dr.

Kamal Taori, Shri R.B.S. Rawat, Dr. Prabhat Kumar, Dr. N. Satish Chandra, Shri D.K. Srivastava, Shri B.A. Khan, Shri Bharat Lal, Shri D.D. Goel, Shri V.P. Pasrija, Dr. S.K. Singh, Dr. S.P. Sati, Shri A.K. Kashyap, Shri Babu Lal, Shri S.P. Singh, Shri O.P. Rathi, Shri Ranvir Singh, Shri Rajesh Patel, Shri V.S. Lal, Shri K.N. Kandwal, Dr. P.K. Das, Smt. Ranjana Sarmah and Shri A.K. Das for their assistance and support.

I am highly indebted to my collegue and friends in NCDM, IIPA mainly Shri Aamir Ali Khan, Dr. D.N. Kaushik, Shri Rahul Kaushik, Shri Sandeep Patil, Shri Chander Shekhar, Shri C.S. Raut, Smt. Krishna, Shri Pyarey Lal, Shri Ahmed Kamal, Shri Amar, Shri Manoj Kumar, Smt. Santosh, Shri Ansar Ali, Shri Rajendra Kumar and others for providing necessary assistance.

The cooperation and encouragement of my family members, my parents, elder brother, wife Mrs. Pratibha and children – Tanushri and Kanishk are equally important and need due acknowledgement.

Last but not the least, I am thankful to Shri Ashok Kumar Mittal of Concept Publishing Company for their excellent efforts in publishing the book.

SATENDRA

CONTENTS

INTRODUCTION

Natural hazards are not new to the world. Since its origin on the Earth, man has been struggling hard against these odds of nature. In fact natural hazards, like other natural resources are mere natural phenomena that have the potential to cause damage to human beings. Ancient historical evidences are indicative of traditions and cultures adopted by man to survive through variable climatic, ecological and hydrological situations in resonance to the natural system. Fortunately or Unfortunately the present scientific wisdom and advancement in technology has opened up many avenues and possibilities to explore and exploit the nature to man's advantage even at the cost of its protection and preservation. Ruthless exploitation of nature in the recent past has increased the incidences of natural calamities resulting to real catastrophes. It is the human interventions and its endeavours towards development that these natural hazards turn into disasters, causing enormous devastation to life and property. The impact of these disasters on human life is multifarious, affecting it in all aspects – domestic, social, economic and the like.

Due to its geological setting, geographical position and other natural reasons, newly evolved Uttranchal State has been experiencing natural disasters year after year. Adding fuel to the fire are the various men induced activities, viz. unscientific developments, extensive deforestation, prevailing agricultural practices, increasing population pressure and so on. A combination of all these factors along with natural causes have created a disbalance in the overall ecology of the area, which directly or indirectly contributes to make the area vulnerable to various disasters.

Uttranchal is a unique region exposed to earthquakes, landslides, forest fires, floods, avalanches and soil erosion. The impacts of these disasters on the socio-economic conditions of the people of the State are quite diversified. Besides hindering the developmental efforts, these disasters are adding many more woes to the people of the State. Despite intensive efforts at both government and non-government level, these calamities continue to claim huge loss to life and property in the State.

It is a fact that losses from these catastrophes cannot be fully prevented, but by applying the appropriate disaster management practices their impacts can be minimized up to a large extent. The present book is an attempt to critically analyze the situation prevailing in the State. To know the factual position the author has carried out an extensive survey in some disaster affected parts of the State and views of various stakeholders have been collected to arrive at an appropriate and more effective solution to the problem. The author has also critically examined the present strategies and approaches for Disaster Mitigation and has suggested a Model for Disaster Management by adopting innovative ways of linking disasters with development plans and policies.

1

DISASTERS
An Overview

The term 'Disaster' owes its origin to the French word *Desastre*, which is a combination of two words 'des' meaning bad and 'astre' meaning star. Thus, the term 'disaster' refers to 'Bad or Evil Star'. In earlier days disasters were considered to be an outcome or outburst of some unfavourable star.

Ideally, a disaster may be defined as "an event concentrated in time and space which threatens a society or a relatively self-sufficient subdivision of a society with major unwanted consequences as a result of the collapse of precautions which had hitherto been culturally accepted as adequate" (Turner, 1976).

Disasters are extreme events which cause great loss to life and property. They pose a serious threat to the normal life as well as the process of development and strike with sudden violence, tearing bodies, destroying lives and structures and throwing apart families. Natural disasters, which are both sudden and powerful, damage national economy and cause hardships to a large section of the population. They are the single largest concern for most of the nations as they take a heavy toll of human life, destroy belongings and infrastructures and have far-reaching economic and social consequences for communities. Thus, the impact of disasters on human life is multi-dimensional, affecting it in all aspects – domestic, social, economic etc.

DISASTERS IN INDIA

Among the top ten countries in terms of average annual loss of life due to natural disasters, all except Australia are developing countries. India, amongst those nations is the most vulnerable to natural hazards. Due to its geographical position, climate and geological setting, India has been experiencing natural disasters every year. In India natural disasters claim a toll of 4888 lives, affect 59 million people, destroy/damage more than 2 million houses and convert many thousand hectares of land into infertile land annually (UN, World Disasters Report, 1994).

The country is highly vulnerable to droughts, floods, cyclones, avalanches, forest fires, and landslides. Out of 35 states/union territories in the country, 24 are disaster prone. This sub-continent is among the world's most disaster prone areas with:

> 55per cent of the total country land vulnerable to earthquake,

8 per cent area prone to cyclones, and

5 per cent vulnerable to floods.

One state (West Bengal) of the country is prone to four common disasters, i.e. flood, drought, cyclone and earthquake, seven states face three types of disasters, ten face two types of disasters and six states face one type of disasters.

In the recent past the frequency of natural disasters in India has increased drastically. Earthquakes of Gujarat, Chamoli, Jabalpur, Latur; landslides in Garhwal and Kumaon; cyclones of Gujarat, Andhra Pradesh and Orissa; tornadoes of Balasore and Midnapore etc. are some of the examples of recent catastrophes in India. Natural disasters in the country are resulting into colossal loss to life and property. Table 1.1 below gives an idea about the annual damage caused due to these disasters and lives lost :

Table 1.1: Damage caused by Natural Hazards in India during the last decade

Year	Number of people affected (in crores)	Number of houses and building partially or totally damaged	Amount of property damages (Rs. in crore)
1990	3.17	1019930	171.0
1991	3.477	1190109	190.0
1992	1.909	570969	205.0
1993	2.624	1529916	580.0
1994	2.353	1051223	183.0
1995	5.435	2088355	473.0
1996	5.499	2376693	543.0
1997	4.438	1103549	n.a.
1998	5.217	1563405	n.a.
1999	5.017	3104064	n.a.
2000	4.162	2736355	1020.90

Source : Ministry of Agriculture, GOI, New Delhi.

Floods, earthquakes, cyclones, hailstorms etc. are the most frequently occurring natural disasters in the country. The life lost due to these natural disasters has been displayed in Table 1.2. During the year 2000-2001, the country faced the most severe earthquake of the known history claiming around 20,000 lives. During the same year, the loss of the life due to floods was also very high and about 3000 people were killed by this natural calamity in different parts of the country (Fig. 1.1).

Table 1.2 : Human lives loss due to várious disasters in the country

Year	Flood	Cyclone/ Flood	Hail-storm	Earthquake	Total
1990-91	1320	979	–	–	2299
1991-92	1185	304	–	768	2257
1992-93	1193	497	–	–	1690
1993-94	1690	318	–	7938	9946
1994-95	2038	247	59	–	2344
1995-96	2072	361	31	–	2464
1996-97	2069	1719	40	–	3828
1997-98	1560	216	247	39	2062
1998-99	2567	1292	–	106	3965
1999-2000	1896	10589	–	–	12585
2000-2001	3048	–	–	>20000	>23048

Source : Ministry of Agricultural, GOI, New Delhi

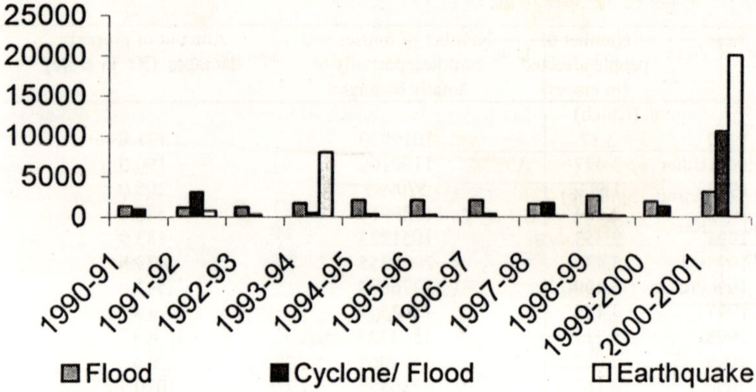

Fig 1.1 : Human lives lost due to three types of common Disasters in India

Among these, while flood is the annually occurring phenomenon, earthquake is the most damaging. January 26, 2001 earthquake in Gujarat has not only shaken the entire country, the colossal loss due to this natural calamity has also been stated as the worst in the learning memory of the country. The impact of this natural hazard is so sudden and unwarned that its prediction and making preparation to save life and property is almost impossible. As mentioned, 55 per cent area of the country is prone to earthquake and out of this

(a) 12 per cent area is prone to severe earthquakes such as in Gujarat.

(b) 18 per cent area is susceptible to earthquakes like in Latur/Uttaranchal.

(c) 25 per cent area is exposed to relatively less severe earthquakes as in Jabalpur and its adjoining areas (Fig. 1.2).

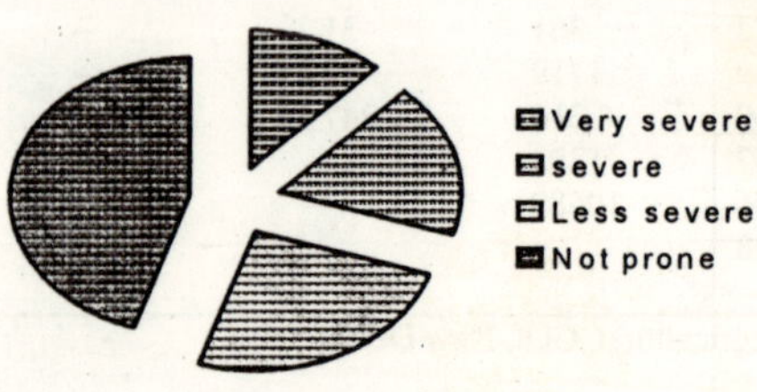

Fig 1.2 : Area prone to earthquakes in India

Table 1.3: Major earthquakes in the Country – (Historically)

Year	Area	Date	IST time hr.m.s.	Magnitude M	Deaths
1819	Gujarat (Kutch)	Jan 16	Mid Night	8.0	Several thousand
1833	Bihar	Aug 26	–	7.7	Hundreds
1897	Assam (Shillong)	Jun 12	16:36	8.7	1600
1900	Kerala (Palghat)	Feb 8	–	6.6	
1905	Himachal Pradesh (Kangra)	Apr 4	6:20	8.0	20000
1930	Assam (Dhubri)	Jul 3	02:33:34	7.1	Many
1934	Bihar – Nepal	Jan 15	14:13:26	8.3	14000
1941	Andamans	Jun 26	–	8.0	Many
1943	Assam (NE)	Oct 23	22:53:17	7.2	N.A.
1950	Assam (NE)	Aug 15	19:39:28	8.6	1500
1956	Gujarat (Anjar)	Jul 21	21:02:36	7.0	Hundreds
1956	U. P. (Bullandshahr)	Oct 10	–	6.7	Many
1958	U.P. (Kapkote)	Dec 28	–	6.3	Many
1960	Delhi	Aug 27	21:28:59	6.0	
1963	Kashmir (Badgam)	Sep 2	07:04:32	5.5	Hundreds
1966	Western Nepal	Jun 27	–	6.3	N.A.
1966	U. P. (Moradabad)	Aug 15	–	5.3	N.A.
1967	Nicobar	Jul 2	–	6.2	N.A.
1967	Maharastra (Koyna)	Dec 11	04:21:19	6.5	200
1970	Andhra Pradesh (Bhadrachalam)	Apr 13	–	6.5	N.A.
1970	Gujarat (Broach)	Mar 23	07:23:03	5.7	N.A.
1975	Himachal Pradesh	Jan 19	–	6.5	N.A.
1988	Bihar – Nepal	Aug 21	04:39:10	6.6	1003
1991	Uttranchal (Uttarkashi)	Oct 20	02:53	6.6	715
1993	Maharastra (Killari)	Sep 30	03:55:47	6.3	7928
1997	Jabalpur	May 22	04:22:31	6.0	38
1999	Chamoli	March29	12.35	6.8	103
2001	Gujarat	Jan 26	8.45	7.9	>20000

After earthquakes, flood is the second most severe natural hazard affecting one or the other part of the country every year. The country receives an annual rainfall of 1200 mm, 85 per cent of which is concentrated in 4 months, i.e. June to September. Due to this intense and period specific rain, all the rivers of the country are fed with huge quantity of water, much beyond their carrying capacity. The carrying capacity of the rivers is further reduced due to sedimentation and drainage congestion. As a result of deforestation and other unscientific developments in the hilly regions, the problem of sedimentation during rain has increased tremendously. In India, every year almost 8 to 10 million-hectare area is flooded, which causes great loss to life, crops, property and environment. Floods very frequently occur in Ganges basin in North and North-Eastern part and Brahmaputra basin in the Eastern part of the country. In all, country's 40 million-hectare area is prone to floods and 8 million hectares is annually affected by floods on an average.

Landslide is another disaster which causes immense loss in the hilly terrain of the country. Landslide is basically the down slope movement of earth or surface material due to gravitational forces. The whole of the Himalayan region, extending from North–West to South-East experiences the maximum landslide damages. Along with the Himalayan hill range, Western Ghats also frequently observe this disaster of varying intensities. The earthquakes in Himalayan region also trigger major landslides. The environmental degradation due to deforestation has further intensified the problem of landslides in the hilly regions. In recent years, landslides have become an annual phenomenon during rainy season in Himalaya due to these reasons. The heavy monsoon rain and cyclones in Western Ghats cause intensive landslide in the area. Landslides along with resulting extensive loss to life and property also create damages to various infrastructures, i.e. roads, bridges and other means of communication.

Rajasthan, Gurajarat, Madhya Pradesh, Chhatisgarh, Bihar, Jharkhand, Bengal, Orissa, Andhra Pradesh, Tamil Nadu and Karnataka are the states which are frequently affected by drought situation. Around five crore population of the country is annually affected by drought. Less than average rain fall, decreasing water bearing capacity of the land (due to increased salinity, and deforestation), damaged natural drainage pattern etc. are the most common factors leading to drought and drought prone situation in various parts of the country. In the country, around 70 per cent of the total sown land in prone to droughts, which hit it one or the other time. Though in the past, country has experienced severe drought conditions many times but 1987-88 was one of the worst droughts after independence. Recently, during 1999-2000, 2000-2001 and 2002 also many states of the country were worst affected by this calamity.

India with a long coastline of 8041 km. is exposed to on an average 5-6 tropical cyclones from the Bay of Bengal and Arabian Sea annually. These cyclones are created by intense low-pressure areas in the atmosphere, due to which wind blows with a very high speed in circular motion resulting into cyclones. Horizontally this area extends from 500 to 1000 km and vertically from surface to 12-14 km above. Cyclones are very common in pre-monsoon (May-June) and post monsoon (October–November) seasons in the country. As per records available during the last century, around 300 cyclones have hit the country coast.

Andhra Pradesh (1996), Gujarat (1998) and Orissa (1999) cyclones are the recent cyclones which caused colossal loss to life and property. The other damaging cyclones that hit the country coast are as follows :

Worst Cyclones in India – Historically

Year	**Death**
1737	3 lakhs
1833	50000
1847	75000
1864	50000
1874	80000
1946	750
1971	10000
1973	5000
1977	10000
1979	700
1990	928
1998	1261
1999	10086

Forest or bush fire is a major hazard for forest cover in the country. As per Forest Survey of India report, 50 per cent of the forest cover of the country is fire prone, out of which 6.17 per cent is prone to severe fire damage causing extensive loss to forest vegetation and environment. Average tangible annual loss due to forest fire in the country is estimated to worth Rs. 440 crores. The coniferous forests in the Himalayan region are very susceptible to fire and every year there are one or more major fire incidences. The other part of the country dominated by deciduous forest are also damaged by fire upto an extent.

Forest fires cause extensive loss in terms of ecology, economy and society. The main damage is caused due to loss of timber, bio-diversity, wildlife habitats, fuel-wood and fodder, water and other natural resources. They also adversely affect the global environment, soil condition and natural regeneration. It is worth mentioning that in India 90 per cent of the forest fires are man-made (intentionally or unintentionally).

Another type of disaster that is usually not much noticed, is soil erosion, which is a direct consequence of environmental degradation. In the recent past due to extensive loss to forest cover and other so called developmental activities, soil erosion has increased tremendously, causing gradient loss to fertile soil. This phenomenon has also reduced the water carrying/bearing capacity of rivers, ponds and tanks and thus increased the frequency of floods from these water bodies. In hilly terrains, particularly in Himalayas, soil erosion has really reached an alarming stage which needs immediate attention and treatment.

DISASTERS IN UTTRANCHAL

Though each and every part of the country is more or less prone to natural hazards, some selected portions or regions of the country are more susceptible to natural/man made hazards. The Uttranchal region of the country, due to its geological set up is also a region where natural/man made hazards are very common and frequent. During the last 100 years, four earthquakes with intensity 8 or more on Richter Scale have hit the Himalayan ranges. Though in general the main cause of these disasters are natural yet the human induced activities are also responsible to a large extent for accelerating their gravity and magnitude. Human activities in such sensitive and fragile areas cause interference in the environmental balance resulting to disruption of the ecological balance which further lead to soil erosion, floods, landslides, forest fires, etc. The data of Table 1.4 below gives an idea about the seriousness of the problem in the State.

Table 1.4: Loss Due to Various Natural Hazards In Uttranchal

Year	Life Loss	Cattle Loss	Household damage	Crop Hectare	Approx. loss (Rs. in lakhs)
1970	200	–	–	–	–
1971	10	440	–	–	10.77
1972	7	22	–	–	1.25
1973	3	169	–	–	8.68
1974	9	25	–	–	0.77
1975	1	85	–	–	7.05
1976	1	21	–	–	7.00
1978	3	22	46	140.00	7.75
1979	14	164	562	777.00	138.96
1980	15	564	725	–	–
1981	5	2	–	–	63.65
1982	7	207	287	–	6.83
1983	11	136	–	7933.00	14.27
1984	1	74	177	–	–
1985	–	7	18	–	–
1986	14	216	445	–	327.81
1987	–	–	–	7.00	–
1988	8	71	334	–	–
1989	14	71	656	120.20	–
1990	20	76	1111	486.00	370.64
1991	36	142	462	2000.00	212.15
1991	723	4000	70000	N.A.	3700.00
1998	384	1002	3000	45785.00	18200.74
1999	100	Thous-ands	50000	–	–

PROBLEMS IN MANAGING DISASTER

Most of the disasters are not completely unavoidable and hence they are to be faced. The best approach to minimise the impacts of these disasters is to manage them in a better and scientific way. The damage from natural hazards can be minimized by introducing appropriate preparedness measures – including both early working and preparedness on the part of vulnerable community. In general, there are three stages in disaster management, namely, pre-disaster, emergency and post-disaster. The pre-disaster stage includes reducing the vulnerability or susceptibility of a society or community to ensure minimal losses in the case of a disaster. The emergency stage refers to fulfil the needs and provisions of the victims affected by a natural hazard. The most important phase of disaster starts with the passing of the emergency phase and it covers the rehabilitation of the affected communities. Rehabilitation does not merely mean rebuilding/repairing the houses, roads etc. or financial assistance to affected population but it has much wider implications. In true sense it aims at total reconstruction of physical and social infrastructure as well as economic and social upliftment of the people of the region. This aspect of rehabilitation is very much desired in a region where disasters are very common and frequent features like in Uttranchal which forms a part of the seismic belt.

The Uttranchal region of Himalaya is geologically very sensitive zone. In this region, every year, one or other types of disasters like earthquakes, landslides, floods, forest fires etc. occur very frequently. Though at the time of disaster, various rescue and relief operations are carried out and plans for long term strategies are formed, yet the long term strategies are easily forgotten as memory fades. It is observed that disaster management in the area is just like fire fighting and very negligible or conscious attempt is made for long term strategies. Partial failure of the administration and other agencies to counter the situation results in further deterioration of the condition. Unemployment, diseases, scarcity of livelihood, food and water shortage, shelter/housing problem, failure of communication and other infrastructures, environmental degradation etc. are some major problems which are being faced due to one or the other form of disasters in the area. In the recent past, mainly due to increasing population pressure and various other man made/natural factors, the intensity and severity of disasters have increased many times and subsequently the problem of rehabilitation has become more serious, particularly in this region of the country.

Realising the seriousness of the problem and its adverse impact on the socio-economic status of the people of the region, it is high time that some appropriate strategic approach is applied for proper disaster management in the area.

2

DISASTER IN HILLS

Indian subcontinent due to its physiographic, climatic and prevailing socio-economic conditions and geological setup is one of the most disaster prone regions of the world. Though every year one region or the other is affected by some natural disasters, hill regions being more fragile and unstable are more exposed to such calamities. As per the definition and classification of Planning Commission, an area having an elevation of more than 500m above mean sea level is ctategorised as Hill Region. Nearly 98 (ninety-eight) districts in the country fall within this category. These regions are regularly exposed to earthquakes, landslides, forest fires, avalanches, flash floods etc. Mostly the reasons are natural yet their intensity and frequency increase manifolds due to human induced activities. Thus the hill regions of the country, characterized by a wide variation in physiography, geology, climate, fauna and flora and having varied socio-cultural traditions, are a unique geographical entity having one thing in common, i.e. their increased susceptibility to natural hazards.

Ecologically being very unstable and fragile in nature, slight disturbance in hilly terrain may lead to exaggerate adverse impacts of natural hazards. The ecology of hilly regions being more fragile needs organised scientific planning for developmental activities. In view of the severity of the problem it is essential that special importance is accorded to hilly regions while dealing with the issue of disaster management.

HILL REGIONS IN INDIA

Physiographically India comprises of four major regions, namely,

(i) The Great Himalayan zone,
(ii) Plain of Ganga, Yamuna and Brahmaputra,
(iii) Desert, and
(iv) The Peninsular India.

A significant portion of the country comprises of hilly terrain. The major hill ranges starting from North to South of India are:

- Himalayan hill ranges
- The Arawalis
- The Satpuras
- The Deccans
- The Western Ghats and
- The Eastern Ghats.

These hill ranges covering quite significant geographical area are spread out over the states of Jammu & Kashmir, Himachal Pradesh, Uttranchal, Arunachal Pradesh, Manipur, Meghalaya, Mizoram, Nagaland, Sikkim, Tripura, West Bengal, Assam, Goa, Jharkhand, Maharashtra, Karnataka, Kerala, Tamil Nadu and Union Territories of Andaman-Nicobar and Daman & Diu. These hill ranges, having unique bio-diversity and plenty of natural resources also play a significant role in determining and regulating the climatic regime and rainfall in the country. All these hill regions though varying in rock and soil composition, topography and structures have one thing in common, i.e. their fragility, which makes them susceptible to various natural hazards. Rapid soil erosion, landslides, flash floods, forest fires etc. are the common form of problems to which these regions are exposed.

The hill regions of the country have a unique closed eco-system, involving various components linked with each other with a very fragile and delicate bond. Slight disturbance created due to human induced activities may break these delicate bonds which may lead to a disaster. Though this fragility of hill eco-system is a common feature for all the hill areas of the country but some mountainous eco-systems like Himalayas are extremely sensitive to human interference.

RESTLESS HIMALAYAS

Himalayan ranges extending from Hindukush in North-West to Burmah in South-East for a length of around 2400 kms. make a natural mountain barrier of 250 to 300 km in width and 500 to 8000 metre in height in the northern part of Indian subcontinent. These ranges characterized by two syntexial bands near Nanga Parbat in West and Wamcha Bairwa in East is one of the youngest and the highest mountain ranges of the world.

In comparison to other mountain ranges of country quite young in age, this mighty Himalayas have been a centre of attraction for pilgrims, saints, poets, artists, philosophers and scientists. Besides its aesthetic, philosophical and religious value, Himalayas due to its extensive natural resources in the form of forests, minerals, water sources and other natural resources have been a source of life for the people of our country.

The most significant gift from the Himalayas for the Indian subcontinent is its functioning as a climatic regulator. The Himalayan mountain ranges, working as a barrier are responsible for monsoon rains and unique climatic condition of six seasons of the subcontinent. The mountain ranges also protect the land lying in its south from the cold waves of Siberia. The Northern Indian subcontinent is dependent on Himalayas for its water needs. The rivers originating from Himalayas carry large amount of water to the plain land. On an average Ganga, Brahmaputra and Sindhu River systems originating from Himalayan Glaciers flow annually bring 1147.00 x 109 M^3 water (Y.K. Murthy, 1981). Besides rainwater, Himalayan glaciers have huge quantity of water (1400 km^3) stored in the form of ice and snow also (J. Bahadur, 1985).

Himalayan region is bestowed with very rich natural resources besides giving the tonic of life-water. Around 30 per cent of the total geographic area of Himalayas is covered by good quality forests. The floral species found in Himalayas are very rare and show much diversity. The common vegetation of this unique ecosystem varies from close evergreen forest of Bhabhar-Siwalik belts in the South through mixed deciduous trees with grassland in middle to Arctic type vegetation in the North. The main species found in Himalayas from South to North are Saal (*Shorea robusta*), Sheesam (*Dalbergia sissoo*), Haldu (*Adina cardifolia*), Sain (*Terminalia tomentosa*); Chir pines, Oaks, Rhododendron, Alders, Blue pine, Tilonj (*Quercus dilata*), Silver Fir, Bhojpatra or birch, Fir, Junipers and Grasses.

The Himalayan forests are endowed with a rich fauna and the species range from elephants, tigers, panthers, bears, wide varieties of deer, ghural (*Nemorhaedus goral goral*), black bear, Himalayan tahr and hundreds of species of birds along with other common wild life species. Mineral wealth, hot springs etc. are other natural resources, which make Himalayan region a unique and important part of Indian subcontinent.

Mighty Himalayas, extending in arc shaped mountain range for more than 2400 kms. in length with two syntexial bands separates the Indian subcontinent from the rest of Eurasia. Longitudinally on the basis of physiography and geology, Himalayas can be subdivided into four distinct parts, i.e. Lower or Shiwalik Himalaya, Lesser Himalaya, Great/Central Himalaya and Tethys or Trans-Himalaya. These four subdivisions of Himalayas are marked by four prominent geotectonic features, i.e. Himalayas Frontal fault, Main Boundary Thrust, Main Central Thrust and Trans-Himalayan Fault (Fig. 2.1). These tectonic features also have a relationship with Himalayan origin. This unique life-giving ecosystem of the world is also unique in its structural and physiographic complexity, which is resultant of various phases of deformation, the mountain system has undergone since its origin. It is really surprising to know that just 100 million years ago this highest mountain range of world was lying below the deep ocean. Since its first embryonic stage, the evolution and uplifting of Himalayas has been a continuous process, which is still ongoing. The scientific investigations reveal that this great mountain, looking very stable from outside is still active in its depth and uplifting. These deep-seated tectonic activities in Himalayas have made it very unstable and

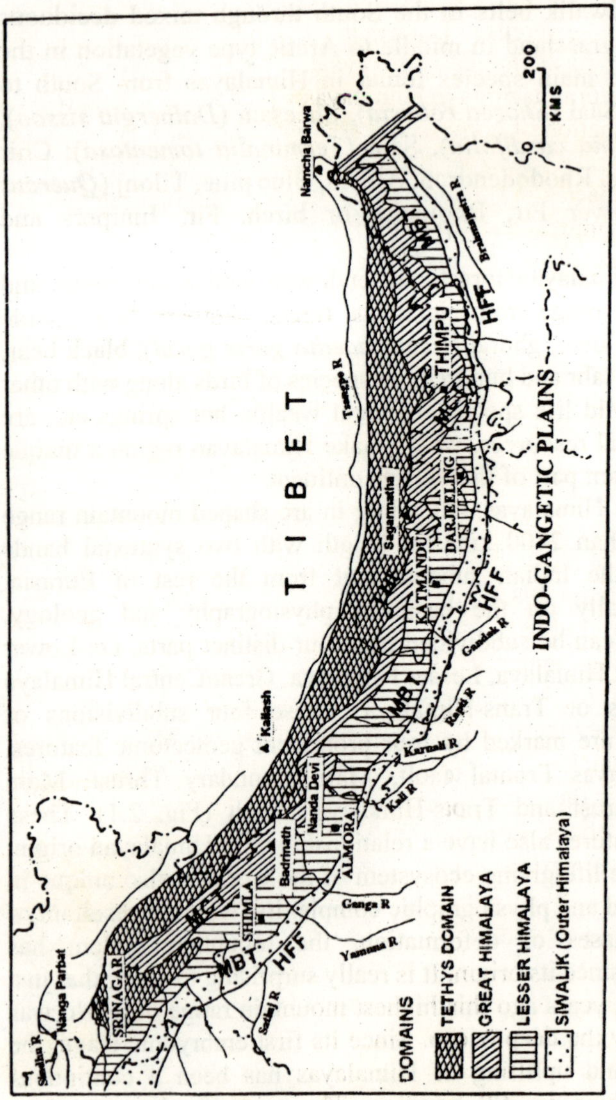

Fig.2.1 : Subdivisions of Himalayas marked by four major tectonic features.
HFF — Himalayan Frontal Fault MCT — Main Central Thrust
MBT — Main Boundary Thrust THF — Trans Himalayan Fault
(After K. S. Valdiya, 1998).

fragile resulting to increased susceptibility to natural hazards. Though the main reason for the natural hazards in Himalayan region are natural, their impact has tremendously increased due to human interference. Earthquakes, landslides, soil erosion, forest fires, flash floods, snow avalanches etc. are some of the common natural hazards in Himalayas which are being generated by a combination of both natural and human induced activities in the region. To manage these catastrophes and lessen their adverse impact on human life and as well as environment, it is essential to understand the underlying causes and the reasons for their origin.

THE SHATTERED CRUST

As per the modern thinking, the earth formed about five billion years ago from the very hot gases that over time cooled and became denser. While solidifying, the earth divided into three distinct layers. The inner most central part of the earth is of solid nickel and iron (20 per cent of the earth radius), surrounded by a larger part of molten nickel and iron (35 per cent of the earth in radius). Around this metabolic centre lies the mantle (45 per cent of earth in radius), formed of molten rock with a viscous, molasses-like material. This mantle part of the earth is surrounded by "asthenosphere" and "lithosphere". The lithosphere is the outermost layer of the earth and on an average is 100 kms thick. The outermost part of the lithosphere is the "Crust". It is the "crust" part of the earth that makes "continents" and ocean floors. The thickness of this "crust" is around 30 km in continental parts and about 5 km under the oceans (Fig. 2.2).

The outer most layer of the earth, the lithosphere is not a single body, instead it is cracked like an "egg shell". These cracked parts of the lithosphere are termed as "tectonic plates, " which are floating over the viscous, semi-liquid molasses like structure or mantle. There are seven large and twelve small tectonic plates, which are continuously in motion (Fig. 2.3). The energy for their motion comes from deep hot interiors of the earth. The heat energy from the hot core part of the earth is released in the form of convection currents. These currents, continuously in motion give sufficient energy to push the tectonic plates and bring in motion (Fig. 2.4).

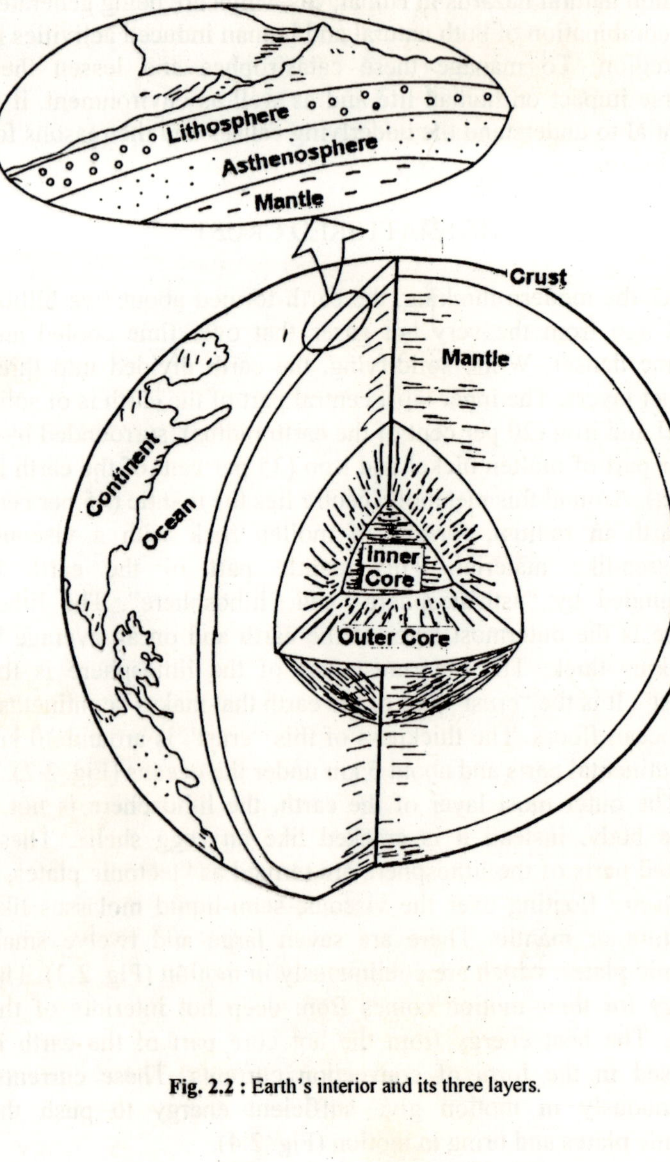

Fig. 2.2 : Earth's interior and its three layers.

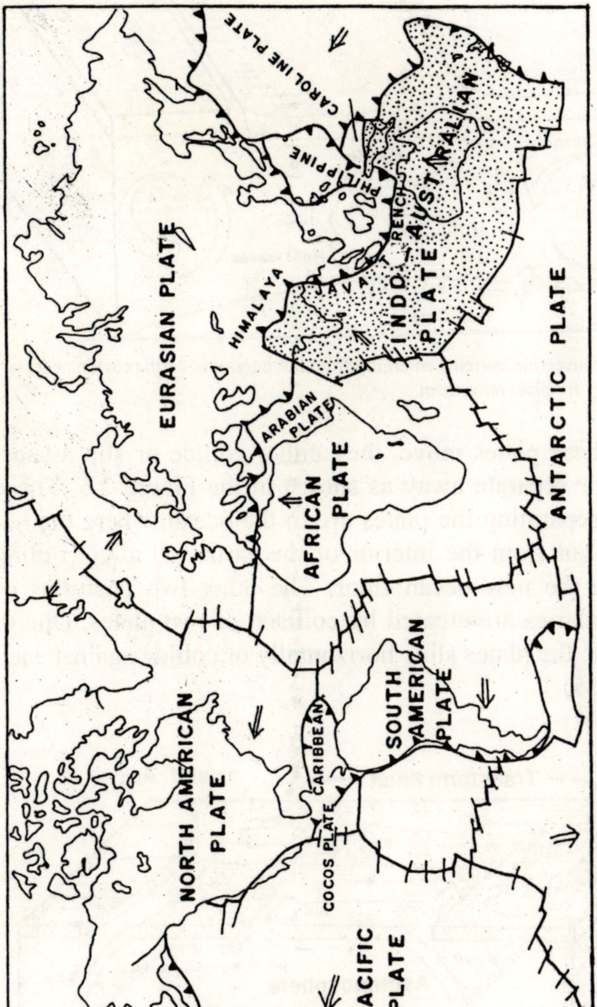

Fig. 2.3 : Tectonic Plates and their movement.

Thrust or Subduction zone

Direction of plate movement

Mid oceanic ridges and transform fault.

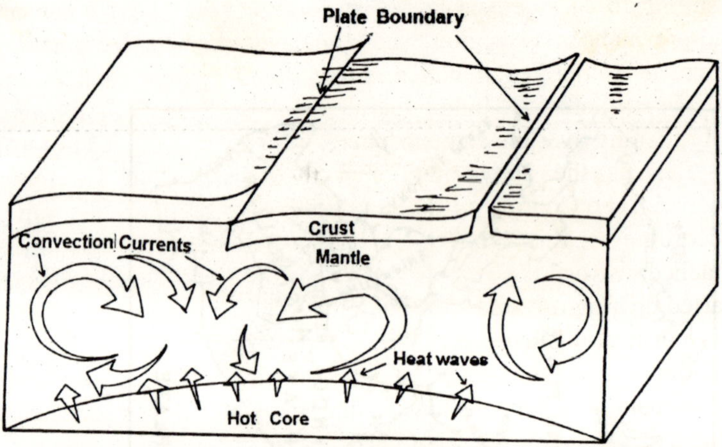

Fig. 2.4 : The convection currents emerging from hot interior of earth provide necessary energy for plate movement.

When these plates move, they either collide or slip against each other or separate away as shown in the Figure 2.5. These boundaries separating the plates are in the ocean, where the hot lava comes out from the interior of the earth and after cooling down forms the new ocean floor. The other two positions of plate's boundaries are created by collison of two plates. Due to this collison, the plates slide horizontally or collide against each other (Fig. 2.5).

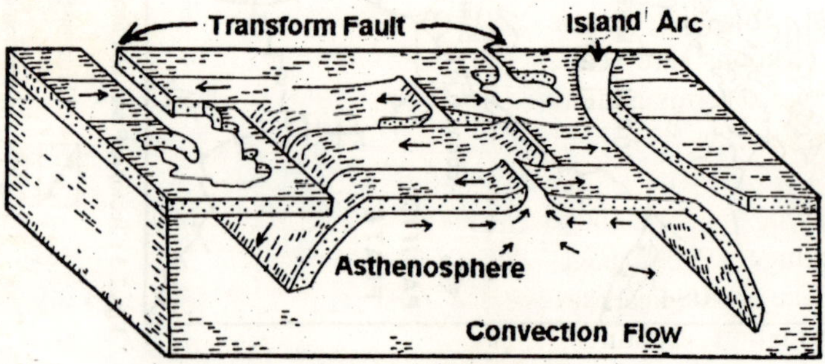

Fig. 2.5 : Convection currents and plate boundaries.

The movement along the plate boundaries make the region lying nearby unstable and various tectonic movements take place resulting to earthquakes, volcanic eruptions etc., very common and prevalent in the region. The Himalayas characterize a region where two continental plates are colliding against each other. These two plates, the Indo-Australian and the Eurasian plates are both floating over the asthenosphere.

Besides the above-mentioned theory i.e. Plate Tectonic Theory, "The Continental Drift Theory" also supports this view. According to this theory, the Indian subcontinent was once attached to Australia and millions of years ago the subcontinent started drifting towards North at a rate of 20 cm per year. Due to this northward movement, a time came when the subcontinent collided against the Asian continent. Due to this collision, the Indian continent happens to pass underneath the Asian continent. But due to its lightweight, the Indian continent could not submerge or sink into the asthenosphere, instead due to continuous pressure toward North, this plate slided between the asthenosphere and the Asian-Plate. Due to this sliding the part of Asian-Plate and the sediment lying between these two plates rose high and formed the great mountain range of Himalayas.

However it is to be noticed here that the story of Himalayas uplifting and plate-movement is not yet over. The Indo- Australian plate is still in movement phase and creating pressure on Eurasian-Plate. Due to this pressure, the Himalayas are still uprising. Besides uplifting of the Himalayas, the pressure of plates is creating stress on the rocks forming the mountain (Fig. 2.6). Due to this stress, the rocks are deformed in various patterns, i.e. tilting, breaking and moving away after rupture. These deformations are called faulting, folding and thrusting in geological terms and are basically the ways to release the stored energy in the rock bodies, created due to continuous increasing stress as a result of plate movement. Whenever this energy is released, the rock bodies forming the land here shatter and roll, resulting to earthquakes.

The earthquakes are very common in the vicinities of large deformation structures, i.e. "Thrusts". Thrusts are the rupture planes running miles in distance in the rock bodies along which the broken fragments of rock move apart. The three major thrusts/faults of Himalayas, also demarcating the four geomorphological divisions of Himalayas extend longitudinally

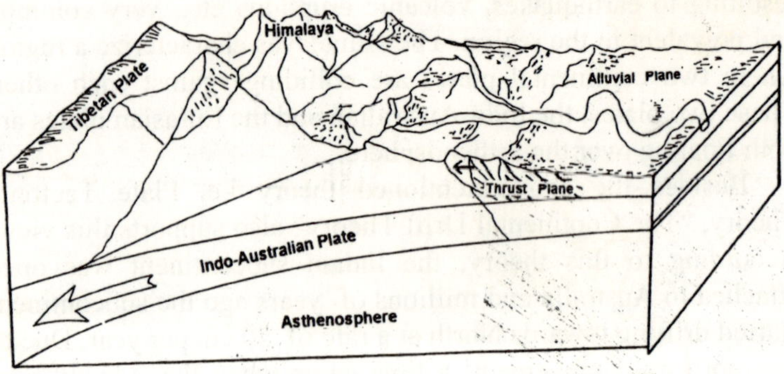

Fig 2.6 : Uplifting of Himalayas

along the whole length of mountain range and are very deep seated (Fig. 2.7). As per new geological investigations, the thrusts are not simple planar features, instead they are represented by many sub-planar features called imbricates, which further slice the rock bodies lying between them. The imbricates run almost parallel to the thrust plane but at higher angles.

This is not all about the structural complexity of Himalaya, there are fault planes also present in the rock bodies, which are diagonal to the thrust plane and dip at higher angles. This complex phenomenon of thrusting and faulting of a part of Lesser Garhwal Himalaya is shown in Figure 2.8.

The recent investigations in the field of Himalayan geotectonic reveal that the Indo-Australian plate still continues to drift northward at the rate of 5 to 6 cm. per year. As the Eurasian or Tibetan plate is stagnant at its own place, the Himalayas lying between these two plates is being squeezed and stresses are continuously being stored in its rocks. Part of these stresses is occasionally released along weak fractured zones causing smaller earthquakes. But a major portion of stress is still remained trapped and continues to buildup. Due to these stresses the main tectonic features of Himalayas, i.e. Himalayan Frontal Fault, Main Boundary Thrust, Main Central Thrust and Trans Himalayan Thrust are being reactivated which is evidenced by various distorted geomorphic features in Himalayas, i.e. uplifted river terraces, change in river gradient etc. The frequent landslides, tremendous increase in soil erosion, rock falls along different fault planes etc. are the other evidences, which support

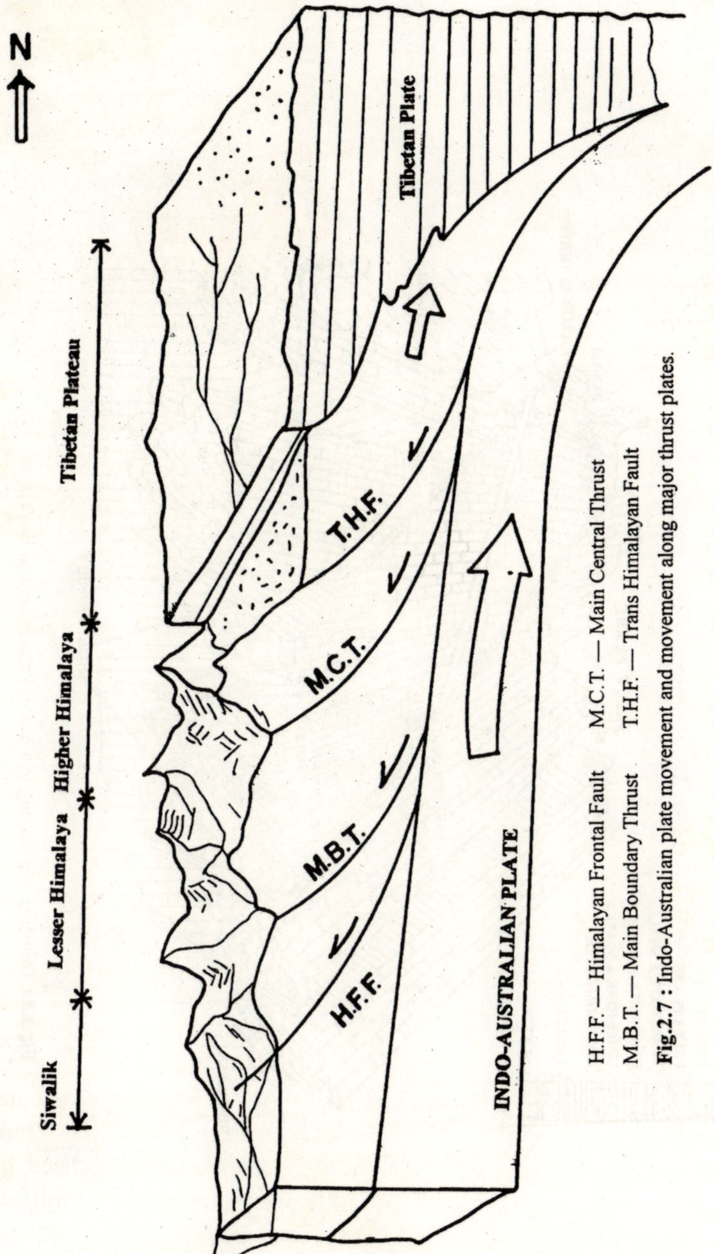

H.F.F. — Himalayan Frontal Fault M.C.T. — Main Central Thrust
M.B.T. — Main Boundary Thrust T.H.F. — Trans Himalayan Fault

Fig.2.7 : Indo-Australian plate movement and movement along major thrust plates.

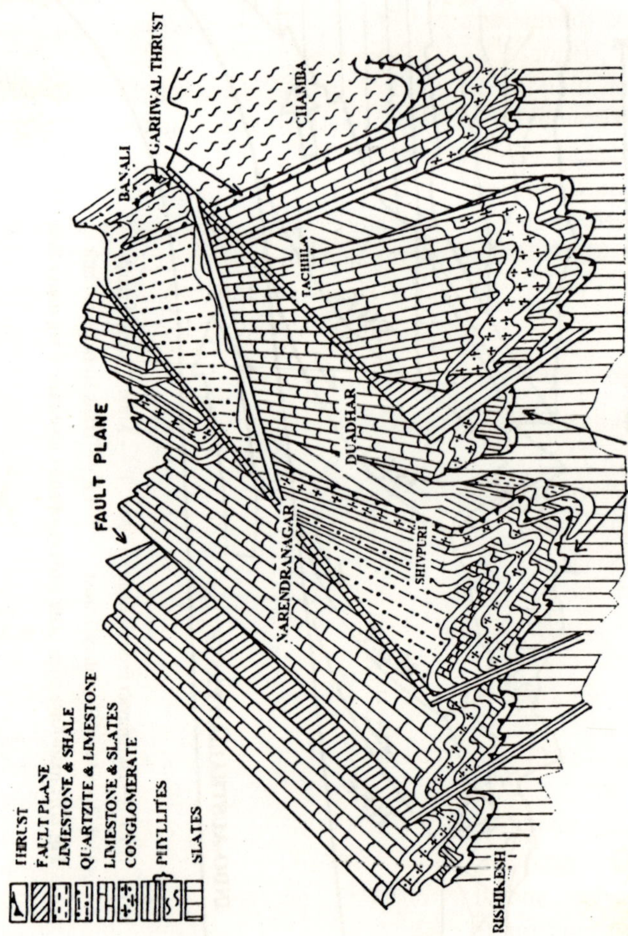

Fig.2.8 : Thrusting and faulting in a part of Lesser Garhwal Himalayas

the reactivation of the tectonic features in Himalayas. Among the four major tectonic features, the Main Boundary Thrust is the most active feature along which movement is evident in many parts, i.e. Darjeeling, Ladhuja valley of Nepal-India border and Balia valley near Nainital (Valdiya, 1998). Beside the tectonic features discussed above, which have deep seated origin, the on ground or physiographic features of Himalayas are also responsible for its increased fragility. The southern and northern slopes of Himalayan ranges have wide contrast while considering their susceptibility to natural hazards. The southern slopes of Himalayan hills have relatively less vegetation making them more susceptible to soil erosion and rock falls. On the other hand, the northern slopes of the hills are gentler in slopes and are less exposed to sun. These features along with thick soil cover and increased water retention capacities of these slopes allow good vegetative cover. These slopes are thus well protected by thick forest comprising of different species of trees, shrubs and grasses.

ENVIRONMENTAL DEGRADATION AND DISASTERS

The discussion in preceding paragraphs clarifies that Himalayan eco-systems due to its geological and physiographic characteristics is very fragile. Slight disturbance by other factors can disturb the eco-balance easily and this is what has happened during the last few decades. Man for his ever-increasing needs and greeds has exploited the Himalayan natural resources beyond the safer limits, resulting into catastrophic consequences. An unwarranted increase in soil erosion, landslide, floods etc. are due to unscientific exploitation which has been carried out under the label of development in these most fragile and unstable mountainous ranges. Large scale deforestation, construction of roads and hydropower station, without taking into consideration the geological and environmental aspects are some of the primary reasons for this destruction. Secondly, the population growth and urbanization, unscientific agricultural practices on sensitive slopes, dependency on forest for fuel and fodder, extensive grazing in forest area, indiscriminate industrialization and large scale building construction for tourism industry etc. are the other major human induced activities which have really shaken the foundation of eco-balance in Himalayan region. Among the factors mentioned above deforestation is the major cause of environmental degradation, which resulted in increased vulnerability of the Himalayan region to natural hazards. Himalayan forests, rich in flora and fauna have been brutally exploited by man for many decades. But after independence a huge portion of Himalayan forest has been earmarked for the sake of green revolution. Thousands of hectares of forest have been cleared especially in Terai belt of Himalayas to provide agriculture land to freedom fighters, army personnel and others for their rehabilitation. This shortsightedness of the policy makers has really caused a great loss to the Himalayan ecosystem. Besides, during the last two-three decades due to population increase and lack of other livelihood resources for this increased population, the dependency on agriculture has increased in Himalayan area. This has forced the villagers to encroach upon forest land. The Jhoom Cultivation in North-Eastern states has been an age old traditional agriculture practice, which has damaged large forest areas in this region. Forest fire, grazing, fuel and fodder collection, road construction and other developmental projects have been the major factors responsible for deforestation in Himalayas. Though after enactment of Forest Conservation Act of 1980 (No forest land can be diverted for non-forestry purposes without concurrence of Central Government) there has been a remarkable decrease in forest land diversion but so many other activities directly or indirectly connected with human need and greed are badly damaging the forests in these areas. According to Forest Survey of India (State of Forest Report, 1999) the total forest cover in the 98 hill districts of the country is 251.219 sq. km. constituting 37 per cent of the total geographic area, which is very less against a goal of 66 per cent as laid down in the National Forest Policy. The major factors responsible for the shrinking of the forest area have been:–

- Increased human and cattle population and over exploitation around forestland and overgrazing.
- Deforestation due to human activities – Agriculture (including shifting cultivation), Multipurpose projects,

Irrigation, Industries, Mining, Quarrying for minerals, Construction of roads, Erection of transmission lines, and Clearing for encroachments (industrialization, urbanization and human settlements) etc.

- Illicit felling, over-felling, forest litter removal, lopping for fodder and fuel-wood.
- Forest fires, etc.

The negative impacts of deforestation and forest degradation are enormous, affecting the overall welfare of the people, and causing heavy social cost (Fig. 2.9). Categorization of these negative impacts include :

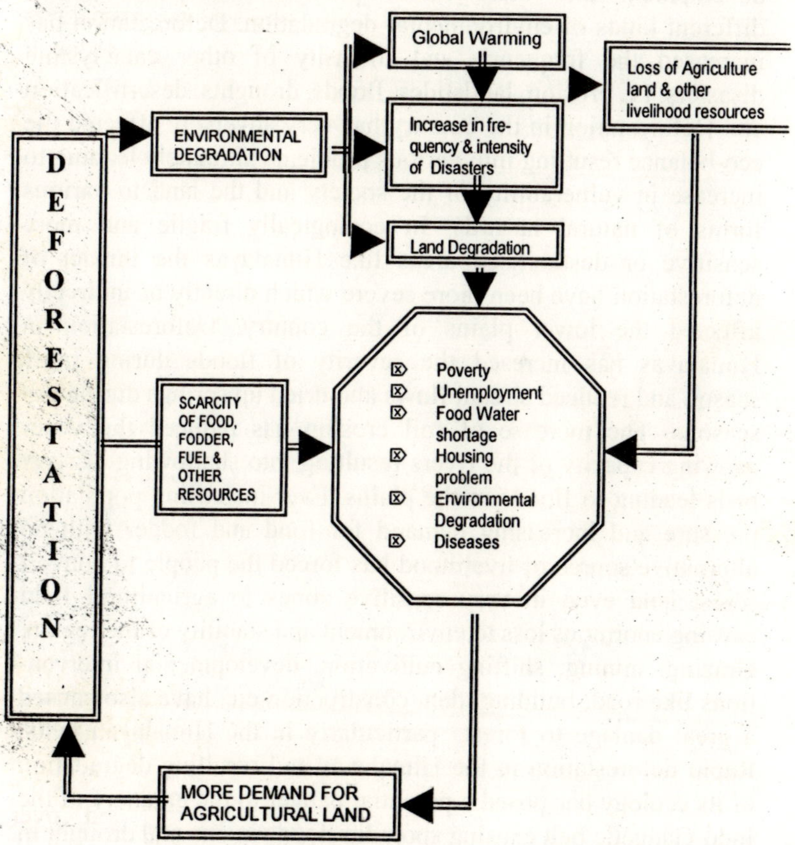

Fig. 2.9 : Adverse Impacts of Deforestation

- Environmental impacts: Loss of ecological stability, damage to the ecological foundations of agriculture; loss of bio-diversity; reduction in carbon sink capability; effects of climate change; floods, drought and related losses; damage to watershed; silting up of reservoirs; soil erosion; desertification; changes in hydrological regime.
- Economic impacts: Reduction in agricultural productivity and crop yield; scarcity for forest produce; closure/underutilisation of forest industries.

The large scale deforestation in the country along with faulty development and management practices have resulted to different kinds of environmental degradation. Deforestation has increased the frequency and intensity of other cataclysmic disasters, i.e. erosion, landslides, floods, droughts, desertification etc. Deforestation in the country has very adversely affected the eco-balance resulting into various problems ultimately leading to increase in vulnerability of the society and the land to various forms of natural hazards. In ecologically fragile and more sensitive or destabilised areas like Himalayas the impact of deforestation have been more severe which directly or indirectly affected the lower plains of the country. Deforestation in Himalayas has incresed the severity of floods during rainy season and reduced stream flows and dried up springs during dry seasons. The increase of soil erosion has reduced the water carrying capacity of the rivers resulting into shallowing of river beds leading to floods in the plains. Ever-increasing population pressure and increasing demand for food and fodder with no alternative source of livelihood has forced the people to convert forest land even in very sensitive zones to agricultural field causing enormous loss to environment and stability of the region. Grazing, mining, shifting cultivation, developmental interventions like road, building, dam construction etc. have also caused a great damage to forest particularly in the Himalayan belts. Rapid deforestation in the Himalayas and resulting degradation of its ecology has posed a potential danger to the greenery of the Indo-Gangetic belt causing sporadic floods in one and drought in other area. About two third agricultural land of the country is affected by drought and about one-fifth is very frequently exposed to floods. Deforestation and other allied land degradation activities such as water logging, flooding, ravines, shifting cultivation, mining, salinisation, water logging, soil erosion, landslides and rock falls, desertification etc. have affected more than fifty per cent of the total geographical area of the country.

Poverty and vulnerability are inextricably linked and mutually reinforcing each other. The Poor for their survival are dependents on natural resources, mainly forests. This dependency of the poor on forests has caused tremendous loss to forest resources. While on one hand the deforestation leads to environmental degradation and increases the intensity and frequency of natural disasters, simultaneously it also enhances the people's vulnerability to natural hazards.

The worst impact of deforestation is the manifold increase of soil erosion and landslides. The mountains consisting of fragile rocks either due to mineral composition or due to fractures and shears in them are worst affected by deforestation. The loss of tree cover loosen the soil and rock material, otherwise bound by the roots of the trees disallowing it to be eroded by water and wind. The problem has become very serious in some parts of Himalayas where due to deforestation and soil erosion the major portion of the fertile topsoil is lost and the area is approaching to desertification. The natural appearance of xerophytic plants in some Himalayan areas is certainly a matter of concern for the country. In comparison to relatively stable areas, the problem of soil loss and slope failures is much more serious in tectonically active zones of Himalayas. Some pockets of Himalayas with an alarming rate of soil erosion are identified by scientists near Kathmandu – Kankani area in Central Nepal, where 126 km^2 of ground is lost every year through mass movement at the rate of 1000 m^3 / km^2 (Ives, J.D. and Messerli, B., 1984). Similarly in the Shiwalik hills of Hoshiyarpur, Punjab the seriously eroded land has increased from 195 km^2 in 1852 to 2000 km^2 in 1980. In Sindhu Valley the rate of erosioin varies from 2 to 12 mm/year (Burbank, D.W. et al., 1996).

According to G.P. Gupta, 1975, on an average the Himalayan mountains region is losing its soil cover at the rate of more than 1.00 mm per year. In central sector of Himalayas the sediments yield of rivers is 16.43 ha. metres per 100 km^2 catchment area per year (Gupta, G.P.,1975). This large scale soil erosion by the flowing rivers has led to multifarious problem in the Himalayan region and the adjoining downstream plains. The shortage of water in one area and floods in other are common as a result of large-scale soil erosion and mass movement. The situation further gets aggravated when this soil is deposited in the streams or lakes. Lakes like Dal and Wular in Kashmir, Naini Lake of Nainital (Uttranchal) and Sukhna lake of Chandigarh are shrinking due to the problem of sedimentation.

Thus we see that deforestation in Himalayan region has not only accelerated but also initiated disasters. This phenomenon as discussed earlier has multiplied the adverse impacts on the society and the land as far as the disasters are concerned. Deforestation, while on one hand accelerates the frequency and intensity of natural hazards on other hand it increases the vulnerability of society and the region to natural hazards and thus the risk.

The main concern, based on the available information is that despite increase of the plantation area due to efforts of various organisations including forest department through tree planting activities, loss of natural forests continues to take place. Tree planting and social forestry activities cannot fully compensate for the loss of natural forests, because they have very different attributes. Another concerning point is that the remaining natural forests (and forest plantations) are becoming progressively degraded due to overuse and lack of protection. The deterioration of the quality, stocking condition and productivity of forests is a matter of serious concern, as is deforestation.

Along with deforestation and forest degradation, the plantation of some exotic species is also having adverse impact on Himalayan environment and ecosystem. The invasion by pines in Himalayas has adversely affected the water tables, ground bio-mass, undergrowth of other smaller species etc. Due to this reduced undergrowth, the ecosystem of pine forest is not wild life friendly. Deforestation and degradation of forests have lead to adverse environmental impact. The invasion of forest vegetation like *Lantana camara* and *Euphorbia roylaena* has really created an alarming situation. These vegetations do not allow the growth and survival of other plants and thus degrade the forest quality.

Unscientific development practices adopted in Himalayas have been yet another major factor causing immense loss to environment of this fragile ecosystem. After independence and especially after China War in 1962 the main emphasis of the Central Government was to increase connectivity in Himalayan region through roads. During this period even the interior villages were connected by roads. But the most unfortunate part of this development had been that these roads were constructed without proper scientific investigation. This activity has generated huge amount of debris and other waste, which ultimately deteriorated the environmental conditions and shattered the eco-balance of the region. The blasting carried out to clear mountains for making new roads also results in landslides and rock falls. Beside roads, other developmental projects, i.e. hydropower, irrigation, railway tracks etc. have also caused irreparable loss to the environment of the region increasing the risk for human society by natural hazards.

Industrialization and urbanisation are also other major causes for environmental degradation in Himalaya. After independence availability of natural resources (forest, minerals, raw materials etc.), electricity, communication, cheap labour etc. encouraged prospective industrialists to establish industries in various towns and cities of Hiamalayan region. Sri Nagar, Jammu, Shimla, Solan, Bilaspur, Dehradun, Haridwar, Almora, Gangtok, Darjleeng, Tezpur, Guwahati, Shillong and many other towns developed various industries, which have resulted to environmental problems like pollution, deforestation etc., further exposing and making the region more susceptible to natural hazards.

Urbanization in Himalayan belt has also been responsible for increased vulnerability to disasters. With the urbanization, the demand for various natural resources increased leading to their brutal exploitation and consequent environmental degradation. Increased demand for residential accommodation forced the people to build houses in hilly terrain without following the specific norms or guidelines stipulated for such areas. It has been observed that mostly in newly developed/developing towns or cities the buildings constructed are mere copies of plain areas without due consideration to local seismicity, ecological or environmental aspects. These concrete and brick structures proved very fatal during earthquakes in the past. During Chamoli earthquake the traditional buildings made up of local materials proved to be relatively safe than the newly constructed structures. The concrete structural collapse proved to be very fatal during 1991 and 1999 earthquakes in Uttranchal. Deforestation, pollution, demolition, soil erosion, etc. are other problems associated with urbanization in hilly regions of Himalayas.

Summarizing the above arguments we can dare to make a conclusive statement that Himalayan region due to its natural set up (geology, geomorphology, climate etc.) is by itself very vulnerable to natural disasters. The human interference leading to environmental degradation has made the condition worst by increasing the vulnerability to disasters. Human induced activities are the prime reasons of environmental degradation and increase in the risk to disasters in hilly terrain. The risk due to these disasters may be estimated from the life lost in such areas during the IDNDR (1990-1999).

Date	Event	Area affected	Deaths
1990	Floods	Entire Country	882
20.10.1991	Earthquake	Uttar Pradesh (Now Uttranchal)	2,000
4.9.-2.10.1992	Floods	U.P, Himachal, J&K, Sikkim	1,500
8-31.7.1993	Floods	Ganga,\Brahmaputra regions	953
28.9.1993	Flash flood	Uttar Pradesh	260
1994	Floods	Entire country	720
1997	Flash flood	Himachal Pradesh	n.a.
17.8.1998	Floods, landslide	Uttar Pradesh (Now Uttranchal)	384
29.3.1999	Earthquake	Uttar Pradesh (Now Uttranchal)	100

Source : Ministry of Agriculture, GOI, New Delhi.

The most frequent of natural disasters observed in hill areas are landslides or rockfalls. The Himalayas including north-eastern states experience maximum number of landslides in the world due to wide variations in geology, geomorphology, rock structure/ texture and climate. The landslides are common near tectonically weak rocks, i.e. affected by faults, thrusts or shears, which make the rocks weaker and susceptible to erosion and landslides. The rock type also plays a decisive role in initiating landslides. Soft and porous rocks with slippery breaking plains (i.e. slates, shales, phyllites etc.) are easily washed away by rain water in comparison to hard and solid rocks, i.e. quartzite, granite etc.

The rainfall is also an important factor for frequent landslides in Himalayan region. A large part of Himalayas receives more than 200 centimetre rainfall per year. Among the activities induced by human being, deforestation and road construction are the most damaging and responsible for mass movement. In Himalayas around 44,000 km of road construction has produced millions of tons of debris which frequently slide and block the roads during rainy seasons. The high seismicity of Himalayan region is also responsible for some of the major landslides in the region. The shock waves generated by the earthquake accelerate the ground movement and trigger the mass movement in weaker areas. During 1950 the landslide in Arunchal Pradesh was probably triggered by an earthquake in the region.

Poor drainage system may be another significant cause for landslide, specially slumps. Lakkar Bazar of Shimla, the area on east of Joshimath, Sher-ka-Danda (Nainital) are some of the areas, where rock bodies have slumped in the recent past (Valdiya, 1987). Recently during 1998 in Gharwal and Kumaun regions of Uttranchal landslides claimed hundreds of lives and destroyed properties worth millions of rupees. In the last decade due to deterioration of environmental conditions and large-scale deforestation the frequency and intensity of landslides have tremendously increased. The landslides themselves causing immense lose to property and life also initiate other types of disaster, i.e. floods in rivers. The rock debris generated by movement of land mass in some of the cases may block the river flow for considerable longer periods by constructing natural check dams. If these dams survive for longer duration, sufficient water is stored and breaching of the dam may cause tremendous loss in the down stream areas. Historical evidences suggest that in the past various Himalayan regions have experienced such devastating floods causing immense loss to life and property. Alaknanda river, a tributary of Ganga and originating from Satopant and Bhagirathi Kharak glaciers in the past has experienced such floods very frequently.

Beside Himalayas the other hilly terrains of peninsular India also face the trauma of landslides. The Eastern and Western Ghat hills are also equally affected by the natural calamity of floods, landslides and rockfalls. Areas near to Godawari and its tributaries very frequently experience landslide and rockfalls. Floods are a very common phenomenon in the Godawari valley. The areas nearing the river have observed devastating floods during 1886, 1900, 1907,1953 and recently in 1986. During the latest flood in 1986 the water level of Godawari rose 22 feet high affecting lakhs of people from more than 700 villages. The floods claimed nearly 80 human lives and killed thousands of cattle.

During May 1990 Vadera area near Visakhapatnam in Andhra Pradesh was affected by heavy landslide and flood due to continuous heavy rainfall for three days. This catastrophic event affected large chunk of habitation effecting around 2000 villages. Nearly sixteen people were killed and 2500 houses completely and 10,000 partially damaged.

Along with Eastern Ghats, the Western Ghats area are also frequently affected by these catastrophic events. Landslides, flash floods etc. are very common in Nilgiris of Western Ghats. As the land forming the peninsular India is geologically more stable compared to the Himalayan region, the major reasons for these catastrophic events are man made or induced due to human interference in exploiting the nature.

During the last few decades a large-scale deforestation has been carried out in these regions. As per an estimate in East Godawari alone more than 10,0000 hectares forest has been cleared for various purposes. Road construction and developmental activities are major causes for environmental degradation and consequent increase in intensity of natural disasters.

Seismically whole of the Himalayan region is very active and falls in zone IV and V. In the Himalayan region the largest number of epicenter are located near two major tectonic features, i.e. Main Boundary Thrust and Main Central Thrust. Besides these two, other smaller features, i.e. transverse faults are also loci of most of the earthquakes in the region. The major earthquake in Himalayan belt are shown in Table 2.1.

Table 2.1 : Himalayan belt earthquakes.

Year	Richter Scale	Focal Depth (km)	Locality
1720	–	–	Delhi
15 July, 1803	–	–	Mathura, Badarinath
6 June, 1828	–	–	Srinagar
30 May, 1885	–	–	Badgam, Kashmir
12 June, 1897	8.7	18-25	Meghalaya
4 Apr., 1905	8.6	44–100	Kangra, H.P.
12 Dec. , 1908	7.5	–	Northern Burma
28 Aug., 1916	7.5	–	Bajang, N.W. Nepal
8 July, 1918	7.6	21–25	Srimangal, Bangladesh
4July, 1930	7.1	25–32	Dbubri, Assam
15 Jan., 1934	8.4	39–79	North Bihar
30 May, 1935	7.6	–	Quetta, Pakistan
20 Oct., 1937	–	–	Dehradun, U.P.
7 Nov., 1937	–	–	Srinagar, Kashmir
23 Oct., 1943	7.2	–	NE Assam
27 Nov., 1945	–	–	Makran, Pakistan
10 July, 1947	–	–	Bhadarwah, Jammu
29 July, 1947	7.9	–	NE Assam
15 Aug., 1950	8.7	28–50	Eastern Arunachal
18 Feb., 1955	–	–	Quetta, Pakistan
29 Sep., 1960	6.0	30–40	Delhi
12 Jan., 1965	6.1	–	Central Nepal
27 June, 1966	6.0	–	Dharchula-Bajang
29 Sep., 1973	7.1	–	NE Assam
19 Jan., 1975	6.8	18–22	Kinnaur, H.P.
31 Dec., 1984	5.4	5	Kachar, Assam
20 Oct., 1991	6.6	–	Uttarkashi, Uttranchal
29 Mar., 1999	6.8	–	Chamoli, Uttranchal

As mentioned earlier the main cause of the earthquake in Himalayan region is the movement of Indo-Australian plate towards north. However, the recent investigation reveals that the storage of water in dams may also increase the seismicity of the area.

The distribution of epicenters in Himalayan region shows maximum density in north-eastern part, which is probably due to under thrusting of Indo-Australian plate below the Burma-Andaman-Indonesia plate (Valdiya, 1984). The second highest concentration of earthquake epicenters is observed in the north-western region is due to movement along one major fault, i.e. Chaman fault. The rate of displacement along this fault has been of the order of 2 centimetre per year during the last 1 lakh year (Lawrence and Yeats, 1979). Though the outer part of Himalaya shows less frequency of epicenters, yet the magnitude of earthquake events is very high. The Kashmir valley, Doda area in Jammu, Kinnaur, Ladakh, Dharchula near Indo-Nepal border, Central Nepal, Central Bhutan, selected portion of Arunchal Pradesh etc. are some of the high seismic zones of outer Himalayan range. In most of the cases the major cause behind higher seismicity is the presence of many transverse and active faults along which movement of rocks is taking place.

Besides landslides and earthquakes, floods and flash floods are other natural calamities in hill areas which cause a lot of damage. In Western and Central Himalayas, the causes of floods are associated with landslides, which block the river flow and build natural temporary barriers. The breach of such dams cause devastating floods in the down stream regions. The major cause of floods in Himalayan region is the increase of soil erosion and sediment deposition in river channels, shallowing them and reducing their water carrying capacity. Due to some natural and other human induced activities the soil erosion by Himalayan rivers is higher in comparison to other rivers of the world. Annual sediment load of three major Himalayan river systems is given in Table 2.2.

Table 2.2 : Himalayan River System : Annual Sediment Load

River System	Annual load (mt/year)			Erosion Rate in catchment (t/sq.km/yr.)
	Dissolved	Suspended	Total	
Ganga	84	329	413	549
Yamuna	17	125	142	392
Brahmaputra	51	597	648	953

(After Subramaniam, 1987)

Among the various river systems, the Brahmaputra is the most floods prone. Flood is a common hazard in Brahmaputra valley causing large-scale devastation and adverse impact on socio-economic setup of the region. Due to this river around 45 per cent of Assam state is prone to floods. The main reason of flood in Brahmaputra river system had been large scale deforestation in the north-eastern hill states. The region endowed with rich forest wealth covering 163.799 sq.km. has shown a gradual forest loss during the last few decades. As per the State Forest Report, 1999 of Forest Survey of India, the total forest loss in North-Eastern region during the period 1991 to 1999 has been of 2012 sq.km. Statewise forest cover along with the changes during the past five assessment years is shown in Table 2.3.

This immense forest loss and degradation of dense forest has made the north-eastern area very fragile and prone to erosion. The heavy rain in the region has resulted into large scale soil erosion and its subsequent deposition in river channels resulting aggressive floods.

Table 2.3: Changes in forest cover of North-Eastern States (State of Forest Report, 1999)

States	Forest cover (1999 assessment)	Change during different assessments			
		1991–93	1993–95	1995–97	1997–99
Arunachal Pradesh	68,847	–96	–40	–19	+245
Assam	23,688	–243	–447	–237	–136
Manipur	17,384	–64	–63	–140	–34
Meghalaya	15,633	–106	–55	–57	–24
Mizoram	18,338	–156	–121	+199	–437
Nagaland	14,164	+27	–57	–70	–57
Tripura	5,745	+3	0	+8	+199
Total	**163,799**	**–635**	**–783**	**–316**	**–278**

The major flood in northern Ganga plane in North India is due to Himalayan rivers. Ganga and Yamuna river systems due to huge amount of sediments eroded from the hills have shallowed and it has reduced their water carrying capacity resulting into heavy floods in plane areas. Flash floods, forest fires, snow avalanches etc. are other catastrophic events, which have affected the hill areas of the country.

From the above discussion it is clear that both natural and human induced reasons are responsible for present poor state of hill regions in the country. The unscientific development in the hills has resulted into large-scale devastation. At the present state of devastation it is feared that if adequate preventive measures are not taken up immediately, many regions in the Himalayan belt may turn into desert in the near future.

Considering the magnitude of the problem it is required that necessary disaster management plans need to be formulated and implemented in hill areas on a priority. The first step in this regard is to carry out detailed geo-environmental studies for the hill regions. The study should include the assessment of various parameters, i.e. geology, lithology, physiography, structures, water resources, land use pattern, fauna and flora, mining, road and other development structures, agriculture practices and details of natural hazards. Relevant information generated scientifically will be of immense use while preparing disaster management plan for hill areas. The other important aspects which are to be given due consideration is linking of development with disaster management. It is of utmost importance that the development process in hill areas should give due importance to improve environment quality and disaster reduction. It will be quite reasonable and cost effective if the current developmental programmes being run by various departments and ministries are slightly modified or tailored in such a way so that they along with traditional development practices also take care of disaster management.

3

UTTRANCHAL
At a Glance

GENERAL

The general physiography of a region forms a base for its planning and development. Thorough knowledge of both physical and economic aspects becomes more crucial, while dealing with fragile and unstable regions like Himalaya. Uttranchal due to abrupt diversity in topography, climate, vegetation, life and culture, etc. depicts very complex and varied characteristics. This diversity of the region has made it very rich in physical, natural and cultural heritage.

Uttranchal is a new state carved out of Uttar Pradesh and consists of 13 districts. Lying between latitudes 28° 44′ and 31°25′ and longitudes 77°45′ and 81° 1′E, the State encompasses an area of 53,179 sq. kms and supports a population of 70,50,634 (1991 census).* Comprising mostly of hilly regions, the State in the North is bordered by Indo-Tibet water parting with Southern boundary of districts, namely, Saharanpur, Muzaffarnagar, Bijnaur, Muradabad, Rampur, Bareilli, and Pilibhit. In the West bounded by the rivers Tons and Pabber, the State extends further upto river Sharda (Kali) in the East.

Administratively, the State consists of two divisions, viz. Kumaun and Garhwal which are further divided into 7 and 6 districts respectively (Fig. 3.1). The thirteen districts of state comprise 95 developmental blocks which have 73 small and big towns and 16,583 revenue villages.

---

* As per provisional data of 2001 Census, the population of Uttranchal is 84,79,562.

General data on the State :

S. No.	Item	Details
1.	Geographical area	53485 sq. kms.
2.	Population	7.05 million (1991 Census)*
	(a) Male	3.641 million
	(b) Female	3.409 million
	(c) Rural	5.416 million
	(d) Urban	1.634 million
	(Rural and urban population ratio 76.83 : 23.17 per cent)	
3.	Administrative units (1999)	
	(a) Districts	13
	(b) Tehsils	49
	(c) Towns	73
	(d) Blocks	95
	(e) Nyay Panchayats	673
	(f) Gram Sabhas	6561
	(h) Revenue villages	16583

PHYSIOGRAPHY

The Uttranchal has distinct and varied physical features, varying from fertile Terai plain land along southern most part to very high snow covered hilly region in North, Uttranchal State comprises of five latitudinal zones with ill defined boundary line i.e. the Terai–Bhabar, the Shiwaliks, the Lower Himalaya, the Higher Himalaya and the Trans-Himalaya (Fig. 3.2). Consequently these five geomorphic regions represent five geological zones also and are demarcated by four major thrust planes, i.e. Himalayan Frontal Thrust, Main Boundary Thrust, Main Central Thrust and Trans-Himalaya Thrust (Pant, 1995).

The Terai – Bhabar Belt

The Bhabar belt of Uttranchal represented by a narrow belt of fertile land is today one of the most developed parts of the country. This land of the region once very densely forested has been diverted to agricultural use after independence and is inhabited by migrant population from Pakistan, retired army

* Provisional data of 2001 : Total population – 84,79,562
Male – 43,16,401
Female – 41,63,161

personels and freedom fighters to whom this land was allotted from Government of India as a special case. Once very thickly forested this land is now classified as the most fertile zone of the country.

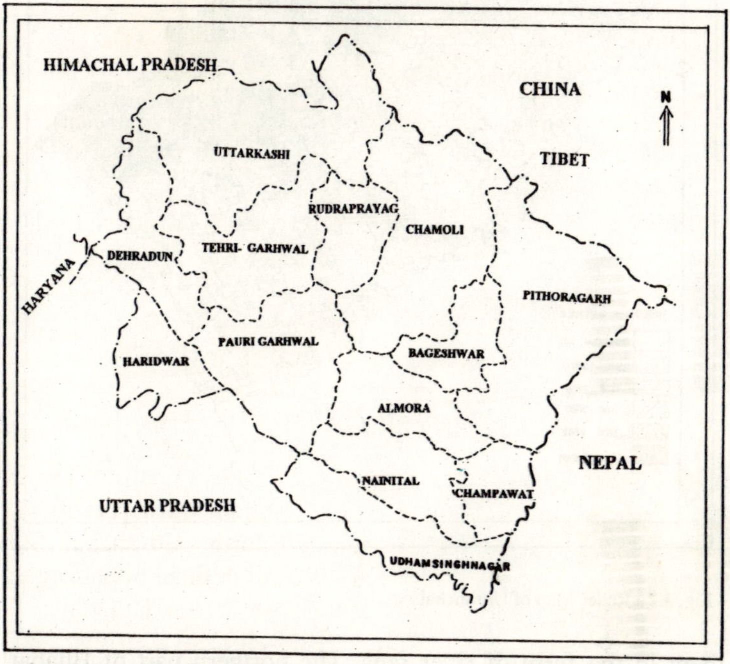

Fig. 3.1 : Map of Uttranchal.

This pocket 10-25 km wide starting in west from Dehradun district extends upto Nainital Terai belt in the east. On a whole, the northern boundary of the region is marked by low lying Shiwalik hillocks, and in south it gradually merges into fertile land of Uttar Pradesh. The Bhabar Terai tract is traversed by various rivers, i.e. Yamuna, Ganga, Ram Ganga, Sharda and their small rivulets. This is the region where these rivers after a long and tiring journey of hills, first time land on the plain which causes a sudden reduction in their speed and load bearing capacity. Due to this reduction in speed and load bearing capacity of rivers, they deposit the heavier loads transported by

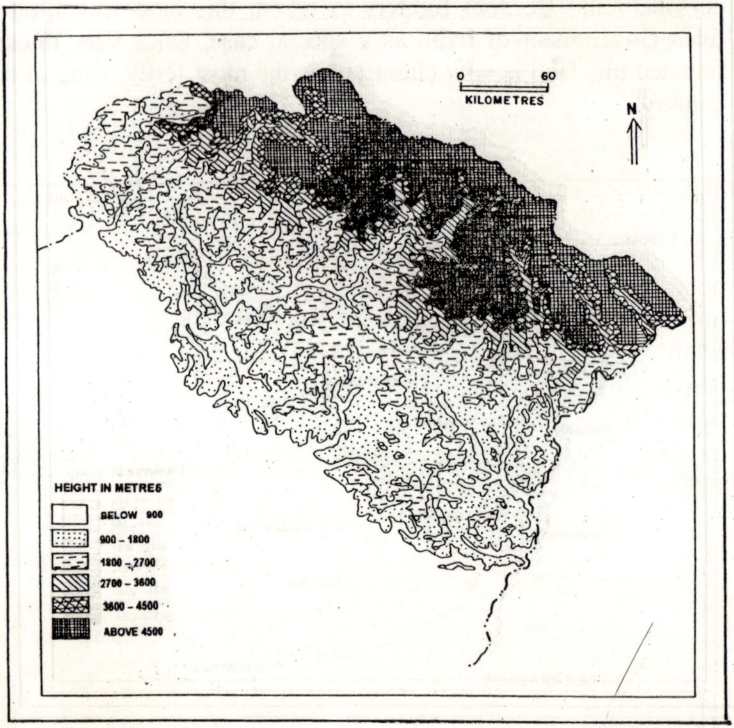

Fig. 3.2 : Relief Map of Uttranchal.

them in the form of river fans. The northern part of Bhabar – Terai belt is marked by many such fans comprising of coarse material up to the size of a big boulder. This makes the region topographically bit rugged in northern part. The southern part of the belt is comparatively plain and comprises of fine grained alluvium deposits.

The Shiwaliks

The northern boundary of Bhabar is marked by low-lying hilly region traversed by almost plain latitudinal areas known as 'doons'. There are five 'doons' in Uttranchal, namely, Dehra, Chaukhamba, Kothari, Patli and Kotaduns from west to east. The hillocks of Shiwalik belt varying from 700 to 1200 meters in height usually comprise of very loose and fragile rocks like sandstone, shale etc. The region is thickly forested and has two major national parks of the country. Due to thick vegetation cover and water scarcity, the area is very sparsely populated.

The Lesser Himalayas

The Lesser Himalayan belt with an average width of 70-75 kms is more massive mountainous tract of different rocks. The area is one of the most densely populated region of Uttranchal and is marked by large number of fertile river valleys and many famous urban centers, i.e. Ranikhet, Almora, Nainital, Lansdowne, Pauri, Sri Nagar, Tehri, Uttarkashi, Chamba, Mussoorie, Gopeshwar, Joshimath etc. Due to availability of water resources and tolerable climate, the area has to face the explosive population pressure which has adversely affected the environment of the region. Deforestation, forest fires, landslides, gully and soil erosion, floods etc. are the major outcome of this environmental degradation in the area.

The Higher Himalayas

The northern boundary of Lesser Himalayan Belt is marked by sudden altitudinal changes in the mountainous ranges. The belt with a width varying between 30-50 kms is marked by very high snow covered peaks (5000 m to more than 7000 m.). Some important peaks of the region include Bander Punch (6815 m), Gangotri (6615 m), Kedarnath (9940 m), Chaukhamba (7318 m), Kamet (7756 m) and Nandadevi (7815 m). The area is further marked by various important glaciers, forming permanent source of water for various river systems. They are Pindari, Milani, Gangotri and Khateling. To summarise, the area is marked by extensive glaciers, snow covered highly elevated sharp peaks and ridges, deep river gorges and snow bound moraines consisting of huge boulders and other transported material.

Trans Himalayas

The northern extreme Uttranchal consisting of Trans Himalayan mountain ranges is a rain shadow zone. This area bordering Tibet, due to its extreme climatic condition and very low rainfall, is very thinly populated.

DRAINAGE PATTERN

Due to its water bearing rivers and rivulets, Uttranchal is of very strategic importance for the country. These rivers form main water source for whole of the northern India. Yamuna, Ganga and Kali rivers and their subsidiaries drain the state (Fig. 3.3). Yamuna, originating from Yamunotri and Saptrishi kund flowing through Uttrakashi and Dehradum forms one important water source for major towns like Delhi, Agra, Bulandshahr, Faridabad and some portion of Haryana. Tons is the other major water bearing river system of the State. Ganga forms the main river system of Uttranchal and its two major tributaries, i.e. the Bhagirathi and the Alaknanda originate from Chaukhamba peaks. Alaknanda is the main river of Ganga system and has its origin from Devtal (Alakpuri Glacier). Flowing in the form of very small water body, Alaknanda increases in size with confluence of many rivers, i.e. Saraswati, Dhauliganga, Girthi Ganga and Rishi Ganga. The other important tributaries of Alaknanda are Birhi Ganga, Mandakini, Pinder and Mandakini etc.

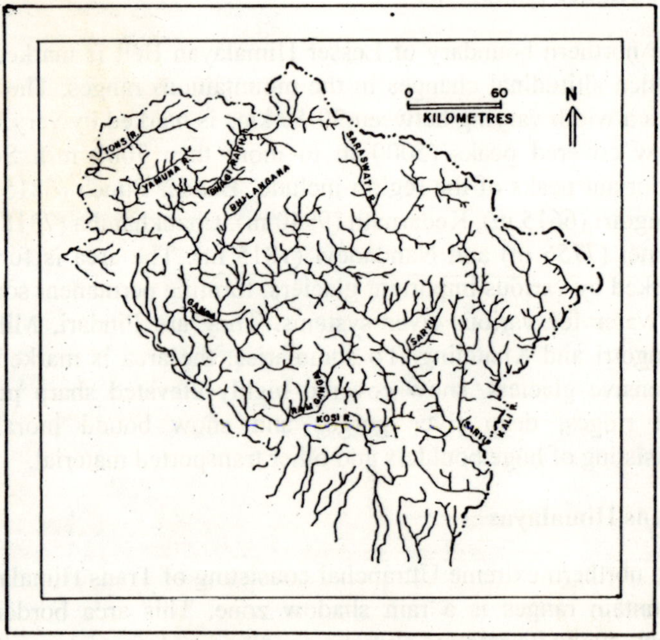

Fig. 3.3 : Drainage pattern in Uttranchal.

The other subsystem of Ganga, i.e. Bhagirathi originates from Gaumukh, which meets another river Jahanvi near Bhaironghati. The Bhagirathi in the initial stage flows almost in north-south direction upto Maheri and then suddenly changes its flows in east-west direction upto Dunda and then from Dunda upto Devprayag it flows in north-west, south-east direction. The major tributary of Bhagirathi, i.e. Bhilangana origins from the confluence of Khatling-Phatling glaciers and joins it at Tehri. Nayar, another major tributary of the Ganga draining Dudhatoli–Pauri Ridge joins it from the west. Ramaganga is one other major river system flowing almost in central part of Uttranchal. The upper tributaries of Ramaganga originate from Chorkhal-dhar and Khamkarkhet ridges of Dudhatoli ranges. Flowing through the districts of Almora and Garhwal, the Ramganga meets Mandal and Palain in the way and enters the Bhabar region at Kalagarh.

In the Kumaon region of Uttranchal, the longest river system prevailing is Kali river system. The river originating from Kalapani near Lipulekh pass meets its main tributaries Kuti, Dhauli, Gauri, Saryu, Lohawati and Ladhiya. Flowing through Pithoragarh district the Kali river descends in plain and is termed as Sarda river.

Other Water Resources

Along with above-mentioned river systems, the area is characterized by many other sources of water, i.e. glaciers, hot springs and lakes. Yamunotri, Badrinath, Tapovan, Gaurikund, Madhyamaheshwar etc. are the famous hot water springs in which water temperature varies from 50 to 80°C. Satopanth, Lokpal Kund, Roop Kund, Hemkund, Rasuki Tal, Chaurabari Tal, Beni Tal, Dumari Tal, Nainital etc. are the major natural lakes of Uttranchal.

Geological and many geomorphologic evidences strongly indicate that during the Ice Age, most of the Uttranchal region was covered under snow. The present glaciers, present on northern peaks are remnants of the past gigantic glacier of the Ice Age. The important glaciers of Uttranchal are Gangotri, Kedarnath, Chaurabari, Satopanth, Kosa, Raikana, Mana, Bamini, Nandadevi, Khatling, Pindari, etc.

CLIMATIC FEATURES

Climatically, the Uttranchal state depicts major contrast, starting from very hot humid climate in Terai-Bhabar belt, the climate varies upto very cold alpine (freezing point) in the northern most part. Elevations, slope aspects, proximity of glaciers, forests etc. are the various factors that influence the climate of the region in Uttranchal. These factors make the climatic pattern very complex. Depending upon these factors, the climate conditions vary from valley to valley and from one side of mountain to another side.

The Terai Bhabar region of the State has very hot and humid climate. The mean temperature during the winter in this belt is around 20°C and in summer it crosses 40°C. The average temperature generally decreases with altitude. Subtropical between 800-1200 m, temperate from 1200 to 2000 m, cool temperature between 2000 and 2400 m, between 2400 and 3000m elevation cold temperate and above 3000m it is very cold freezing alpine climate.

Monsoon in the region commences around in the last week of June and remains upto the end of September. The annual rainfall rate shows extensive variation from east to west and from north to south. Average annual rainfall is about 150 cm in the Bhabar–Terai belt. It generally shows a decreasing trend towards north. The Lesser Himalayan region receives annual rainfall of around 90 cms.

Nainital is one of the most rainfed region where annual rainfall reaches upto 250 cms. From January to March, the highest peaks of Uttranchal receive heavy to medium snowfall which affects the climate of whole State and even the plains of Uttar Pradesh, Delhi and Haryana.

NATURAL VEGETATION / FOREST COVER

Uttranchal is a forest dominated state. As per the Forest Department report published (Uttranchal State Forest Statistics – 2000), 64.81 per cent of the total geographical area of the state is covered under forests, which forms an enormous wealth of the state (Table 3.1). The rich forest cover have variety of forest species. Soil, rock type, relief and climate aspects, attitude etc. are the main factors controlling the vegetation type in different regions of the State. The total forest cover of the State is 34661.52 sq. km. This forest as per the legal status belongs to 7 major categories (Fig. 3.4).

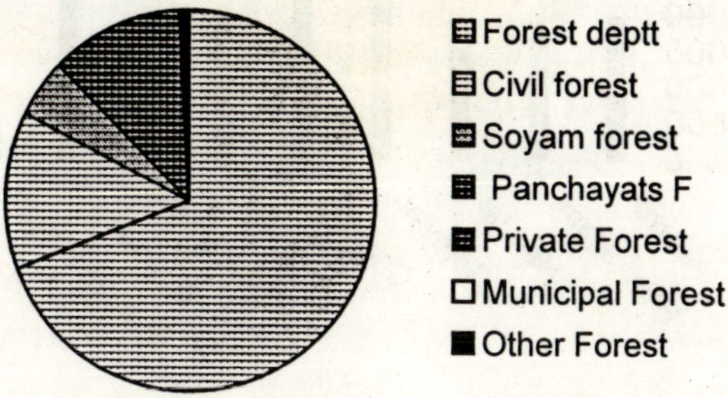

Fig 3.4 : Legal status of Forest in Uttranchal

(a) Forest managed by Forest department - 23988.76 sq. km.
(b) Civil forest under Revenue department - 4585.88 „
(c) Soyam forest under Revenue department- 1749.17 „
(d) Forest under Panchayats - 4046.58 „
(e) Private Forest - 62.36 „
(f) Municipal and Cantonment forest - 59.57 „
(g) Other Forest - 169.20 „
Total - **34661.52** „

Table 3.1: Districtwise distribution of various major categories of forest (Area in sq.km.)

S. No	District	Area under Forest Department			Other forest area		
		Total	Reserved forest	Area under civil and soyam forests	Panchayati forests	Private cantonment municipal and other Forest	Total forest area
1	Almora	1471.97	1471.97	1244.24	1204.75	18.73	3939.69
2	Pithoragarh	1377.98	1377.98	831.47	1092.98	1.07	3303.50
3	Nainital	2625.07	2594.80	112.83	286.84	0	3024.74
4	Garhwal	2393.80	2375.89	1450.87	651.53	16.46	4512.66
5	Chamoli	3639.13	3639.13	946.47	618.02	6.78	5210.40
6	Tehri	2781.16	2781.16	1261.36	16.38	0	4058.90
7	Dehradun	1512.94	1460.75	417.72	98.28	87.97	2116.91
8	Uttarkashi	6800.41	6783.96	70.09	77.80	160.12	7108.42
9	Udhamsingh nagar	1011.11	1010.55	0	0	0	1011.11
10	Haridwar	375.19	330.68	0	0	0	375.19
	Total	**23988.76**	**23826.87**	**6335.05**	**4046.58**	**291.13**	**34661.52**

Source : Forest Department, Uttranchal Pradesh.

Note : Figures of Bageshwar, Champawat and Rudraprayag districts are included in their parent districts.

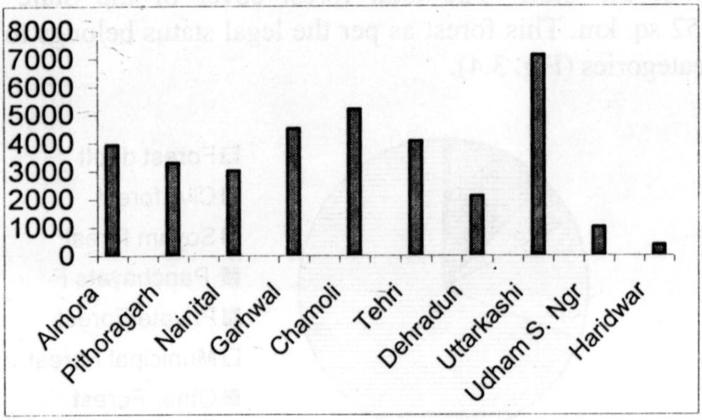

Fig. 3.5 : Total Districtwise Forest Cover of Uttranchal (Area in Sq. km).

The major portion of the forest is under the control of forest department (69.20 per cent). On the basis of most widely used classification of Champion and Seth the forest distribution in the State is as follows (Table 3.2):

Table 3.2 : Various types of forest cover (Under Forest Department) in Uttranchal

S. No.	Type of Forest	Forest Area (Ha)
1.	Tropical moist deciduous forests	309918.00
2	Riveraine and swampy forests	652.00
3	Tropical dry deciduous forests	94053.00
4	Tropical thorn forests	158.00
5	Subtropical Chir-pine forests	448348.00
6	Himalayan dry temperate forests	6132.00
7	Himalayan moist temperate forests	537381.00
8	Subalpine forests	29172.00
9	Moist alpine scrub forests	107510.00
10	Dry alpine scrub	7862.00
11	Others	0
A	Barren, snow covered, rocky and unutilisable land	542536.00
B	Plantation and unclassified forest area	315154.00
	Total	**2398876.00**

Source : Forest Department, Uttranchal Pradesh

The major species found in the forests are - Sal, Teak, Sissoo, Eucalyptus, Chir Pine, Catechu, Deodar, Blue pine, Fir and Spruce, Oak and other miscellaneous species. The specieswise classification of forest area, managed by Forest department is as follows (Table 3.3) :

Table 3.3: Specieswise forest distribution

S. No.	Species	Area (Ha)	Percentage
1	Sal	256367	10.7
2	Teak	21625	0.9
3	Sissoo	24726	1.0
4	Eucalyptus	39907	1.7
5	Catechu	11192	0.5
6	Chir pine	412166	17.2
7	Deodar	24675	1.0
8	Blue pine	17534	0.7
9	Fir and Spruce	96921	4.0
10	Cypress	5242	0.2
11	Oak	217874	9.1
12	Miscellaneous / mixed	735440	30.7
13	Unproductive, barren etc.	535207	22.3
	Total	**2398876**	**100.0**

Source : Forest Department, Uttranchal Pradesh

Wildlife of Uttranchal

Along with forest, the state is very rich in wildlife species also. There are 6 National Parks and 6 wild life sanctuaries in the state. Their location, area and year of establishment is given in Table 3.4.

Table 3.4 : National Parks and Wild Life Sanctuaries (W.L.S.) of Uttranchal

S. No	Name	Year of establishment	Area in Sq. Km	Location (District)
A	**National Park**			
1	Corbett National Park	1936	521	Garhwal, Nainital
2	Nandadevi National Park	1982	630	Chamoli
3	Valley of Flowers N. Park	1982	87	Chamoli
4	Rajaji National Park	1983	820	Haridwar, Dehradun, Garhwal
5	Gangotri National Park	1989	1553	Uttarkashi
6	Govind National Park	1990	472	Uttarkashi
	Total		**4083**	
B	**Wildlife Sanctuaries**			
1	Mussoorie W.L.S.	1993	11	Dehradun

(Contd.)

Table 3.4 (Contd.)

S. No	Name	Year of establishment	Area in Sq. Km	Location (District)
2	Kedarnath W.L.S.	1972	957	Chamoli
3	Govind W.L.S.	1955	481	Uttarkashi
4	Askot W.L.S.	1986	600	Pithoragarh
5	Sona nadi W.L.S.	1987	301	Garhwal
6	Binsar W.L.S.	1988	46	Almora
	Total		**2396**	

Source : Forest Department, Uttranchal Pradesh

POPULATION DISTRIBUTION

Due to diverse ecological and environmental condition, the population distribution and land use pattern is very uneven in Uttranchal. The population of Uttranchal is mostly concentrated in Terai Bhabar belt and doons. Haridwar, Dehradun and Udhamsingh Nagar are the districts with population more than one million.

The districtwise population as per 1991 census is given in following table:

Table 3.5 : Districtwise population distribution*

S. No.	Name of district	Population (91 Census)	Decadal growth rate (1981-91)
1	Dehradun	1025679	34.64
2	Tehri	500689	16.46
3	Uttarkashi	239709	23.65
4	Pauri	682535	6.90
5	Rudraprayag	179339	25.00
6	Chamoli	354999	25.00
7	Udhamsingh Nagar	1009950	35.44
8	Nainital	510542	35.44
9	Almora	607920	10.57
10	Bagheswar	228697	10.57
11	Pithoragarh	416496	15.75
12	Champawat	169594	15.75
13	Haridwar	1124488	26.80
	TOTAL	**7050637**	

(Growth rate of newly created district is not available, hence the growth rate of old districts are shown here.)

* On the basis of data provided from Uttranchal Resident Commissioner Office.

More than 83 per cent population of Uttranchal lives in small villages having population of 500 or less, there are 11 doons having population more than 5000.

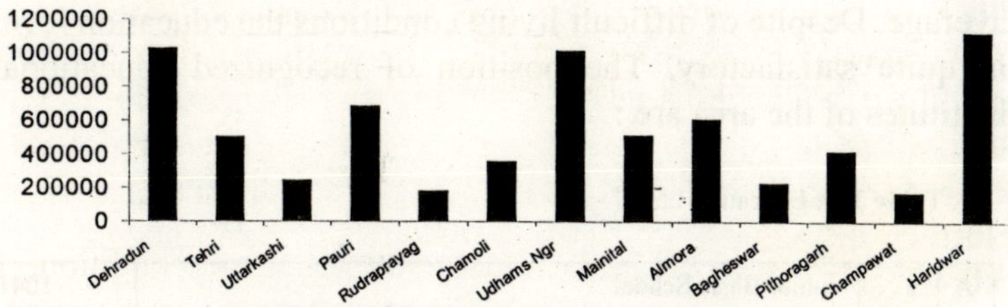

Fig. 3.6 : Districtwise population of Uttranchal (1991 census).

The classification of habitat villages according to population in Uttranchal is as follows :*

a	Less than 200	8084	51.59 per cent
b	200-499	5029	32.09 per cent
c	500-999	1631	10.40 per cent
d	1000-1499	435	2.79 per cent
e	1500-1999	199	1.27 per cent
f	2000-4999	250	1.59 per cent
g	Above 5000	41	0.26 per cent

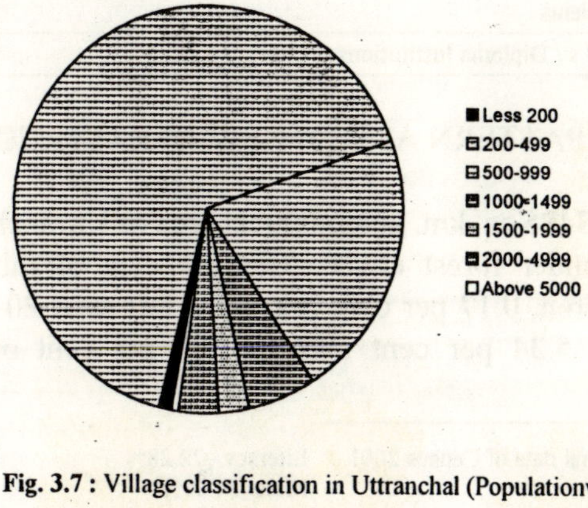

Fig. 3.7 : Village classification in Uttranchal (Populationwise)

* On the basis of data provided from Uttranchal Resident Commissioner Office.

Out of total population of 70.50 lakhs 17.49 per cent are Scheduled Caste and 3.00 per cent are Tribal population. The rural, urban ratio is 76.83 per cent : 23.17 per cent. As far as literacy is concerned, only 57.8 per cent population is literate.# In rural areas more than 50 per cent population is literate on average. Despite of difficult living conditions the education level in quite satisfactory. The position of recognized educational institutes of the area are :

Table 3.6 : Education Level*

A	a	Junior Basic School	10411
	B	Teachers	26204
	c	Student Boys	531302
	d	Student Girls	419302
B	a	Senior Basic School	2242
	b	Teachers	10058
	c	Student Boys	252280
	d	Student Girls	165710
C	a	Higher Secondary School	1329
	b	Teachers	20545
	c	Student Boys	210170
	d	Student Girls	211910
D	a	Degree College	42
	b	Teachers	1338
	c	Students	66133
E	a	I.T.I.s / Diploma Institutions	81

LAND USE PATTERN AND OTHER INFRASTRUCTURES

Out of total 53485 sq. km. geographical area of Uttranchal, 62.30 per cent is under forest cover. 5.73 per cent of this land is cultivable barren, 0.17 per cent is current fallow, 1.20 per cent other fallow, 5.34 per cent barren, 3.02 per cent other land

As per provisional data of Census 2001 Literacy –72.28%
Male- 84.01%
Female – 60.26%

* On the basis of data provided from Uttranchal Resident Commissioner Office.

additional to cultivable, 4.12 per cent is pasture and 3.93 per cent under orchard and other trees. The total sown area in Uttranchal is only 14.18 per cent of the total geographical area of the State.

The number and area of operational land holding as per 1991 census are as follows* :

S. No	Holding	Number	% of Total holding	Area (Ha)	% of Total Area
a	0.02 to 0.50 Hec	414626	48.60	96140	11.54
b	0.50 to 1.00 Hec	183515	21.51	127881	15.36
c	1.00 to 2.00 Hec	145846	17.07	203160	24.29
d	2.00 to 4.00 Hec	81269	9.53	221198	28.58
e	4.00 to 10.00 Hec	25978	3.04	144516	17.35
f	Above 10 Hec	2096	0.25	39989	4.80
	Total area of land holding	853132	100.00	832894	100.00

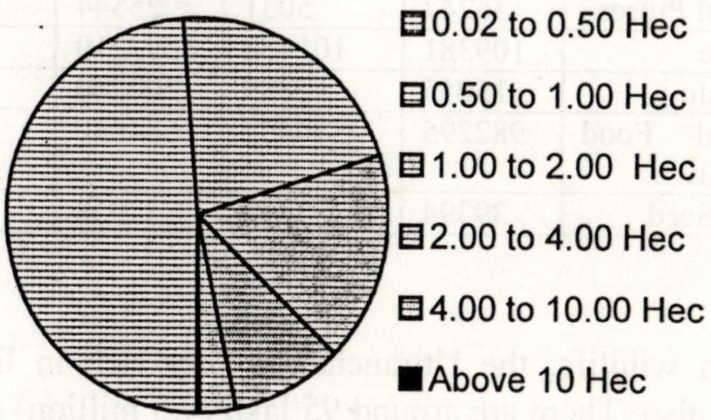

Fig. 3.8: Operational Land holding in Uttranchal (1991 census).

Other relevant data about land use, i.e. irrigated land, chief agriculture and horticulture crops etc. is given below* :

A	Irrigated Area		
	i	Net Irrigated Area	318531 Hec.
	ii	Gross Irrigated Area	519806 Hec.
	iii	Net Irrigated area to Net sown area	56 %

* On the basis of data provided from Uttranchal Resident Commissioner Office.

B	**Irrigated Area By Different Sources (In Hectare)**		
	i	Canal	150506
	ii	Tube well	
	A	Government Tube Well	31532
	B	Private Tube Well	186840
	iii	By well	37336
	iv	By other sources	76879

Chief Crops*

S. No.	Item	Total area (Hec)	Irrigated Area	Production M.T.	Estimated surplus (M.T.)
1	Rice	283769	173516	565012	50362
2	Wheat	388125	194232	747306	232656
3	Maize	29662	738	37320	—
4	Barley	29801	1068	37320	—
5	Sanwa/Bajra	71882	6	87178	—
6	Manduwa	140767	184	183031	—
7	Total Cereal	946048	369596	1659096	—
8	Total Pulses	36247	5031	25544	—
9	Cane	109381	101488	6592219	—
10	Potato	15055	2889	302220	—
11	Total Food Grain	982295	374627	1684640	—
12	Oil Seed	39394	7854	37958	—

Livestock

Along with wildlife, the Uttranchal is very rich in livestock population also. There are around 95 lakh (9.5 million) cattle in the State which form an integral part of the rural economy. The distribution of livestock is given below* :

S. No.	Livestock	No. in '000
1	Cow family	2112
2	Buffaloes	1046
3	Sheep	360
4	Goats	1098
5	Other livestock	4890
	Total	9506

* On the basis of data provided from Uttranchal Resident Commissioner Office.

Other Infrastructures

Other infrastructure available in the State, i.e. Electricity, Industrial work, Transport and Communication facilities, Drinking water facilities etc. are as follows:

A.	**Registered Industrial Unit under the Industrial Act 1948 (1990-1991)***	
i	Registered units	1029
ii	Working units	644
iii	Average working labour per day	54329
iv	Cost of industrial production	Rs. 1451 crore
B. Working Industrial Units (1996-1999) Nos.*		
i	Khadi Industries	4809
ii	Small Industrial Units	9225
iii	Working Person '000 No.	193
C. Industrial Estates		
i	Persons in Employment	4345
ii	Production Cost ('000 Rs.)	74352
Electricity (1997-1998)		
a	Electrified villages	12311
b	Percentage of Electrified villages	78.6%
Transport & Communication (1995-1996)*		
I	**Mattled Road Length**	
A	P.W.D	12708 km
B	Local Bodies Roads	1353
C	Other Department Road	2593
II	**Communication**	
A	Post Offices	2695Nos.
B	Telegraph Centre	543
C	P.C.Os.	5095
D	Telephone	55316

* On the basis of data provided from Uttranchal Resident Commissioner Office.

Animal Husbandry Facilities (1994-1995)*

a)	Veterinary Hospitals	299
b)	Livestock Service Centre	586
c)	Artificial insemination	436
d)	Sheep Development Centre	116
e)	Poultry etc.	845422

Drinking Water Facilities/Problem Village (1996-97)*

(a)	Habitat village	15669
(b)	No. of village where drinking water is available	11940
(c)	Villages with scarcity of water	3729

* On the basis of data provided from Uttranchal Resident Commissioner Office.

4

UTTARANCHAL AND ITS VULNERABILITY

Uttranchal has a very rich natural resource but still it is exposed to many problems which have both natural and man-made origin, hampering the development process in the region. The frequency and intensity of natural disasters in Uttranchal is one of the major problems. Disasters in the form of earthquakes, landslides, flash floods, soil erosion, forest fires etc. have caused tremendous loss to the region and the society. At large the whole region of Uttranchal State, starting from Gangetic plain in south and extending upto high snow covered peaks in north, is one of the most unstable and sensitive zones of the world. This unstability and sensitivity of the region has resulted into many casualties in the area. The statistical data shows that various forms of disasters are very common and frequent in Uttranchal. Though for most of the disasters, the causes are natural, the intensity and impact of these disasters are tremendously increased by many man-made activities. A combination of the factors natural and man-made is responsible for these disasters in Uttranchal.

NATURAL CAUSES

Natural causes for disasters in Uttranchal are deep-rooted within the earth's crust which form the region. It is the natural geological setting of the region which make it very susceptible and prone to disasters. Though the whole of Himalayas is very sensitive and active, Uttranchal due to its complex geological factors is more prone to disasters. This instability of Himalayas can be best understood by "Plate Tectonic Theory", which has already been discussed in Chapter 2. The various tectonic features like thrusts, faults, shear zones etc. are very common in Uttranchal part of Himalayas. The major tectonic features of Himalayas, i.e.

Himalayan Frontal Fault, Main Boundary Thrust, Main Central Thrust and Trans Himalayan Thrust, that are characteristics of this mountain range are very prominent in this part (Fig. 4.1). The ever-increasing pressure of Indo-Australian plate is activating these thrusts and other associated tectonic features. This has made the region very unstable, fragile and prone to natural hazards. The instability of Uttranchal has been further increased by the presence of one more tectonic feature, i.e. Delhi-Haridwar ridge. Geophysical investigations reveal that the Aravalli mountain range starting from Rajasthan is not finishing at Delhi and it extends up to Himalayas. This ridge beyond Delhi is submerged below alluvium and penetrates below the Himalayan rocks. As this ridge is lying on Indo-Australian plate and this plate is moving northward, consequently the Delhi- Haridwar ridge is mounting enormous pressure on Himalayan rocks in Uttranchal.

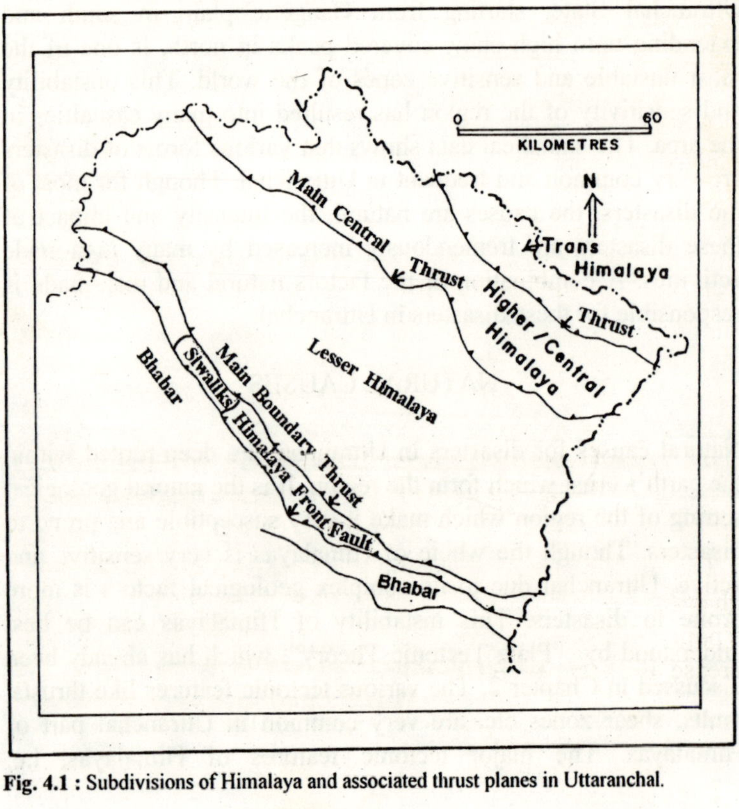

Fig. 4.1 : Subdivisions of Himalaya and associated thrust planes in Uttaranchal.

The collision of these two mountain belts, i.e. Delhi-Haridwar and Himalaya is responsible for making the Uttranchal region more unstable and susceptible to natural hazards. The 1991 earthquake of Uttranchal was also said to be the result of the northward movement of Delhi-Haridwar ridge into the Himalayan range. The geologists believe that any further movement of this ridge may cause serious seismic activities in Uttranchal.

MANMADE CAUSES

As discussed earlier, the basic reason for disasters in Uttranchal is natural due to seismic factors. These natural causes make the region very unstable and fragile. This instability and fragility of the region makes it very susceptible and prone to natural disasters. Slight disturbance in this eco-balance either due to human induced activities or other natural causes result into havoc that leads to disasters. Unscientific development and land use pattern, deforestation, increasing human and cattle population pressure, forest fire etc. have further increased the vulnerability of the region to disasters.

Population Growth

Increasing population pressure in Uttranchal leading to ecological disturbance is the basic reason for making it vulnerable to natural. While comparing with other hilly states of the country, the population density of Uttranchal is the second largest after Tripura. As per 1991 census the population density in Uttranchal is 143 per cent higher than that of Himachal and 173 per cent more than that of Jammu and Kashmir (Table 4.1 and Fig 4.2).

The growth rate of population in Uttranchal has been very high among the hilly states of the country. From 1901 upto 1991, the population of Uttranchal (excluding Haridwar) has shown an increase of 257.6 per cent (Table 4.2).

Table 4.1 : Geographical Area, population and population density of different Himalayan states of the country*

S. No.	States	Area (Sq.Km.)	Population (1991 Census)	Density (Per Sq. Km.)
1	Uttranchal	55485	7050634	132
2	H. P.	55673	5111079	92
3	Sikkim	7096	405505	57
4	Arunachal Pradesh	83143	858392	10
5	Nagaland	16579	1215573	73
6	Manipur	22327	1826714	82
7	Mizoram	21081	686217	33
8	Tripura	10486	2744847	262
9	Meghalaya	22429	1760626	78
10	J & K	222236	7718700	76

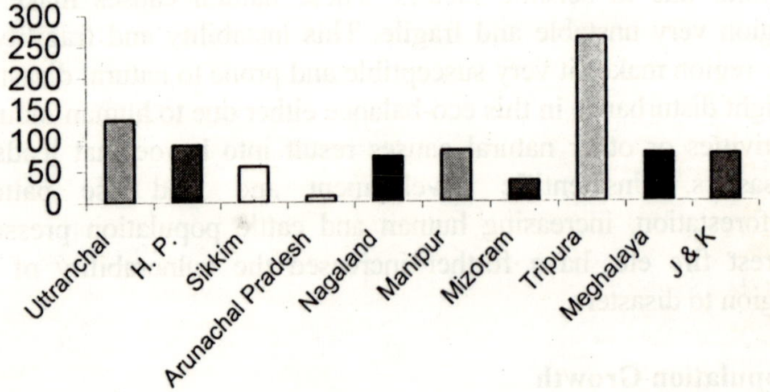

Fig. 4.2: Population density of different Himalayan states of the country

Table 4.2: Population increase/decrease since 1901 in Uttaranchal (excluding Haridwar)

Census year	Population (in lakh)	Percentage increase or decrease	
1901	16	+	-
1911	18	-	11.0
1921	18	+	0.6
1931	19	+	8.3
1941	22	+	13.7
1951	25	+	12.3
1961	31	+	23.3
1971	38	+	23.0
1981	48	+	26.5
1991	59	+	21.5
Growth during 1901-91	(+)43	+	257.6

Source : Anon, 1981a, 1991b and 1991c; Pant, 1996a.

---

* On the basis of data provided from Resident Commissioner Office, Uttranchal

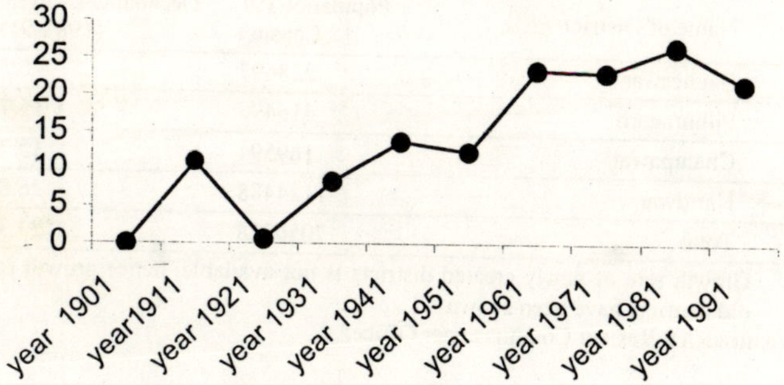

Fig 4.3 : Population percentage increase/decrease of Uttranchal (excluding Haridwar).

The large size of population is restricted to Dehradum, Udhamsingh Nagar, Haridwar and Nainital. The total population of these five districts out of 13 districts of Uttranchal is around 52 per cent of the total population (Table 4.3). This 52 per cent of the state population reside in only 22 per cent of the geographical area of the state. Thus the population density is very uneven in the state. The population is more concentrated in Bhabar-Terai and Lesser Himalayan belt. The growth rate in different districts of the state is also uneven and contrasting (6.9 in Pauri to 35.44 in Nainital/Udhamsingh Nagar). The decadewise growth rate in various districts is elaborated below :

Table 4.3 : Decadal population growth rate of Uttranchal

S. No.	Name of District	Population (91 Census)	Decadal Growth rate (1981-91)*
1	Dehradun	1025679	34.64
2	Tehri	500689	16.46
3	Uttarkashi	239709	23.65
4	Pauri	682535	6.90
5	Rudraprayag	179339	25.00
6	Chamoli	354999	25.00
7	Udhamsingh Nagar	1009950	35.44
8	Nainital	510542	35.44
9	Almora	607920	10.57

(Contd.)

Table 4.3 (Contd.)

S. No.	Name of District	Population (91 Census)	Decadal Growth rate (1981-91)*
10	Bagheswar	228697	10.57
11	Pithoragarh	416496	15.75
12	Champawat	169594	15.75
13	Haridwar	1124488	26.80
	Total	7050728	23.38

- Growth rate of newly created districts is not available, hence growth rate of old districts have been shown.

Source : Uttranchal Resient Commissioner Office.

Note : The growth rate is much more in four Terai-Bhabar Districts (i.e. Dehradun, Nainital, Udhamsingh Nagar and Haridwar) than other districts and region.

The extensive growth in population in Uttranchal has adversely affected the environment in general. This increase in population has increased the demand for jobs subsequently. In search of job opportunities the people are forced to undertake agricultural activities in more sensitive areas, which ultimately leads to disturbance of sensitive ecological regions (Fig. 4.4). The increase in population has also led to more developmental activities, i.e. road, building construction etc. accelerating the factors responsible for disasters in the region.

Unscientific Development

Vulnerability or susceptibility of a region or society to natural hazards is basically the result of the prevailing conditions. The prevailing conditions of a region or society are the consequence of the development pattern. Therefore the development pattern ultimately works as a decisive factor for the vulnerability of a society or region to natural hazards.

The well-known sociologist Enrico Quarantelli (1986) in this regard has rightly quoted "*All disasters are primarily the result of human actions. A disaster is not a physical happening, it is a social event. Disasters are in one sense the manifestation of the vulnerability of a social systems (and) prime attention should be given for doing something about such vulnerabilities*".

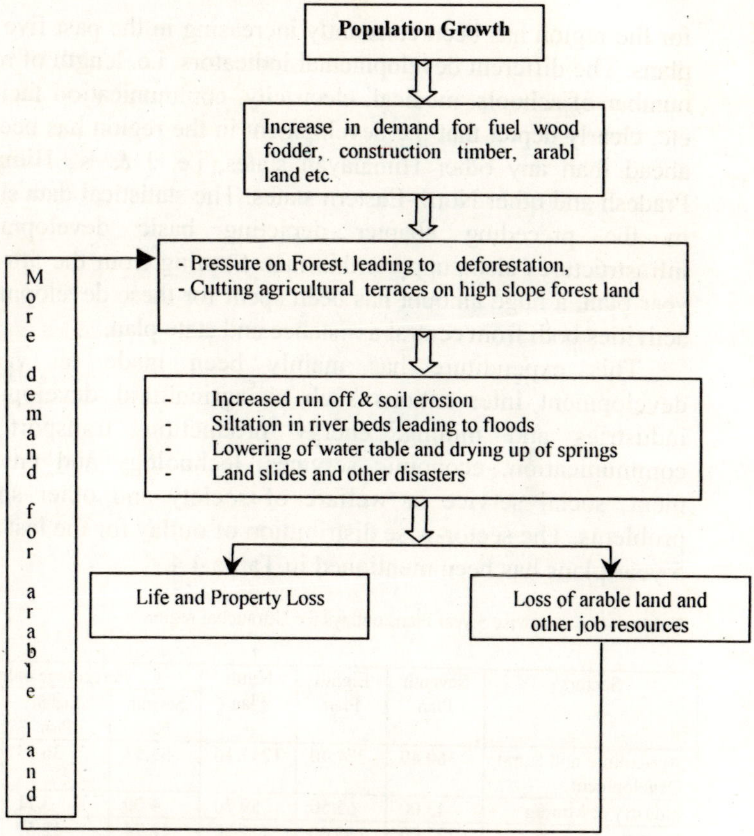

Fig. 4.4: Impact of Population growth on disasters

If seen minutely and critically, development and vulnerability are inextricably linked. As it is the vulnerability that turns a natural hazard into natural disaster, the development and disasters have very close and intimate relationship. It is the nature and kind of development that makes things bad to worst.

This relationship or link between disaster and development is very much visible in Uttranchal. After independence, various activities have been carried out in the region for the sake of development. The green revolution, mining, road/buildings/dam construction etc. are the so-called developmental activities which directly or indirectly affected the vulnerability of the local community and region to natural hazards.

If viewed in term of so called development, Uttranchal does not present a picture of an underdeveloped region. The plan outlay for the region has been constantly increasing in the past five year plans. The different developmental indicators, i.e. length of roads, number of schools, medical, electricity, communication facilities etc. clearly depict that the development in the region has been far ahead than any other Himalayan states, i.e. J & K, Himachal Pradesh and other North-Eastern states. The statistical data shown in the preceding chapter depicting basic developmental infrastructures also supports this fact. Starting from the 5th five-year plan, a huge amount has been spent for these developmental activities both from central assistance and state plan.

This expenditure has mainly been made on various development interventions such as agricultural development, industries and mining, energy production, transport and communication, economic services, technology and environment, social service or welfare of society and other special problems. The sector-wise distribution of outlay for the last three 5 year plans has been mentioned in Table 4.4.

Table 4.4 : Sectorwise 5 year Plans outlays for Uttranchal region

Sectors	Seventh Plan	Eighth Plan	Ninth Plan	Percentage outlay		
				Seventh Plan	Eighth Plan	Ninth Plan
Agriculture and Rural Development	360.49	774.40	1247.16	33.53	36.53	28.15
Industry & Mining	43.00	65.50	59.70	4.00	3.11	1.35
Energy	137.00	265.00	411.00	12.74	12.59	9.28
Transport and Communication	176.00	297.50	1052.00	16.37	14.13	23.75
Economic Services Science, Technology and Environment	22.77	94.08	88.12	2.12	4.46	1.99
Social Services	297.00	488.00	1340.21	27.63	23.18	30.25
Welfare of Labour, Disadvantaged population and Social Security	38.24	119.52	110.30	3.56	5.68	2.49
Special problems	-	-	121.51	-	-	2.74
Total	1075.00	2105.00	4430.00	100.00	100.00	100.00

Source : Ninth Five Year Plan (1997-2002), Uttrakhand Sub-Plan, Uttar Pradesh, Lucknow.

The above data depict that out of total allocation about 62.5 per cent allocation has been for agriculture including rural development, industry, mining, energy transport and communication. It would not be incorrect to state that all these developmental activities in the region have been carried out at the cost of environmental degradation and the vulnerability of the region to hazards. This so called development has extensively damaged the forest, wildlife, the watersheds, drainage patterns, fertility of the soil and in brief has disturbed the already fragile ecological balance of the region. This unscientific development has really increased the vulnerability of the region to natural hazards.

The reason behind this is that during the developmental planning of the region, the need for a exclusive development approach to this region has been ignored keeping in view its geological instability and fragile eco-balance. Instead, in the initial stages the development pattern in the area has been similar to the plain areas of the erstwhile Uttar Pradesh.Though after third plan some specific provisions were made for the region, even then the environmental aspects were almost neglected. This negligence of policy makers and implementers and to some extent the local communities, has made the region more disaster prone and the price is being paid in the form of life and property loss by the local inhabitants of the region even today.

Road Construction

In the hilly terrain, the construction of roads is the main factor disturbing the ecological balance. Along with the stability of the region, it also causes serious damage to drainage pattern (both underground and surface), increases soil erosion and leads to mass movement of the soil and rocks (Fig- 4.5). The problem accelerates further if the road construction is carried out without taking into consideration the geological, geomorphological and ecological aspects. Major destruction due to road construction is the result of ignoring all these aspects. This leads to excavation of steep and unstable slopes, felling of trees, dumping of debris down the slope neglecting the damage to drainage pattern of the area.

In Uttranchal after independence, main emphasis has been given on road construction for better communication (a basic need

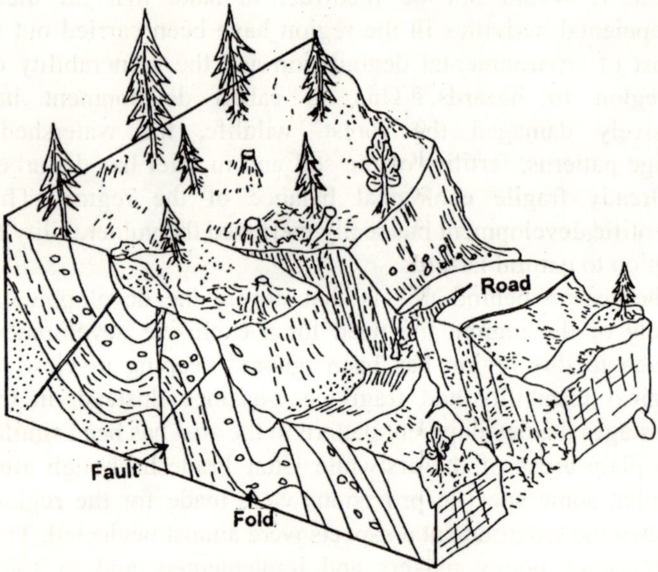

Fig. 4.5 : Road construction in hilly terrain without taking into consideration the geology and geomorphology is very damaging.

for developing an undeveloped region). The construction of roads in Uttranchal accelerated after 1962 Chinese and 1965 Pakistan aggressions in India. For defence purposes, many new roads even upto interior places like Song, Munsiayari, Chirbatiya, Rik-shal, Bungidhar, Gangotri, Salakhet, Thalisain, Gotgarh, Netwar, Patkot, Mandoli, Jaurasi, Arakot, Betalghat, Kunyakhanak, Mandal, Nagachul, Khal etc. were constructed. Total 16,654 km of mattled and 2593 km of non-mattled roads have been constructed or developed in the region. Most of these roads have been made without giving due consideration to the geologi-cal/ecological aspects. The roads leading to Badrinath and Gangotri are the best example of such roads, which have been constructed in very sensitive zones with thrust, faults/shears etc. in proximity. Hence these roads are very frequently affected by various types of mass movement and are prone to severe soil erosion.

Road construction is very damaging in hilly terrain, particularly in sensitive zones like Himalaya. Scientists have estimated the erosion from road sites to be ten times more than from agriculture fields, 200 times more than grass land and 2000 times more than forest cover. The environmentalists on the basis of various researches have revealed that one-kilometre length of road construction requires removal of 60,000 m^3 of debris from the site. If calculated for the entire length of the mattled road of Uttranchal, i.e. PWD 16654 kms (mattled road = 12708, local bodies = 1353 km and other departmental roads = 2593 km) the debris removal for mattled road comes to 16654 x 60000 m^3 = 999240000 m^3. This huge amount of debris removal gives an idea about the damage, the construction of roads has done to the environment and stability of the region. Unfortunately, most of these roads are constructed without giving much consideration to geological, geomorphological and other environmental aspects. Hence their unscientific development has turned the region into a boiling pot. The consequence of this hurriedly taken decision has been evidenced in the form of frequent landslides and tremen-dously increased soil/sediment erosion in the hilly terrain. According to erosion data collected by Swaniston and Swanson (1978) in road areas of USA, the erosion rate of such areas tremendously increases in comparison to forest covered areas (Table 4.5).

Table 4.5 : Erosion data for road and other areas of USA (after Swaniston and Swanson 1978)

Site	Period of Record (Yr)	Area (%)	Number of slides	Erosion rate m^3 Km^3 / Yr	Erosion Rate relative to Forested area
Stequaleho Creek, Olympia Peninsula					
Forest	84	79	25	71.8	1
Clear cut	6	18	0	0	0
Road R/W	6	3	83	11825	X 165
Alder Creek, Western Cascade Range, Oregon					
Forest	25	70.5	7	45.3	1
Clear cut	15	26.0	18	117.1	X 2.6
Road R/W	15	3.5	75	15565	X 344
Selected Drainage, Coast Mountain, SW British Columbia					
Forest	32	88.9	29	11.2	1
Clear cut	32	9.5	18	24.5	X 2.2
Road R/W	32	1.5	11	282.5	X 25.2
H. J. Adrews Experimental Forest, W. Cascade Range, Oregon					
Forest	25	77.5	31	35.9	1
Clear cut	25	19.3	30	132.2	X 3.7
Road R/W	25	3.2	69	1772.0	X 49

The results of road construction are very much obvious in many parts of Uttranchal. The Kaliasor landslide near Srinagar is the most evident example of such endemic phenomena. The frequent landslides (10 medium and small landslides) on Dehradun-Tehri road, creating 500 m^3 of debris and one chronic landslide in every 10 km stretch (Banasal and Mathur, 1976), is another prominent example of such calamities, which are the result of human induced activities. Tanakpur-Tawagthat of Kumao, Pakhi-Gulablobi pilgrim roads etc. in the Ramganga valley are the other roads, where major landslides occur very frequently. These landslides and erosions are the direct consequences of road construction, which cause great loss to environment and stability of the region.

Agricultural Practices

Out of total area of 53,485 sq. km in Uttranchal only 12,61,925 hectares (14.18 per cent) is used for agricultural purposes. This land use is the prime source of livelihood for more than 80 per cent of the total population of the state. Around 85 per cent of the total sown area of Uttranchal is primarily on terraced slope and is rain-fed. Agriculture in this fragile and difficult terrain is neither economic nor eco-friendly. The total production from this land is not even adequate for the whole population of the State. Despite the constraints and hardships in carrying out agriculture in the hilly terrain, the people are forced to depend on it due to non-availability of other livelihood sources. The increasing population pressure, which has forced the people to move to more sensitive and unstable areas on steeper slopes to make agricultural fields, has further deteriorated the situation. This compulsion has further worsened the condition and the vulnerability of the local population to disasters has increased many folds. Carrying out agriculture on steeper slopes has led to serious problems of landslides and soil erosion. The 1998 landslides, which claimed hundreds of lives in Uttranchal, was upto an extent the consequence of such unscientific agricultural practices. In Madhymaheshwar river valley, many villages were blown away by landslides which initiated from the agriculture fields lying on steeper slopes above the villages.

The Agricultural cropping practice which do not have enough resilience and capacity for protection has tremendously increased the soil erosion from the fields hundred times greater. The unscientific ploughing, i.e. parallel to the slope without contour terraces and drainage/ditches has also been responsible for soil erosion and deterioration of land. Due to scarcity of land and increasing population dependent on agriculture, ignoring the old practice of leaving marginal levees on terraces and making drainage has further increased the vulnerability of land to soil erosion. To summarize, the unscientific agriculture practice in Uttranchal and increasing dependence of population for livelihood on agriculture has made the area prone to various forms of disasters.

Deforestation

Vegetation cover serves as a carpet and is very helpful in checking soil erosion. The main benefits of the vegetation are in the form of –

- Foliage intercepting rain drops falling directly on soil,
- Root holding and stabilizing soil on rocky foundation, and
- Decayed vegetation, i.e. humus binding soil aggregates together.

Plate 1 : Deforestation has aggravated to landslide problems many times in Uttranchal.

India in total has 76.50 million-hectare area under forest cover, very diversified and rich in plant and animal species. Despite its richness in variety of fauna and flora, the forest cover in India is very less when compared to its total population. This forest resource has to meet the demand of 1000 million people and 470 million cattle of the country. As such the forest of the country has to meet the need of 16 per cent population of the world with its meagre 1.8 per cent of the total world forest cover. The same forest has also to cater for 19 per cent of total cattle population of the world.

The increasing population (both human and cattle) and its increasing need has put tremendous pressure on natural resources. Forest, the easily accessible natural resource, has been worst-affected due to this increasing pressure. Beside this individual needs of people, i.e. fuel wood, timber, minor forest produces, agriculture land etc., various developmental activities like irrigation and hydro power stations, roads, buildings, mining etc. have also adversely affected the forest cover. Though deforestation has adversely affected almost the whole of the country's ecology and environment, the situation in Uttranachal is bit serious. As per the State Forest Department Report, during last two decades around 26,000 ha. forest land has legally been transferred for various developmental schemes in Uttranchal (Table 4.6 and Fig. 4.6).

Fig. 4.6 : Diversion of forest land for various developmental schemes in Uttranchal *(Area in Hectare).*

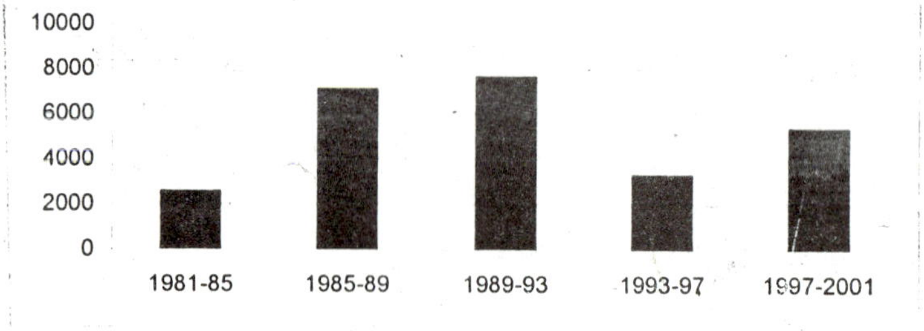

It is worth-mentioning here that the above data literally refer only to legal transfer, other illegal encroachment which is mainly for agriculture, housing and other allied activities is much more as compared to the legal transfer.

Besides this diversion/encroachment, the forest in Uttranchal has suffered tremendous loss due to the forest produce exploitation by human population. Both timber and other minor forest produce extraction have also adversely affected forest of Uttranchal. Along with illicit felling and theft from forest, various forest based industries of Uttranchal and Uttar Pradesh are getting their raw material supply from the forest of the region. Such industries include sugar mills, soap and other chemical factories, paper mills, match industries, katha factories, plywood, sports goods, toys, pencil, packing case industries etc. Besides, some industries are getting their timber and other minor forest produces, i.e. resin, fuel wood, khair bamboo, tendu leaves, grasses and cane from the forests of Uttranchal.

The exploitation of forest by these industries is mainly due to the faulty policies. For example, the sugar mills which easily have other source of fuel, due to meager profit are using wood in their furnaces. In the similar way resins, which have many alternatives, is still being extracted in large quantity from the forest trees, causing much damage to forest cover. The plywood, match and toys industries, which can easily be switched over to other raw materials, are also totally dependent on forest and are equally responsible for its exploitation.

Beside industrial exploitations and diversion of forest land for developmental scheme, illicit felling and forest produce collection by local inhabitants (in the absence of other livelihood source) is also one of the major contributors for reduction in the forest cover. The forest fire (90 per cent human induced) are also responsible for the degradation of forests in Uttranchal. Among the causes mentioned above, forest fire is the most damaging factor in Uttranchal. Along with causing direct economic loss of timber and other forest produce, forest fire has greater negative impact on forest regeneration, soil, ecology and environment of the region.

Thus, the forests of Uttranchal are under tremendous pressure from all directions and as a result are diminishing at an alarming rate. During the last 4-5 decades, the forest cover has

Table 4.6 : Forest land transferred for various developmental projects in Uttranchal during last two decades (Area in hectares)

Year	Irrigation projects	Hydro Power projects	Road construction projects	Communication projects	Mining projects	Drinking water schemes	Other schemes	Total (in ha.)
1981-82	3.5310	–	2.1700	–	–	–	767.92150	773.62250
1982-83	14.0812	–	134.4806	163.8080	–	2.07500	422.90770	737.35250
1983-84	17.4733	85.0000	97.6973	31.5732	2.2000	3.60490	6.65540	244.20410
1984-85	10.7799	0.4800	75.3265	517.0440	2.0000	3.00090	203.65440	812.28570
1985-86	5.9995	–	61.4492	67.7640	–	–	1.96500	137.17770
1986-87	332.3854	1302.5110	210.4734	95.6120	–	4.61780	146.76320	2092.36280
1987-88	6.5200	3050.4306	4.3816	6.1000	–	0.26000	53.10400	3120.79620
1988-89	10.7190	157.2960	1.9250	10.9400	1547.0000	10.10180	29.06750	1767.04930
1989-90	19.4998	6.5600	90.6816	200.5690	4380.2800	23.64230	9.17360	4730.40630
1990-91	6.9200	628.8780	231.3799	202.8300	1513.7390	4.04470	2.76730	2590.55890
1991-92	2.5700	1.9680	7.4819	2.7170	–	3.01050	0.96200	18.70940
1992-93	1.2300	–	17.6158	3.3810	–	2.29440	283.87300	308.39420
1993-94	7.0325	–	102.3404	321.6418	–	7.37310	706.30540	1144.69320
1994-95	1.5150	–	175.1047	819.9718	–	11.14990	6.96300	1014.70440
1995-96	7.3073	0.1235	159.7618	5.8140	–	8.40500	6.01100	187.42260
1996-97	3.2241	449.2308	112.9286	111.9257	258.0000	16.98040	10.63480	962.92440
1997-98	1.3194	–	79.0725	1.6955	44.3400	13.51270	14.32550	154.26560
1998-99	30.7155	–	219.7958	74.4172	–	10.93110	156.00380	491.86340
1999-00	4.4410	9.5668	573.5149	682.2626	2450.5500	11.06730	156.68830	3888.09090
2000-01	0.5500	20.5020	635.7108	7.1340	7.5290	11.95037	162.28791	845.66408
Total	**487.8139**	**5712.5467**	**2993.2923**	**3327.2008**	**10205.6380**	**148.02217**	**3148.03431**	**26022.54818**

Source : Forest Department, Uttranchal Pradesh.

decreased tremendously and due to increasing population pressure per capita forest areas has come down to 0.49 hectare (as per 1991 census).

This diminishing forest cover in the state has destabilized the ecological balance of the region, which was already very sensitive and prone to natural hazards. The obvious negative impact of deforestation hád been on the soil cover. As mentioned earlier, the forest cover play a very significant role in checking soil erosion. Scientific researches have proved that a barren land is many times more susceptive to soil erosion in comparison to land covered with forest. Broad leaf trees like Oak in the forest, intercept the maximum rain water to hit the ground directly. The interception by these broad leaf trees has been measured 34 per cent, while for the needle leaf pine trees it is around 22-27 per cent (Ghosh *et al.,* 1980). The tree leaf litter on the ground also helps in intercepting the rain water. The roots of these trees hold the soil and prevent soil erosion and mass flow.

The deforestation in Uttranchal has extensively increased the soil erosion, which is evident by the frequent landslides, siltation in river and other drainage channels, deterioration of agriculture land etc. The deforestation to a large extent has been responsible for the desertification in some parts of the region. The eroded sediments in the area are filling reservoir and choking the streams. Springs in many parts of the State have dried up or have become seasonal. In the areas east of Nainital 40-45 per cent springs have met this fate (Valdiya, 1987). The floods in hilly region have become a frequently occurring phenomenon. All this has led to drying up of the land and decrease in its fertility. The day is not far that entire crop of fuel wood and fodder will diminish from the State, if the present rate of consumption continues and if alternative arrangements are not made. The invasion of xerophytes plants in some parts of Uttranchal on slopes and river valleys has symbolized the initiation of desertification.

Grazing

India has around 470 million cattle (19 per cent of the total world cattle population), which is directly or indirectly dependent on

76.50 million ha. forest (about 1.8 per cent of the World Forest Cover).

In comparison to other parts of the country, the situation is much more serious in the hilly terrain like Uttranchal, where land is more fragile and susceptible to erosion. In Uttranchal, the total cattle population is around 95 lakhs (forming 2.0 per cent of the country and 0.38 per cent of the total world cattle population). The worst part here is that most of these cattle are directly or indirectly dependent for their fodder or food on the nearby forest (Fig 4.7).

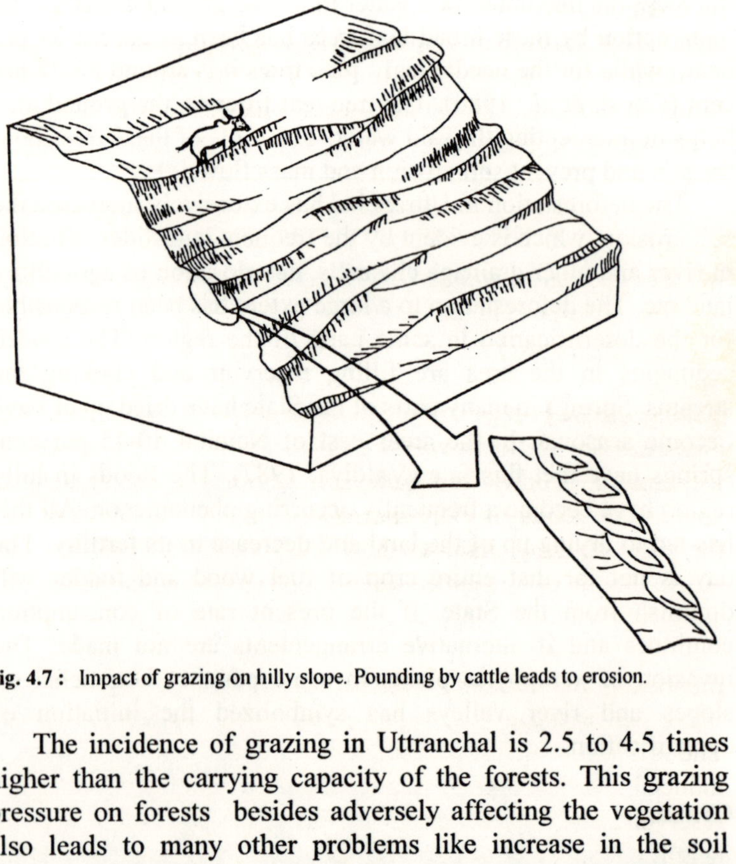

Fig. 4.7 : Impact of grazing on hilly slope. Pounding by cattle leads to erosion.

The incidence of grazing in Uttranchal is 2.5 to 4.5 times higher than the carrying capacity of the forests. This grazing pressure on forests besides adversely affecting the vegetation also leads to many other problems like increase in the soil erosion and landslides, reduction in regeneration, retardation in tree/plant growth, siltation in stream channels and so on. The pounding and troddling by cattle hoofs along with destroying vegetative cover also segregates the soil mantle. The cattle tracks become permanently devoid of grass and vegetation and easily fall prey to gully erosion. This intense grazing ultimately converts the land to desert or initiates desertification which is evident in some parts of Uttranchal.

Dams and Reservoir Construction

Dams or reservoirs are constructed on rivers channels to impound or divert the water for electricity generation, flood control and irrigation. Since dam or reservoir is an artificial structure creating artificial check in the natural flow of the water, its creations considerably affects the ecological balance of the area. This disturbance along with creating environmental degradation of the area also increase its vulnerability to many forms of hazards. The environmental changes, a dam/reservoir creates may be enlisted as :

– The normal flow pattern in equilibrium with the ecosystem is upset.
– The geological and geo-hydrological conditions are altered.
– The riverine and geo-hydrological ecosystems are altered. (Valdiya, 1987).

Taking all these aspects into consideration, it is required that dams are not to be viewed within the restricted framework of technical feasibility and economic gains but are also to be assessed in terms of environmental changes, they produce and the socio-cultural impacts they have on the affected communities. Some of negative impacts of dams construction in sensitive areas are:

Increase in Earthquake Frequency

The scientific investigations have proved that seismicity is induced and increased soon after the accumulation of water in a reservoir. The induced seismisity has direct correlation with the height of the water column. Experiments in various parts of the world have proved that the degree of seismicity and strength of shock waves increase rapidly, if the height of a reservoir is more than 100 metre. The induced seismisity depends on :

- The rate of increase of water level.
- Duration of high water level maintained.
- Maximum height attained.
- Deeper infiltration of accumulated water through faults, fractures, joints and shear zones.
- Existence of deeper tectonic conditions.
- Brittleness of the rock (Gupta and Rastogi, 1974 and Huang Nain,1982)

In Uttranchal region (Garhwal and Kumaon both) there are many major thrusts and faults present along which high stresses prevail. In such conditions construction of dams with height more than 100 m. may be a suicidal attempt. Taking all these aspects into considerations, many prominent geologists of the country have rightly advised to reduce the height and make other necessary amendments in Tehri dam, coming up on Bhagirathi river.

Increase in Erosion/Landslides

The change of water level in reservoir increases the intensity of landslides/soil erosion in the upper streamside. This is due to the change in water table in the rocks/soil along the reservoir. This change in water column also increases the intensity of soil erosion. Due to the change in water table, the soil or the rocks along reservoir loosens and becomes susceptible to erosion by rainwater and wind. The other reason for this increased rate of erosion is the clearance of vegetation in the upstream side. In the down stream side also the increase in the rate of erosion is observed due to dam construction. Devoid of suspended silt, the water released from the reservoir has a strong tendecy for eroding the stream bed in order to satisfy its capacity of bed material (Valdiya 1987).

Loss of forest cover and wild life

The construction of dams results into massive loss of vegetation and wild life. A large part of the forest is drawn under the reservoir. The other loss to forest is due to increased demand of fuel wood and hutments of the labourers involved in dam construction. The wild life of the area is also badly affected by the loss of its habitat. In Uttranchal as per forest department data about 5700 hectare of forest cover is lost due to various hydroelectric projects (Table 4.7).

Table 4.7 : Year wise loss of forest due to hydroelectric project and other irrigation facilities in Uttranchal.

(in hectares)

Year	Irrigation projects	Hydro Power Projects
1981-82	3.5310	–
1982-83	14.0812	–
1983-84	17.4733	85.0000
1984-85	10.7799	0.4800
1985-86	5.9995	–
1986-87	332.3854	1302.5110
1987-88	6.5200	3050.4306
1988-89	10.7190	157.2960
1989-90	19.4998	6.5600
1990-91	6.9200	628.8780
1991-92	2.5700	1.9680
1992-93	1.2300	–
1993-94	7.0325	–
1994-95	1.5150	–
1995-96	7.3073	0.1235
1996-97	3.2241	449.2308
1997-98	1.3194	0
1998-99	30.7155	0
1999-00	4.4410	9.5668
2000-01	0.5500	20.5020
Total	**487.8139**	**5712.5467**

Source : Uttranchal Forest Department.

This loss in vegetation cover has direct adverse impact on the environment and socio-economic conditions of the local inhabitants and make them more vulnerable to natural hazards.

Loss of Agriculture land and uprooting of human communities

Reservoir construction absorbs major fertile agricultural land in the valley. The local population is uprooted and forced to migrate to other places. This migration and shifting of agriculture fields in new areas have direct consequence on the local ecology and environment. The new area inhabited for residential and agricultural purposes is subjected to deforestation resulting into massive soil erosion and landslides.

Socio-economic impacts

The migration of the uprooted population has direct socio-economic impact on the community. The loss of their livelihood resource in the form of agricultural land and other petty business really worsens the condition of the population beyond imagination. For the people, who had been living in an area for generations, it really becomes very difficult to settle in a totally new environment. This leads to high level of frustration in the society which ultimately affects their economic conditions. As poverty and vulnerability are very much inter-linked, such economically vulnerable society becomes more exposed and prone to natural disasters.

TEHRI DAM

The construction of Tehri Dam across the Bhagirathi river has been controversial since its planning stage in the late sixties. The project was approved by Planning Commission in 1972 for Rs.197.92 crores to generate power worth 600MW. However, due to strong opposition from various sectors of the society, the construction could not be started as per schedule.

Though later, the construction of the dam has started yet the safety of the dam is still questionable and under controversy and construction of the dam is being opposed by various sections of the society, i.e. the environmentalists, geologists, seismologists, construction engineers, NGOs etc. The main cause of opposition from these sections is the instability of the region in which the dam is being constructed on. According to Prof. K.S. Valdiya, renowned Himalayan Geologist, this Dam is being built very near to active fault called Srinagar thrust, which has shown many evidences of its activities in the form of upliftment in the recent past. The occurrence of many small earthquakes in the recent past near the vicinity of the thrust has evidenced that energy is being stored along this tectonic structure. The other evidences in favour of the activiness of this thrust are the morphometric analysis of the various geomorphic features, i.e. shifting of river channels etc. It is very surprising to note that the Tehri dam is located just south of this active Srinagar fault. Beside this active Srinagar fault, there are other active thrusts also close to dam site (Fig. 4.8).

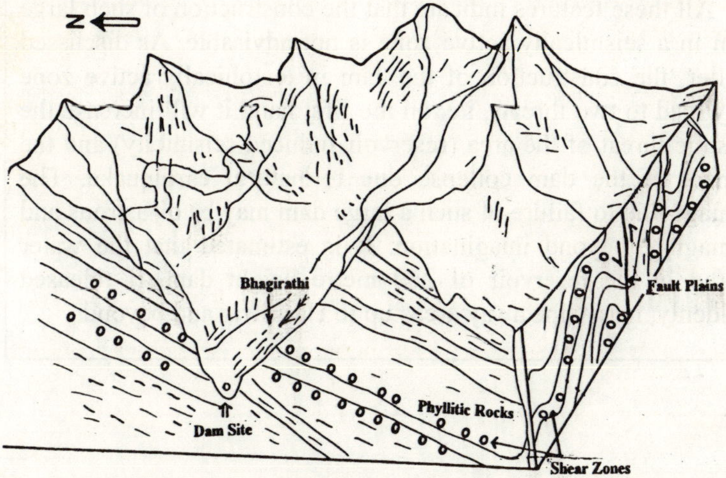

Fig. 4.8 : Geology along Tehri Dam site. The rocks weak in nature are further exposed to fault and shear zones, making it prone to natural disaster in future.

As per the scientists, these faults and thrusts may become active any time due to the stress being stored in them. Though this stress is released occasionally in the form of smaller earthquakes, yet the major part of the stress is being stored along these faults and thrusts. As per an estimate the tectonically much active Garhwal and Kumaun portion has seismically remained quiet for sometime, i.e. around 20 years, with regard to strong earthquakes (intensity > 8.0 on Richter Scale).

The author also carried out extensive geological studies near Tehri and found that along with these major thrust and faults there are many more smaller tectonic features which make the rock bodies of the area very unstable and thus susceptible to any type of natural hazard, i.e. earthquake, landslide etc. Compositionwise also, most of the rock types of the area are limestone, slates, phyllites etc. which are of very soft nature and prone to erosion and weathering by water. The repeated tectonic crumbling of these rock bodies have further weakened them. Due to their vulnerability to water erosion, these rocks are more easily washed away and are to be deposited in the reservoir of the proposed dam. This will increase the stress on the dam and weaken the strength of the dam wall to withstand any shock due to a strong earthquake.

All these features indicate that the construction of such large dam in a seismically active zone is not advisable. As discussed earlier, the construction of the dam in tectonically active zone may lead to two threats, i.e. on the first hand it will increase the seismic threat of the area (reservoir induced seismicity) and the impact of the dam collapse due to natural earthquake. The damage due to failure of such a large dam may be disastrous and damaging, beyond imagination. It is estimated that the water stored in the reservoir of 260 metre height dam, if released suddenly, may wipe away areas up to Haridwar and beyond.

5

DISASTERS IN UTTARANCHAL

Uttranchal as a state has been endowed with very rich natural resources. However, the general topography, the physical features of the area and active geomorphic changes have converted the area vulnerable to natural disasters. Adding fire to the fury are the faulty agricultural practices, extensive deforestation and the prevailing socio-economic conditions. A combination of these factors together with its multiplier effects have created a disbalance in the overall ecology which directly or indirectly contributes to make the area vulnerable to disasters.

Uttranchal is a unique region which is affected by earthquakes, landslides, forest fires, avalanches and soil erosion to a large extent. The fragile conditions and the factors responsible for the same are elaborated in the subsequent text.

EARTHQUAKES

Earthquake is one of the natural hazards which is quite devastating and sudden in its origin. The estimated loss is beyond imagination as it changes the overall scenario of the area within seconds.

During the last two decades there have been more than twenty-two major earthquakes (intensity > 6.00) causing heavy loss to life and property throughout the world (Table 5.1). Unfortunately, out of these twenty-two major earthquakes 4 have hit our country (2 in Uttranchal – 1991, 1999, one in Latur – 1994 and one in Gujarat – 2001).

The effects of the earthquake are usually catastrophic as they cause damage to infrastructures and buildings and result into landslides, fires etc. Taking into consideration the extensive loss due to earthquake, it is imperative to know about their nature and causes and the ways to prevent the same or at least to minimize the overall loss.

Table 5.1: Major Earthquakes in Last Two Decades

S. No.	Date	Place	Intensity	Deaths
1	30.10.1983	Turkey	6.9	1300
2	19.9.1985	Mexico	8.1	9500
3	15.3.1987	Equador	7.0	1000
4	7.12.1988	Soviet Russia	6.9	25000
5	15.8.1988	North-Eastern India	6.8	10000
6	21.6.1990	Iran	7.7	35000
7	16.7.1990	Philippine	7.8	1600
8	1.2.1991	Pakistan / Afghanistan	6.8	1200
9	20.10.1991	Uttarkashi, India	6.6	769
10	12.12.1992	Indonesia	6.8	2200
11	30.9.1993	Latur, India	6.4	7600
12	17.1.1995	Japan	7.2	6430
13	28.3.1995	Russia	7.5	1900
14	28.2.1997	Iran	5.5	1000
15	4.2.1998	Afghanistan	6.1	4200
16	30.5.1998	Afghanistan	6.9	4000
17	17.7.1998	Papua-New Guinea	7.1	2000
18	25.1.1999	Columbia	6.3	1100
19	29.3.1999	Chamoli, India	6.8	103
20	17.8.1999	Turkey	7.4	15000
21	21.9.1999	Taiwan	7.6	2000
22	26.1.2001	India	8.9	20000

Causes of Earthquakes

Why the earth quakes? The question did arise in the human mind since his origin on this planet. From the earliest antiquity man has searched for a way to explain this terrifying natural phenomenon. Almost all religions of the world have attributed one or the other strange cause of this mysterious event. According to Hindu mythology, the earth is balanced on the head of a large cobra, called *"Shesh Nag"* and when it moves, the earth trembles. The native Americans thought that the earth was supported by a giant tortoise and its movement makes the earthquake. The belief of ancient Japan was also somewhat similar, according to which the creature balancing the earth is a mysterious giant crab and so on. The great philosopher of 4th century, Aristotle had slightly different thoughts about earthquake. He believed that they are originated by wind escaping from caves within the bowels of the earth.

Despite a lot of research and investigation in the field of earth science, the complete phenomenon of earthquake is still not very clear. However the scientific developments have made many contributions in this regard. As per the modern thinking, the earth originated about five billion years ago from very hot gases and dust, which over time cooled and became denser. While solidifying it divided into three distinct layers, *core, mantle* and *crust*. The inner most spherical part, the core, made-up of very heavy metals is surrounded by molten molasses like substance forming mantle. The upper most part, the earth crust, which makes continents and ocean floors, is floating over the viscous molten mass of the mantle. According to "*Plate-Tectonic Theory*", the crust is not a single piece of mass, instead it is cracked like an eggshell and split into many floating islands called "*Plates*". The plates are continuously floating over the viscous mass and the energy for their movement comes directly from the deep interior of the earth which is still very hot. Most of the earthquakes originate along the edges of these plates, i.e. *plate boundaries*. Whenever two floating plates collide, one starts sliding down into the depth and melts. The Himalayan region is also an area where Indo- Australian plate is colliding against the Asian - plate. As a result of this collision the Indian plate is intruding below the Asian plate. This movement is still continuing and it is estimated that the speed of movement is 1.6 centimetres per annum. The plate intrusion starts creating pressure against the other plate and consequently energy is stored in the rock bodies of surrounding areas. When this energy reaches at a level more than the bearing capacity of the rock, the rock bodies split and move apart. These phenomena of rock rupture and movement respectively called "*faulting*" and "*thrusting*" and release a lot of energy which tremble the earth surface and earthquake generates.

The Earthquake Waves

When a stone is dropped in still water pond, waves are created which seem to move in all directions from the place of stone dropping. A similar phenomenon happens during the earthquake. When the rock bodies rupture and move, the energy created moves in all directions in the form of waves, called "*seismic*" or "*earthquake - waves*". These waves are of three types : "P", "S", & " L" waves. The "P" waves, which are the fastest, move in the back-and-forth direction. In the second category of waves, i.e. "S" waves, slightly slower in speed, the movement is transverse to the "P" waves. The "L" waves, which restrict themselves along the earth surface and moves with a speed of around 3.5 km. per second are associated with structural damages caused by the earthquake (Fig. 5.1). The seismic waves are recorded with the instrument called "*Seismograph*", which gives exact record of the waves – "*Seismogram*". The exact location in the deep interior where earthquakes originate has been termed "*focus*" of the earthquake and point just vertically above the focus is known as "*epicentre*". The intensity of seismic waves is maximum near the epicentre and slowly decreases as one moves away.

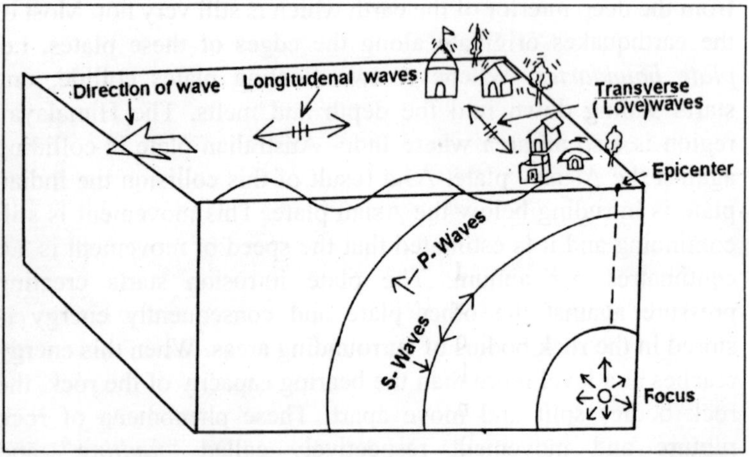

Fig. 5.1 : Different waves generated due to earthquake.

Strength of Earthquakes

The intensity and strength of an earthquake is measured on Richter Scale. The scale, invented by Charles Richter of California categorizes earthquakes on the basis of energy released. The amounts of energy released during different categories of Richter Scale earthquakes are as follows:

Intensity of earthquake (Richter Scale)	Energy released (Amount of TNT)
1.0	170 Grams
2.0	6 kgm.
3.0	179 kgm.
4.0	5 metric tons
5.0	179 metric tons
6.0	5643 metric tons
7.0	179100 metric tons
8.0	5643000 metric tons

As per an estimate, the amount of energy created by an earthquake of 7.5 intensity will equal to the energy released by explosion of one-megaton nuclear bomb. The maximum intensity the earthquake measured till date is of 9.0 which struck Chile in 1960.

Distribution of Earthquakes

The earthquakes are common natural phenomenon on earth surface. As per an estimate the earth surface experiences one or the other earthquake after a gap of 2-3 hours. The frequency of the earthquakes on the surface is not uniform. The areas near the tectonic-plate boundaries are more susceptible to earthquakes in comparison to others. If seen concisely, most of the world earthquakes are restricted along two narrow belts, i.e. Circum-Pacific and Mediterranean/Trans-Asian belts. The Circum-Pacific belt, running along the Pacific ocean covers Alaska, Japan, Philippines, Guinea, New Zeland and North and South American beaches. Sixty-eight per cent of the earthquakes are restricted to this belt only. The second belt, i.e. Mediterranean/ Trans-Asian belt starting from Alps runs through Asia Minor, Baluchistan, Palmir, Himalaya, Tibet and China. One branch of this belt extends up to Baikal Lake of Mongolia and other goes to Myanmar. These belts originally represent plate boundaries where two plates are either colliding or moving away from each other (Fig. 5.2).

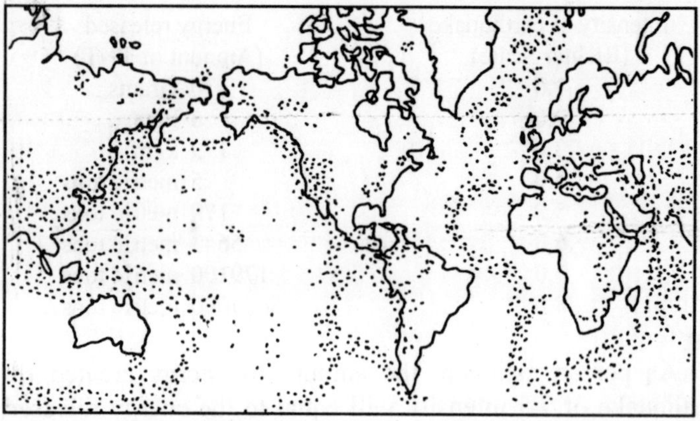

Fig. 5.2 : Earthquake belts distribution at global level (After Arthur Holmes, 1965).

Prediction of Earthquakes

Earthquake is the most unpredictable devastating natural phenomenon for mankind. The statistical data tells that in the last century this catastrophe caused an estimated loss of two billion lives. Despite intensive research and investigation in the field of earthquake science (seismology), it is not yet possible to precisely predict an earthquake. However some estimates can be made about the possibility and rough idea of timing of earthquake in a region, which sometimes may come true. Prediction of earthquakes may save many lives and can reduce the magnitude of loss. (Plate 2)

EARTHQUAKE ZONES OF INDIA

Over half of India is vulnerable to earthquakes. The most vulnerable areas of the country are located in Himalayan and Sub-Himalayan region, Kutch and the Andaman and Nicobar Islands. Just as earthquake prone areas have been identified in and demarcated as such all over the world, India has also been divided in into different zones as per Indian Standards Code, 1893-1975. Indian Meterological Department has prepared

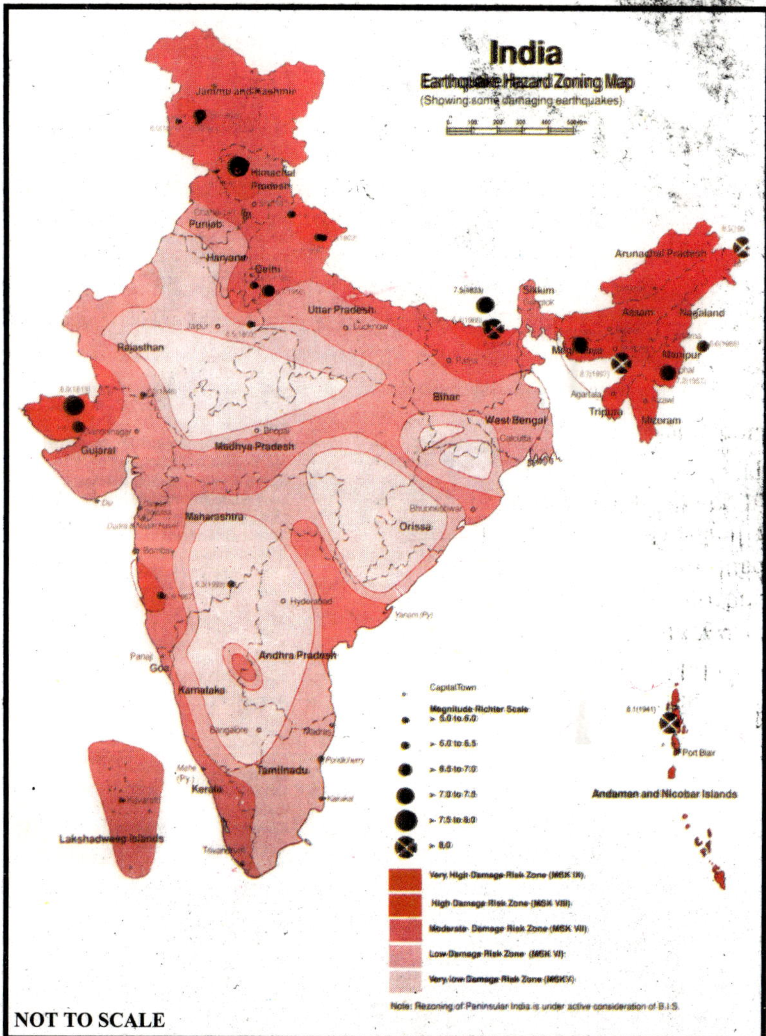

Plate 2 : India (Earthquake Hazard Zoning Map)

Source : Earthquake Catalogue (M ≥ S), J.M.D., G.O.I.

a catalogue of all the earthquakes of intensity of 5.0 and above, which is being updated continually. According to this classification the entire country has been classified into following categories depending upon the degree of seismicity.

1. Kashmir and western Himalayas – This region covers the states of Jammu and Kashmir, Himachal Pradesh and sub-mountanious areas of Punjab.
2. Central Himalayas – This region includes the mountain and sub-mountain regions of Uttar Pradesh and the sub-mountainous parts of Punjab.
3. Northeast India – This region comprises the whole of Indian territory to the east of North Bengal.
4. Indo-Gangetic Basin and Rajasthan – This region comprises of Rajasthan, plains of Punjab, Haryana, Uttar Pradesh and West Bengal.
5. Cambay and Rann of Kutch.
6. Peninsular India including the Islands of Lakshwadeep.
7. The Andaman and Nicobar Islands.

This distribution of magnitudes equal or more than 5.0 in these regions and their average return periods are represented in the following table.

Region-wise Earthquake (M>5.0) Occurrence in India, (1897-1993)

S. No.	Seismic Region	No. of Earthquakes of Magnitude				Return period
		5.0-5.9 25	6.0-6.9 7	7.0-7.9 2	8.0+ 1	2.5-3 yrs.
1.	Kashmir & Western Himalayas					
2.	Central Himalayas	68	28	4	1	1 yr.
3.	North East India	200	128	15	4	<4 months
4.	Indo-Gangetic Basin	14	6	-	-	5 yrs
5.	Cambay and Rann of Kutch	4	4	1	1	20 yrs
6.	Peninsular India	31	10	-	-	2.5-3 yrs
7.	Andaman & Nicobar	80	68	1	1	<8 months

Numbers of earthquakes under 5.0-5.9 are approximate.

(Based on the available data and intensity of the earthquake related features a seismic zone map has been prepared as IS:1893-1984, in which 5 seismic zones have been identified as very high, high, moderate, low and very low damage risk zones as shown in the map.)

It has been observed in few countries that animals sometimes give a faint idea about the future earthquakes. The people in China during 1835 earthquake noticed the unusual behaviour of pet animals. Similarly, just few days before the earthquake of Chile during 1835, the dogs left the city, which was worst affected by the earthquake later. The sudden appearance of snakes in large number in Japan is other such phenomenon, which suggests that the animals have some extraordinary sense or ESP (Eatra Sensory Perception) and sometime may help in predicting the earthquake. Though still no scientific basis has been found for such strange behaviour of the animals yet many researches are being carried out in this regard and it is hoped that some useful results may come out in future.

Beside strange behaviour of the animals, some scientific techniques have also been evolved which may be of some help in earthquake prediction. The measurement of the sea level is also one such technique. The scientists have observed changes in water level of the sea before earthquakes. One another technique in this field is the use of Geodimeter - an instrument used for measuring the rock deformation. The measurement of the rock deformation may give some idea about the occurrence of earthquakes. The measurement of electric resistivity of the rocks may also sometime be helpful in the prediction of earthquake.

Earthquakes in Uttranchal

Seismologically, the major porition of Uttranchal falls in Zones V and IV and thus very susceptible to earthquakes. As discussed earlier, the reason for this seismisity lies deep rooted in the interior of the land forming this region. The tectonic activities, as a result of continuous mounting pressure of Indian plate on Tibetan plate is still going on in this part of Himalaya. These activities are quite evident by frequently occurring earthquakes in this region especially the north-eastern part of Uttranchal Himalaya are very frequently hit by earthquakes of magnitude between 5 and 6. On the basis of an intensive study of this part for earthquakes, the scientists have suggested that most of the earthquakes here result from strike slip and dip – slip movements along various faults and thrusts. The statistical data in this region shows that most of the earthquakes have taken place along 3 major thrust/faults zones.

(a) MBT (Main Boundary Thrust), which demarcates Shiwalik foot hills from rest of Himalayas.
(b) MCT (Main Central Thrust), demarcates Central Himalayas and the Lesser Himalayas.
(c) CCT (Central Countre Thrust) Separating Central Himalayas from Tibetan Himalayas.

The existence of Delhi-Haridwar ridge and its extension upto Himalayas is another major reason for the instability of the region. As discussed earlier, this ridge is playing a very active role in accelerating the frequency and intensity of earthquake in Uttranchal region (Fig. 5.4).

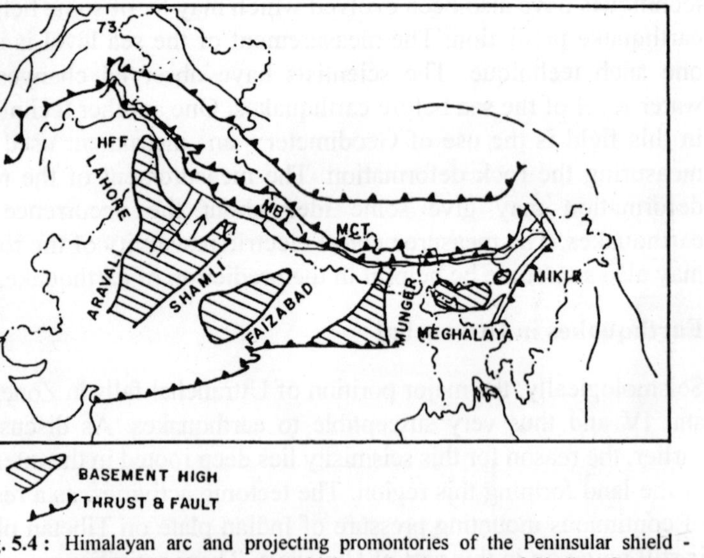

Fig. 5.4 : Himalayan arc and projecting promontories of the Peninsular shield - including hidden basement highs under the sands of Sindhu, Ganga an Brahmaputra. (After K.N. Khattri, 1983 and Khattri and Tyagi, 1982).

Major Earthquakes of Uttaranchal

The Uttranchal Himalaya has a well-known and recorded history where large magnitude earthquakes strike frequently. The entire area is under Zones IV and V of the Seismic Zone Map of India, with very high seismic vulnerability. This area has already faced

36 major earthquakes (m > 5.0 on Richter Scale) in the last one and a half century. During the last century, the region has had 12 earthquakes of magnitude greater than 6.0 on the Richter Scale.

Table 5.2 : Major earthquakes of Uttranchal

Date	Intensity	Place
1 September 1803	9.0	Badrinath
1809	9.0	Garhwal
26 May 1816	7.0	Gangotri
25 July 1869	6.0	Nainital
28 October 1916	7.5	Dharchula
28 October 1937	8.0	Dehradun
27 July 1966	6.3	Kapkot, Dharchula
28 August 1968	7.0	Dharchula
29 July 1980	6.5	Dharchula
20 October 1991	6.6	Uttarkashi
29 March 1999	6.8	Chamoli

Uttarkashi Earthquake, 1991

A earthquake of 6.6 magnitude rocked the Uttarkashi and the surrounding areas on October 20th, 1991 at 02.53 A.M. when the people were in deep sleep. The epicentre of the earthquake was near Uttarkashi town. This tragedy caused widespread damage in many districts of Uttranchal, i.e. Uttarkashi, Tehri, Rudraprayag and Chamoli. About 723 people lost their lives and thousands got injured. About 70,000 houses were damaged fully or partially due to this catastrophy. Many villages were wiped out around Bhatwari-Maneri along Bhagirathi valley, Budha-Kedar-Chamiala in Balganga valley, Ghansayli in Bhilngana valley, and Guptkashi-Ookhimath in Mandakini valley. Uttarkashi town was badly damaged. It was a shallow to intermediate focus earthquake. Agora, a small village near Uttarkashi was its epicentre.

Due to difficult terrain and the damaged infrastructure facilities like roads, bridges, and communication networks, rescue and relief works were hampered. It became very difficult to reach the affected community and to cater the need of first aid, food, warm clothes etc. Considering the handicaps of the local Civil Administration in handling the situation, the services of the Army and other Para Military forces were pressed into action.

Along with this the voluntary organisations, very active in the region were of extreme help to the affected population in providing timely assistance like foods, clothes, shelter etc. More than 1200 NGOs reportedly reached the site.

Destruction caused

Affected Districts	Uttarkashi, Tehri, Rudraprayag and Chamoli
Persons killed	More than 720
Injured	5000 approx.
Affected village	2000
Affected population	4.5 lakhs
Totally collapsed houses	25000+
Semi-collapsed with cracks useless for living	75000+
Collapsed Schools/Inter Colleges	630
Animals killed	4000+
Total loss	Rs. 370 + crores

Chamoli Earthquake, 1999

On 29th March, 1999 at 12.35 a.m. a stronger earthquake measuring 6.8 on the Richter scale struck near the town of Chamoli. The epicentre of this earthquake was approximately 10 kilometres away from the township.

It was an unprecedented earthquake which caused extensive damage to life and property for the people living in Chamoli, Gopeshwar, Nandprayag, Rudraprayag, Joshimath, Ookhimath and other parts of the Garhwal and Kumaun Himalaya. More than 100 people were killed and about 300 injured. In the district of Chamoli 90% of the houses were totally damaged. Other highly vulnerable areas of the Kumaun Himalaya, i.e. Munsyari, Dharchula and Bageshwar were also reportedly affected. In Almora and Bageshwar districts also many people were reportedly injured and property damaged (Table 5.3).

Plate 3 : Cracks developed due to Earthquake

Table 5.3: Damage due to Chamoli Earthquake - March 1999

S. No	Name of village	Loss of property and life
1	Masoli	27 Houses damaged
2	Kevada Malla	11 Houses damaged
3	Matayee	10 Houses damaged
4	Shregad Pokhari	12 Houses damaged
5	Jakhmalla Pokhari	10 Houses damaged
6	Sanala	81 Houses damaged
7	Gopeshwar (SC Familes)	11 Houses damaged
8	Pipalkoti	57 Houses damaged
9	Dogri Kandai	16 Houses damaged
10	Makroli	1 women injured houses damaged
11	Bacher	All houses damaged
12	Rikhuli Shen	2 Houses damaged
13	Dever Khadora	Houses and cowshed damaged
14	Khadora	5 Houses totally damaged 117 houses cracked
15	Tangsa-Gair	10 persons injured in Gair and 15 persons inured in Tangsa, 6 animals injured 1 dead, cracks in houses, 1 totally damaged
16	Gadi	5 persons and 6 animals injured, 1 dead, crack in all houses, 1 damaged
17	Devaldhar	2 children dead, 17 houses totally damaged
18	Sirokhoma	3 House damaged
19	Gangol Gaon	1 death
20	Gram Siro Sinji Pipalkhali	1 girl death, 10 persons injured 2 persons injured 3 persons injured
21	Kunjo Mekot	27 Houses damaged, 1 person injured
22	Chamoli	117 Houses damaged
23	Gopeshwar	37 Houses damaged, 7 dead, 15 injured

It was noticed while studying the response of building structures of the earthquake in Chamoli that new but unengineered buildings were the ones to experience maximum damage, while, engineered buildings withstood the quake. The stone based buildings, which are very popular in the region are very dangerous and a threat to life. The situation demands the urgent need for engineering inputs for design of earthquake resistant buildings, and dissemination of such features to the masses so that construction activity that is usually carried out informally can also adhere to such basic principles. The fact that ancient structures also survived, the earthquake speaks volumes that traditional wisdom on these things, including lifestyles and construction methods, was very sound and responsive to location needs.

Managing the Quake

Though the earthquakes cannot be precisely predicted, the introduction of various measures can reduce the risk of a society or region from this hazard. During earthquake maximum loss is caused due to collapse/damage of houses. Damage to buildings depends upon various factors :

Damage to building = f x (construction and maintenance of building, energy generated by earthquake, duration and acceleration of motion on the ground, the type and character of rocks and soil, distance from the epicentre).

Among the factors mentioned, the construction and maintenance of building and soil and rock type upto some extent are the only variables which can be managed or controlled. Thus to minimize the damage to buildings, it is necessary that these two variables are managed by various measures which can be classified further as long term and short-term. In earthquake prone areas like Uttranchal, these measures are to be adopted very strictly to minimize the damage to buildings. The measures may be enlisted as :

- Buildings are to incorporate earthquake resistant features.

- Public buildings like schools, hospitals, community centres, temples, mosques etc. are to be built as per the prescribed technique for earthquake resistance buildings, so that they can be used as temporary shelters in case of earthquake.
- Retrofitting of weak buildings and other structures.
- Geological investigations and researches in the area and mapping the faults, thrusts etc. tectonic features very precisely.
- Avoiding houses/buildings construction near such tectonic features and on steep slopes which are prone to land slides.

Along with these measures to make buildings earthquake resistant and avoiding constructions in dangerous zones, other measures regarding the community making strong enough to resist the impact of earthquake are also of strategic importance in managing this disaster. Proper education and awareness to public about the process of disaster mitigation, involvement of local people in the developmental process, networking of NGOs, involvement of local research institutes and educational institutes in carrying out research regarding earthquake and its management are the activities which are to be carried out in earthquake prone areas of Uttranchal to reduce the vulnerability of the region and society.

While constructing dams or other large scale construction work in Uttranchal, which is very sensitive and earthquake prone, necessary precautions are to be taken. Dams constructed in such areas should be flexible and self-healing. Concrete dams should be avoided near an active fault, because such fault can break the contact between dam and the foundation. The core of earth dam should be made larger with higher camber and flatter slopes. Minimum four accelerographs must be installed at each site of the dam to record earthquake motion in the dam foundation and measure the response of the dam. Construction of dams without proper precaution may be suicidal in earthquake prone area. Keeping the severity of the problem in view, necessary arrangements and modifications are being made in Tehri dam being constructed at Bhagirathi river in the State.

LANDSLIDES

Landslides may be defined as the downslide movement of the soil, debris or rocks resulting from naturally occurring vibrations, loading with weight, removal of lateral support, change in water content of rock or soil bodies, blocked drainage pattern etc. This mass movement in hilly region may vary in magnitude from soil creep on one hand to instantaneous and huge landslide on the other. Depending upon the nature of the mass movement, landslides may be classified as soil creep, scree creep, solifluction, valley bulge and proper landslide.

Soil creep is the slow downward movement of earth, which is usually imperceptible except by observation of lông duration. It is usually evidenced by the formation of small terraces, soil accumulation on uphill side, tilting of poles and curvature in tree stems.

On higher attitudes of Uttranchal hills, one more type of mass movement occur called "Solifluction". It is basically a form of creep in which snow or water saturated rocks move down slopes. It may carry huge size rock-boulders along with it and deposits them at new places. Its movement is very slow in comparison to other mass movements.

Problem of landslide is very common and frequent in Uttranchal. Almost every year this region is affected by one or more major landslides. In the recent past due to extensive road construction and other developmental activities, their frequency has increased. The development of the road network in the area has paved way for soil erosion and creation of various landslide zones.

Table 5.4: Major Landslides in Uttranchal

S. No.	Disaster location	Year	Life claimed
1	Gudiya Tal	1868	73
2	Nainital	1880	151
3	Birehi River	1893	-
4	Namtal	1898	27
5	Alaknanda	1970	70
6	Khaila village	1977	
7	Bhagirathi	1978	25
8	Mandakini	1979	50
9	Neelkanth	1990	> 100
10	Dewar Khadora	1991	25
11	Piderghati	1991,92,93	59
12	Ookhimath and Malpa	1998	326

Causes and Mechanism of Mass Movement in Landslides

Mass movement in landslides usually takes place by flowing, falling, sliding or combination of these factors. However the first and most important factor here is a trigger mechanism that starts the movement of the mass which was already on the verge of failure. Basically, there are two forces which decide the rock movement, i.e. resisting force and the disturbing force. Whenever the disturbing force exceeds the resisting force, the mass movement starts.

Plate 4 : Landslide causes much more damage to agricultural land. The land covered with debris of landslide.

In general, the causes of landslides may be grouped as internal and external. The internal causes basically define the mechanism within the mass that reduces its resisting force or shear strength. The second category of causes includes the outside factors which are mechanically responsible for overcoming internal shear strength.

Internal Causes

The internal causes of mass movement are decided by geology of the mass. This includes both lithology, i.e. rock or soil type and various structures present in it. Both these factors decide the shearing strength of a mass. The lithology of soil or rock defines

– the minerals present and their chemical composition, the size of the constituents and texture or other factors that attribute its physical and chemical behaviour that ultimately decides the internal shearing strength of the rock or soil body to resist the movement.

External Causes

The external causes of mass movement are the factors which control the external forces leading to mass movement. These causes may be natural or due to the factors induced by human beings.

EXTERNAL CAUSES

Natural causes

- The earthquakes
- Climate or rainfall
- Thawing
- Vegetation cover
- Artesian pressure
- Ground water conditions
- More variation in day and nigh temperature,
- Volcanic eruption

Man induced causes

- Unscientific development (i.e. construction of road/building/ hydropower station etc.)
- Heavy water discharge from the underground water resources
- Deforestation
- Forest fire
- Mining activities
- Artificial explosion or blasts
- Agricultural activities on steeper slopes.
- Blockage in natural drainage pattern

Role of Water

Water plays an important role during landslides, deciding slope instability. Heavy rain/snow melting at higher attitudes, rapid drawn down, rapid change or elevation of water table, seepage from artificial source of water are some important water related factors that ultimately affect the mass movement. While mitigating landslides, all these issues need a detailed investigation and appropriate measures are to be taken, if necessary.

The various impacts of water on mass movement may be summarized as in Table 5.5 :

Table 5.5 : Impact of water on mass movement

S. No.	Nature of water	Nature of rock or soil	Action of water	Result
1.	Rain or snow melt	Clayee or shale type rock bodies with cracks and fissures	The cracks. or fissures are widened and new one formed	Soil or rock creep
2.	Rain or snow melt	All type of rocks containing minerals of Iron and Magnesium and carbonates	Make rock susceptible to erosions.	Weathering
3.	Rapid draw down	Sand and clay	Shrinkage	Seepage from the rock/soil mass and destabilizing it.
4.	Frost	Highly jointed rock and silt	Widen the joint and make top layer of silt rich in water	Rock particles are loosened
5.	Water table elevation	Loose sand	Pure water pressure increases	Liquefaction
6.	Seepage from dams or canals	Sand and silt	Increase in water pressure and loosen-ing of bonds among grains	Rock particles loosened.

Impact of Vegetation

Along with type of material and water content, the vegetation also upto an extent affects the slope stability in hilly terrain. In general, the vegetation impact on landslides is quite positive as the trees protect the surface from weathering, rain and winds and also checks the water run off and soil erosion. The root system of trees works as cohesive substance for soil and prevents it from erosion and loosening. However, in some rare instances forest cover may intensify the landslides. This is the case where the land on the lower part is barren and on top it is thickly forested. This causes an ecological imbalance and the soil or rock bodies just lying under the forest cover become quite heavy with load of water retained by tree roots. This leads to gravity imbalance and the soil or rock bodies from above starts moving downward under its load pressure and gravity. This phenomenon was observed during 1998 landslides in Madhyamaheshwar valley landslides of Ookhimath block of Uttranchal.

The positive and negative impact of vegetation on slope stability may be summarized as follows :

Positive Impacts

- Tree roots bind the soil and thus reduce erosion.
- The leaves evaporate excess water from the soil and reduce water pressure in pores of soil or rocks.
- The tree cover intercepts rainfall from directly hitting the ground and thus evade soil erosion and loosening of soil.
- Tree roots also help in binding the loose rock mass by making firm grip on solid rock mass, which work as anchor for the loose rock bodies.
- Tree leaves intercepts the rainfall and allow part water to evaporate. This reduces the water quantity available for infiltration.

Negative Impacts

- Roots make rock or soil masses porous and thus increasing its water infiltration capacity.
- Evaporation of water from soil through tree foliage results into cracking of land laying below the trees, which increases soil and infiltration capacity.
- High velocity winds may cause uprooting of trees on steeper slopes leading to slope failure.

Man and Landslides

Along with natural causes human induced activities are much more responsible for landslides in tectonically active zones like Uttranchal. Various developmental activities discussed in Chapter 4 have extensively damaged the ecological balance of the zone. Among the activities listed, road construction is quite damaging for the eco-balance. As per an estimate, one-kilometre length of road construction in Himalaya needs 60,000-cubic metre debris removal. By this estimate one can imagine the destruction caused by total 44,000 km mattled and unmattled road constructed in Himalaya. In Uttranchal alone the road length is 16,654 kms. The large amount of debris removed for road construction from the region, which is already prone to land slides is very disastrous. The debris removal also affects the natural drainage system, which further accelerates the problem of mass movement. The rock blasting during construction of road is also upto a large extent responsible for landslides by loosening the hard and stable soil rock mass. Besides road construction, other developmental activities, i.e. buildings, canals, dams also create similar impacts on the stability of rock/ soil masses.

These activities along with debris removal cause much loss to forest cover. In Uttranchal alone as per the information made available by forest department, during the last 20 years 26,022.54 hectares of forest land has been transferred for various developmental activities such as irrigation, hydro power, road construction, communication cables, mining, drinking water pipe lines etc. The above data are only for legally transferred forest land. The illegal encroachment on forest land is also quite significant. The deforestation at large scale has really deteriorated the situation and made the land of Uttranchal prone to landslides.

The unscientific agricultural activities in Uttranchal is another prime factor responsible for large scale migration and movements. The increasing population pressure and lack of other employment opportunities in the region has forced mankind to make new agricultural fields, even on very steep and unstable slopes. Terrace-cutting on these slopes has made them prone to landslides. Landslides of Ookhimath is the recent example of this unscientific agricultural practice leading to landslides. Thus, all these natural and man induced activities have made the problem of landslides very common and frequent in Uttranchal.

Ookhimath and Malpa Landslides (1998)

Two major landslides occurred in the Ookhimath area in Garhwal on 11-12 and 18-19, August 1998. The first slide came on 11-12 August and many people left for the safer places. The heavy rainfall of 18-19 August created fresh slides in the region and one of the most devastating slides occurred along the left bank of the Madhyamaheshwar river. This slide destroyed two villages (Bhenti and Paunder) completely and blocked the flow of Madhyamaheshar river for 12 hours on 19th August, 1998. The river blockage occurred due to incessant rains and landslides.

Plate 5 : Major landslide resulting into river blockage and lake formation in the way of Madhyamaheshwar river during 1998 landslide at Ookhimath, Rudraprayag.

With time nature found its own solution to avert the intending catastrophe, as its water gently overflowed from the rubble, gradually creating its way out of the mass. A total loss of 107 lives, property worth Rs. 41 million and 422 heads of cattle was reported.

Another landslide occurred in Malpa in Pithoragarh district on 17th August, 1998. About 219 people were killed due to the catastrophe and property worth millions of rupees was destroyed. Amongst the deceased there were members of the 12th batch of pilgrims to Kailash Mansarovar. Fresh landslides, heavy fog and incessant rains hampered rescue operations in the calamity hit Pithoragarh district even as the Army and para-military personnel tried shifting through mounds of debris to recover the dead bodies. The details of the deceased in the landslide are as follows :

Sl. No	Number of casualties	Details
1	60 pilgrims	12th batch of Kailash Mansarovar pilgrimage
2	5 employees	Kumaon Mandal Vikas Nigam, Ltd.
3	59 coolies	Kumaon Mandal Vikas Nigam, Ltd.
4	19 workers	Employees of GREF
5	8 members	ITBP
6	4 employees	PWD
7'	16 villagers	Local villagers from five families
8	3 constables	UP Police
9	32 villagers	Villagers from Gunji and Bundi in Malpa
10	12 villagers	Dumling village in Nepal
11	1 Sadhu	

From the geomorphology of these northern regions, it is clear that most of the villages here are located on the debris of old landslides or receding glaciers. In Chamoli district, one-third of the settled villages face the threat of landslides. Similarly, in Uttarkashi and Pithoragarh districts more than one-third of the villages are listed as unsafe.

The destructive drama like in Malpa and Ookhimath is replayed almost every year killing dozens of people and causing unprecedented damage to several villages so that they have become totally unfit for inhabitation. Recent landslides have caused havoc and the terraced fields have been destroyed which cannot be easily renovated or made productive again. The road network remained closed for over 3 months causing indescribable hardship to the villagers who get their basic supplies and provisions from the neighbouring areas. The water source was also disrupted due to landslides as they were breached from several places and the debris choked them. The total damage by these landslides during 1998 is as follows :

Sl. No	Extent of Damage	
1.	Villages affected	893
2.	Population affected	177698
3.	Total area affected (in ha)	98667
4.	Crop area affected (in ha)	45785
5.	Houses damaged :	
	(a) Fully	522
	(b) Partially	2529
6.	Human Lives lost	>326
7.	Cattle killed	1002

Relief measures taken by the Government

The road network was cleared to enable the transportation of the basic necessities and other essentials. Restoration work in other areas was left almost untouched. There was not very much help coming from the local authorities and the pace of restoring the services was very poor and inefficient which was the main cause of resentment by the affected population.

The central team of Government of India recommended a total grant of total of Rs. 60.38 crores (app.) which was needed by the state government for the relief assistance work. This is especially for the construction / repair of irrigation channels, ensuring a regular drinking water supply, compensation to small and marginal farmers, against damage to the houses, for utensils, clothes, cattle etc.

Mitigation Measures

The appropriate landslide management needs a detailed scientific study of the region. A Landslide Zone mapping is the first step in this regard. By this study the areas which are very sensitive and unstable are recognized and mapped, which require necessary treatment. This treatment involves both engineering and non-engineering techniques. In India and abroad various studies have been carried out in this regard. The techniques and methods evolved by these researches may be applied in such sensitive zones to check further deterioration.

Man induced activities are very much responsible for landslides in Uttranchal. Unscientific land use pattern is the major cause for the present deteriorating situation. It is necessary and unavoidable that after carrying out detailed scientific and social study of the whole Uttranchal region, an appropriate land-use regulation is evolved and implemented strictly. This land use regulation should be applied for both the existing and the new settlements and future developments. Social and economic upliftment, generating new local resource based small eco-friendly industries, discouraging agricultural practices on steeper slopes etc. can be other measures which must be introduced to reduce landslide hazards. As will be discussed under the heading "Development and Disaster Mitigation" in Chapter 9, the development pattern of the area must be carried out giving appropriate consideration to various environmental issues in the area.

Some of the indicators suggested by Kockelman (1986) can be applicable for combating landslides in Uttranchal.

Discouraging new developments in hazardous areas by:

Disclosing the hazard prone areas to real-estate buyers
Posting warnings of potential hazards
Adopting utility and public facility service area policies
Informing and educating the public
Making a public record of hazards.

Removing or converting existing development through:

Acquiring or exchanging hazardous properties
Discontinuing non-conforming uses
Reconstructing damaged areas after landslides
Removing unsafe structures
Clearing and redeveloping blighted areas before landslides

Regulating new development in hazardous area by:

Enacting grading ordinances
Adopting hillside development regulations
Amending land-use zoning and regulations
Enacting sanitary ordinances

Creating special hazard reduction zones and regulations
Enacting subdivision ordinances
Placing moratoriums on rebuilding

Protecting existing development by:
Controlling landslides and slumps
Controlling mudflows and debris flows
Controlling rock falls
Operating monitoring, warning, and evacuating systems.

SOIL EROSION

Soil erosion is like tuberculosis which slowly eats out the fertility of soil and turns the land barren. It is a slow process which is hardly noticed in general. Though this is a natural process, in extreme cases it is very dangerous and deteriorating to the environment and the society inhabiting a region. Loss of top soil due to erosion removes high proportion of the organic matter and free mineral fraction from the soil that provide nutrient for the plant growth.

It is basically a part of the process of demolitions responsible for changing the landscape. The process has been continuing on the earth surface since its origin. However soil erosion becomes hazardous when it crosses the safety limit. The human activities accelerate soil erosion beyond this safety limit and thus cause great damage. Water and wind are two agents causing soil erosion.

In Uttranchal state which is drained by large network of river systems (mainly Ganga and Kali river systems), soil erosion by water has become a serious problem. Along with causing great loss to fertile soil and land mass in hilly terrain, the huge quantity of eroded material carried by these rivers are deposited in their basin in plain areas, making them shallow and reducing their water bearing capacity. This ultimately results into floods in the plains of Uttar Pradesh, Haryana, Bihar and other down stream states.

Soil erosion by water is most active where most of the rain water finds it difficult to infiltrate the ground and thus its large part floods over the surface removing the top soil. The erosion by water is generally in two forms, i.e. gully and sheet erosion. While the earlier form of erosion is concentrated to a narrow path, the later one is spread over much larger area, but extends upto lesser depth. Beside this, the water velocity in sheet flow is much less in comparison to gully erosion. Scientific researches have revealed that rills and gullies begin to form when the velocity of flow increases more than 30 cm per second and it is turbulent. Along with velocity of flow, the soil nature also decides the gully formation. This type of erosion is much more dangerous as it carries larger volume of soil than sheet flow. If extensive in scale, gully erosion may give rise to landslides also.

Vegetation and Soil Erosion

In general, as and when vegetation increases, soil erosion decreases. However, the growth of vegetation is directly dependent on rain fall in an area. Farming practice in this region also works as a deciding factor for soil erosion. It is the farming practices in an area which decide for how long the soil will be left free after ploughing and harvesting. During this period, the land is most vulnerable to soil erosion. However, the relation between vegetation and soil erosion is a bit complex and vegetation has both positive and negative impacts on soil erosion.

Beneficial effects of vegetation

1. Vegetation intercepts rainfall from directly hitting the ground. This reduces the impact of rainfall on soil and decreases soil erosion. Some portion of rain water intercepted by leaves is exposed to evaporation and thus less water is left for infiltration in soil.
2. Stems and leaves intercepts the flow of water and air and, therefore, reduce its kinetic energy resulting to less erosion.
3. Roots of plants and trees make strong grip on soil and do not allow it to flow with water or air.
4. Through roots, a large quantity of water is evaporated to atmosphere, leaving less amount of water in soil. This

decreases pore pressure on soil and increases the soil strength.

5. Roots penetrate deep into the rock strata and anchor them, binding soil mantle to stable bed rock.
6. Vegetation cover the ground surface and thus provide protection against erosive flows. The vegetation also absorbs noise and vibration impact of traffic, protecting soil surface from damage.

Adverse impacts of vegetation

Though in general vegetation helps in reducing soil erosion, in certain circumstances vegetation may enhance soil erosion also. Vegetation by absorbing water from the soil open up cracks which increase infiltration. Rain water accumulated on leaves, drips in the form of large drops and increases localized rainfall intensity.

Soil Erosion in Uttranchal

The soil erosion is very serious problem all over the country. More than 170 m hectare of country land had suffered from soil erosion. In comparison to peninsular India, the erosion rate is much higher in the Himalayan belt. The river channels flowing through Himalaya, carry huge quantity of sediments and deposit it in the plain. In Uttranchal, the Ganga and Yamuna river systems erode extensively and carry large quantity of sediments to the plains of Uttar Pradesh and Bihar. The sediment accumulation in these plains has overshot the carrying capacity of the rivers, which causes very frequent floods during rainy season. The sediment deposition has further deteriorated the soil fertility in this part of the county. Rate of erosion in Ganga and Yamuna river basins has been estimated 549 and 392 tons/km^2/yr. respectively (Abbas and Subramanaim, 1983 and Subramaniam, 1987).

In the recent past, the erosion rate in Uttranchal has tremendously increased due to various man-made reasons. Mining, grazing, developmental activities, i.e. roads, canals, buildings constructions, installation of hydro electric power stations, deforestation, unscientific agricultural activities etc. have intensified the soil erosion in hilly terrain of Uttranchal.

Conserving Soil

Soil erosion has become a serious problem in whole of Uttranchal state. Loss of natural drainage system is the major reason for increase in soil erosion. The natural drainage system of Uttranchal has really become much more deteriorated due to various developmental practices mainly road construction. In earlier days the village community used to do *"Shram-Dan"* for clearing and maintaining the natural drainage system. But now this practice has stopped and as a result the hill drainage systems have been adversely affected. There is a urgent need that the drainage system in the hills of Uttranchal is revived, so that the rain water may flow downward without causing much soil erosion.

Plantation of suitable species in barren and landslide affected land is another requirement, which is to be taken care to check soil erosion. Various scientific researches have been carried out by Forest Research Institute (FRI), Dehradun and other research institutes. The techniques suggested by these organisations may be used for protecting an area from soil erosion.

Non-scientific agricultural practices are also very much responsible for soil erosion in hilly regions. On the basis of scientific researches various recommendations are made in this regard, which need to be implemented strictly. The major recommendations are :

- Avoiding agriculture practice on steep and dangerous slopes. The landslide affected area must be discarded for agriculture.
- In hilly regions, agriculture fields are formed in the form of terraces. These terraces may fall if they retain excess water. It is required that excess water from these terraces is immediately drained out. For this, it is very important that terraced slopes are adequately drained. Diversion ditches, terrace channels and grass water ways may be constructed for this purpose.

- Contour farming is another technique which may be used very successfully for soil conservation. It is very successful in deep and well maintained soil, with less slope. For further treatment of soil erosion alternative strips of grass and crop, which help in reducing soil erosion by putting check on water velocity, raindrop impacts and infiltration may be planted.
- Soil erosion may also be checked by multiple cropping pattern, which refers to growing of 2 or 3 crops in sequence in the same year on the same area. This practice keeps the soil covered for most of the time, preventing soil erosion.
- The retention of different crops on same area also improves the soil quality and texture.
- For better results after crop harvesting, the field may be covered by mulch to check soil erosion.
- To deal gully erosion it is beneficial that gullies may be planted or grassed. Small gullies can be filled and at places small check dams may be constructed for larger gullies to prevent soil erosions and widening of the gully.

FOREST FIRES

Forest fires are not new for the forests, they have burned across the earth for millions of years. Evidence of fires that burned in the past exists today as fossilized trees – trees that lived long ago and have, over many years, turned hard like a rock. But in recent past the incidences of forest fire have increased tremendously due to human induced activities.

In comparison to other parts of the country, the forests of Himalayan region due to various biotic and geographic reasons are more prone to forest fire. Being ecologically very sensitive, the impact of fire on forests of Himalaya is more serious and beyond repair. The severity of the problem may be judged from the recent forest fire of 1995 in two states – Uttranchal and Himachal Pradesh, in which along with direct loss of Rs. 1750 million worth of forests, the impacts of fire and its scars on local environment are still visible prominently.

Types of Forest Fire

Forest fires are basically of four types depending upon their nature and size:

Surface Fire : This is the most common type of forest fire. It burns undergrowth and dead material along the floor of the forest and is useful to the vegetation and does more good than harm.

Ground Fire : This fire burns roots and other materials on or beneath the surface. It is more damaging than surface fire because it can destroy vegetation completely.

Crown Fire : This is most unpredictable fire and burns the tops of trees and are spread rapidly by wind.

Firestorm : A firestorm is the most damaging to the forest cover. It is basically an intense fire over a large area. As the fire burns, heat rises and the cold wind from outside rushes in, causing the fire to grow rapidly. More wind inflow makes the fire spin very violently like a storm. Temperatures inside this type of forest fire can reach up to 2,000 degrees Fahrenheit.

Causes of Forest Fire

Causes of the forest fire are both natural and also due to human interventions. Fires occur naturally due to lightning but most fires are caused by the local community. Approximately 90 per cent of forest fires are due to human interventions, both intentional or unintentional. In developing countries like India forest fires have close link with poverty. The people residing within the forests or nearby areas are dependent on forests for their livelihood. They ignite forests mainly for collection of forest produces or clearing the land for agricultural purposes. Some fires are caused due to the poor knowledge and the negligence of the people. Throwing burning *biris* or cooking food etc. are such causes of forest fire. The remaining 10 per cent of forest fires are due to natural processes such as lightning, increase in the temperature during the summers etc. Lightning is the most common natural cause of forest fire. Lightening strikes the Earth about 100 times each second. Its temperatures can sometimes reach more than 28,000°C. In Indian forests, during the summer the temperature rises quite high. The dry leaves and other vegetation may catch fire due to this increase in temperature also.

Components and Variables of the Forest Fire

Components

For a fire to start three components are essential, i.e. oxygen, fuel and heat. These three components of forest fire play an important role in forest fire management. Oxygen must be at least 16 per cent in the air for a fire to start. Fuel is any living or dead material that can burn. Dead plants, dry leaves, pine needles, grass etc. are the fuels that catch fire very easily. The third component for the fire i.e. the heat can be supplied by lightning striking a tree or grass or human induced activities such as forest produce collection, clearing of forest land for agricultural purposes, throwing of lighted cigarettes or *biris,* cooking food in and around the forest etc. These three components of fire are very easily available in the Indian forest and hence the forests of the country are more prone to forest fire.

The Variables

In the case of forest fire, the different recognized variables are - the type of vegetation/forest, the climate of the region, the topography of the area, the training level of the forest officials, the education level and knowledge of the local population about the forest fire, the resources available to detect and suppress forest fire etc. These variables can be further classified under three heads, namely, controllable, uncontrollable and outcome variables.

Controllable Variables

The availability of the forest fire prevention and suppression equipments, the training of forest officials, peoples' participation, the budget of forest divisions and availability of forest fire data etc.

Uncontrollable Variables

The type of vegetation (deciding resistance of forest species to fire), the topography and the climate of the area.

Outcome Variables

The incidence of forest fire (area affected by forest fire).

Fire as a Forest Management Technique

Forest fires are not always harmful. Most of the fires are very useful and essential for a good natural forest management, i.e. development and regeneration of forest vegetation. This utility of the fire was recognised by many ancient civilisations also. These civilisations recognized fire as a part of nature. There are many legends about great fire creature. The Egyptians believed in a brightly coloured bird named the Phoenix which could live for as long as 1000 years. When the bird became old it would end its life by burning in the fire. After the old Phoenix disappeared in the fire, a new bird would rise from the ashes. Thus forest fire was more or less responsible for the rebirth of phoenix. In the similar manner, the foresters use fires as a means to protect natural resources and keep the environment healthy. For proper forest management the foresters study a forest area and write a fire prescription for that area. The prescription indicates when or if a fire will be ignited by trained professionals or when a fire ignited by natural causes will be allowed to burn and up to what duration and extent. After starting the fire, the foresters keep a close vigil on the spread of the fire. This controlled forest fire burns the dry leaves and other fuel material available on the ground and thus make the forest safe from the big fire incidences. The vegetation burned by the fire also provides minerals and salts for the new plants and seedlings and thus helps in regeneration and growth of the new plants and trees.

Dangers of Fire

Though a controlled forest fire is useful for the vegetation, an uncontrolled fire may cause much harm to forest, human life and property. The burning of forest may have severe impact on the environment of an area. Burning of forest vegetation creates harmful gases like Methyl Bromide, which helps in depleting Ozone Layer and consequently the Global Warming. The other gases produced during forest fire are Carbon-Di-Oxide, Carbon-Mono-Oxide, Methane, Nitric and Nitrous-Oxide, Methane and various forms of Hydrocarbons. These gases and chemicals are very dangerous to human beings, cattle and other wild life living in or near the forest. During very dry or windy weather conditions, fire burns much faster. Such fire burns the forest timber and other minor produce and thus causes direct economic loss to the forest property. The houses and other property near the forest are also badly damaged by the forest fire.

The adverse ecological, economic and social impacts of forest fire may be summarised as follows :

- Loss of valuable timber and minor forest produce resources.
- Loss of livelihood for tribal population living within or near the forest.
- Loss of human life (Four women grass cutters were killed in February, 2001 in Gwar village of Uttranchal).
- Depletion of carbon sinks and thus deteriorating the environmental conditions.
- Loss of bio-diversity and extinction of plant and animal species.
- Soil erosion resulting in loss of soil productivity and flooding in the down stream valleys.
- Loss in agricultural land due to erosion and land slide.
- Degradation of water sheds resulting in low rainfall and fall in water table.

- Damage to wild life habitat and their death.
- Damage to natural regeneration and reduction in forest vegetation.
- Increase in percentage of Carbon-Di-Oxide in the atmosphere.
- Degradation of microclimate of the area making it unhealthy for living.
- Increase in incidence of respiratory diseases.

MANAGING THE FOREST FIRE

In the forest fire management there are basically three steps, i.e. *prevention, detection* and *suppression* of forest fire (Fig. 5.4).

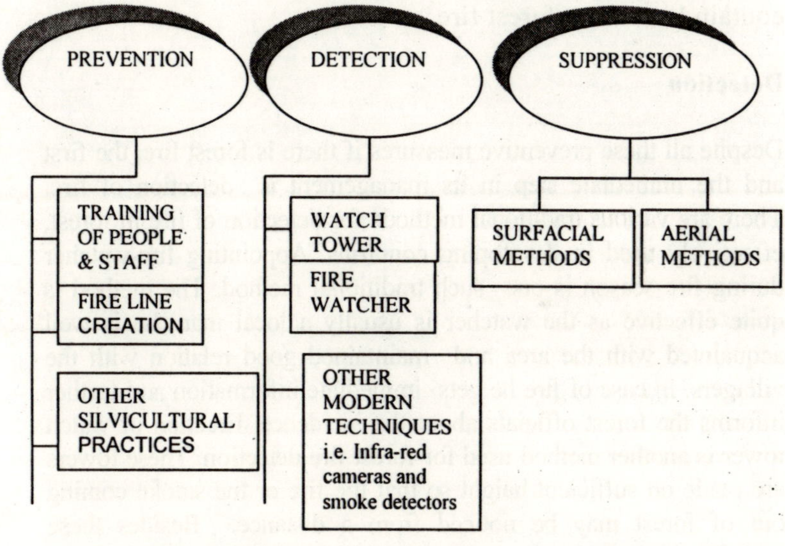

Fig 5.4 : Three essential steps of forest fire management.

Prevention

As prevention is better than cure it is of utmost significance that necessary preventive measures are taken to manage the forest fire in an area. Cutting of forest fire line is a very old and traditional method, which is very successful in preventing the forest fire. In this method fire lines are made by clearing a strip of vegetation in the forest. This helps in preventing the fire spread beyond a limit and thus control its spread. The training of the forest officials and making people aware are the other preventive measures that may prove quite successful in forest fire control. Educating the people about the do's and don'ts to prevent forest fire is very important. They must be made aware of the damages, which fire causes to their environment and health etc. Awareness programmes should be conducted for the villagers at Panchayat and Block levels. Placards may be put at appropriate places and pamphlets distributed showing the causes and damages of forest fire. Various audio-visual means such as film show, radio and TV etc. are to be used for telecasting programmes about the fire. At school level and even college level the syllabus must contain lessons on forest fire.

Detection

Despite all these preventive measures if there is forest fire, the first and the immediate step in its management is detection of fire. There are various traditional methods for detection of fire in forest, effectively used in developing countries. Appointing fire-watcher during fire season is one such traditional method. The method is quite effective as the watcher is usually a local man, he is well acquainted with the area and maintained good relation with the villagers. In case of fire he gets immediate information and further informs the forest officials about the incidence. Erection of watch tower is another method used for forest fire detection. These towers are made on sufficient height so that the fire or the smoke coming out of forest may be noticed from a distance. Besides these traditional methods, recently many new techniques have been evolved for forest fire detection. The use of modern infrared imaging equipment can help fire fighters to locate fire through smoke. Planes equipped with small infrared cameras can detect heat from wildfires at night and in heavy smoke. They can penetrate even the thickest cloud of smoke and show fire fighters where the hotspot exists. A fire's location and direction are mapped and then used to send fire fighters to control the fire.

Suppression

After detection attempts are made to suppress forest fire. There are two general ways to attack a forest fire, i.e. direct and indirect.

Direct

For small, low-intensity fires, the fire fighters cool fire's edges with water, dirt, bushes or chemicals and then scrape a fire line to expose soil and eliminate fuel around the fire. In India traditionally fire is extinguished by use of twigs and bushes. If available, soil or dust/sand is also used for the purpose. Various tools, i.e. rack, Pulaski, flask key, shovel, macklied, garden rack etc. are also used for fighting fire. But in hilly terrain it is observed that the traditional methods are more frequently applied for the purpose. The tools provided by the forest department are heavy and not feasible to carry them at the fire spot due to their weight and the lack of training of the forest officials. Keeping the problem in view, it is required that instead of traditional equipment, some light tools, which can be easily carried in hilly terrain are provided to the forest department to suppress fire in Uttranchal. To suppress fire the role of local population is very important. Though attempts have been made through Joint Forest Management Committees to involve people, still there is much more to be done. The local population is to be assured that the survival of the forest is must for their own survival.

Indirect

For larger fires, fire fighters construct a fire line at a distance from the fire and burn out the area between it and the fire, depriving the main fire of fuel. Initiating an anti-forest fire is another indirect method of forest fire suppression. In this method, a controlled fire is initiated in the forest which spreads in the opposite direction of the main forest fire. When the two fires meet, they automatically suppress each other.

In the developed countries, aeroplanes and helicopters are used for detection and suppression of forest fire. This is very useful to fight a fire, when it is in some remote area. To extinguish fire, chemicals and water carried in large buckets are sprinkled over the burning forest. This method though somewhat costly, is very effective method to fight fire in difficult terrain.

Forest Fire Situation in India with Special Reference to Uttranchal

India constitutes one of the mega bio-diversity zones of the world, abundant with unique and diversified floral and faunal wealth. The country with a forest cover of 76.4 million hectares, contains a wide variety of climate zones ranging from the tropical south to north western deserts, to the Himalayan mountains and the wet north-east. The forests here are endowed with a variety of biomass and biological communities. With increasing population pressure the forest cover of the country is under tremendous pressure and is deteriorating at an alarming rate. Along with other factors, forest fires are major cause of degradation of Indian forests. As per Forest Survey of India Report, about 50 per cent of forest areas in the country are fire prone (ranging from 33 per cent in some states to 90 per cent in the others). Very heavy, heavy and frequent forest fire damages are noticed over 0.87 per cent, 0.14 per cent and 5.16 per cent forest areas respectively. Thus on a whole total of 6.17% of forests damaged in the country due to forest fire.

Forest fires in the country cause immense loss to the environment and the property. Ecological, economic and social impacts of the forest fire in India may be enlisted as loss of timber, loss of bio-diversity, loss of wild life habitat, global warming, soil erosion, loss of fuel wood and fodder, damage to water and other natural resources, loss of natural regeneration, loss of Non-timber Forest Produces (NTFPs). As per rough estimate average direct economical annual loss due to forest fire in the country is Rs. 440 crores.

The susceptibility or vulnerability of the forests of the country to fire varies from place to place depending upon the type of vegetation and the climate. As far as the fire season is concerned, various regions of the country have different normal and peak fire seasons, which normally vary from February to June. In the hills of Uttranchal fire season starts late and most of the fire occurrences are reported between April and June. However in certain circumstances the fire may start bit early also, as seen in the case of year 2000-2001, when the fire was reported in the month of February also. This fire in the Gwar Forest area of Rudraprayag district claimed four lives and injured many more. The fire broke out in the grass field, when some ladies were busy cutting the grass. The probable reason of the fire seems to be the negligence of the people, may be some lighted cigar or *bidi.* Due to fast wind in the valley, the fire did spread very rapidly and it engulfed the grass cutters within no time and caused the tragedy.

Major Forest Fires in Uttranchal and their Impacts

Due to various factors including the vulnerability of species, climate, poor training and awareness of the people and the administration, lack of equipment and funds etc. the forests of Uttranchal are every year badly affected by the forest fire. During 1990s several forest fires occurred in Uttranchal and Himachal Pradesh. Between the years 1995 and 1999, many forest fire incidences occurred in these two states, which affected an area of around 6,77,700 hectares. The direct economic loss to the timber wood by these fires is estimated as approximately Rs. 170 crores. Besides the direct loss, the other damage due to these fires are – loss of soil fertility, soil erosion, loss of employment, drying up of water resources and loss of bio-diversity. These fires also brought a major change in the microclimate of the region in the form of soil moisture balance and increased evaporation.

As far as the causes of forest fire are concerned, in the region there are very few cases of fire due to natural reasons. Majority of the forest fires, in the area are man made. It is widely acknowledged that most of these fires are caused by the people and have close relationship with their socio-economic conditions. Grazing, collection of minor forest produce including fire wood, grasses etc. by villagers are some of the causes of fires in Uttranchal.

The Problem in Forest Fire Management

The problem of forest fire in general is very challenging and multifarious in Uttranchal. The major handicap for handling this issue is non-availability of the data regarding forest fire in the area. It is sad to state that this problem of forest fire has never been taken seriously and efforts have never been made to collect factual data about the forest fire in such sensitive areas. The available data is either skeletal or sketchy or unreliable, as no systematic approach has ever been adopted so far, to collect the same. The data collected by central survey agency of the country, i.e. Forest Survey of India are quite contradictory to the data supplied by the state government.

The second problem regarding forest fire in the region is lack of proper mechanism/system for forecasting forest fire. There is no research institute engaged in research related to forest fire. The research data available with other countries is not relevant and useful to Himalayan conditions for forest fire control and prevention. The other major issue is the way, forest fire is tackled in the region. The non-co-operation of the state, lack of proper training to forest department officials, non-co-operation of the local community etc. are some other major shortcomings which make the condition more grave and serious. Among the causes mentioned above the non-co-operation of the local community and their lack of knowledge about the forest fire is of great concern. It is worth mentioning here that 90% of forest fires are initiated by man (knowingly or unknowingly). In some parts of Himalaya, the grass lands are burnt annually to improve the quality of the pasture-land and to facilitate the collection of various minor forest produces. This practice of annual burning is not closely supervised and regulated, which results in spreading of fire to nearby forest areas causing significant damage and loss to forest cover.

Besides all these, the other shortcomings, which come in the way of handling forest fire in the region is the improper utilisation of the funds by the state forest departments and lack of supervision and monitoring of the scheme by forest fire prevention unit of the state and central government. The various problems in tackling the forest fire may be summarised pictographically, as shown in Fig. 5.5.

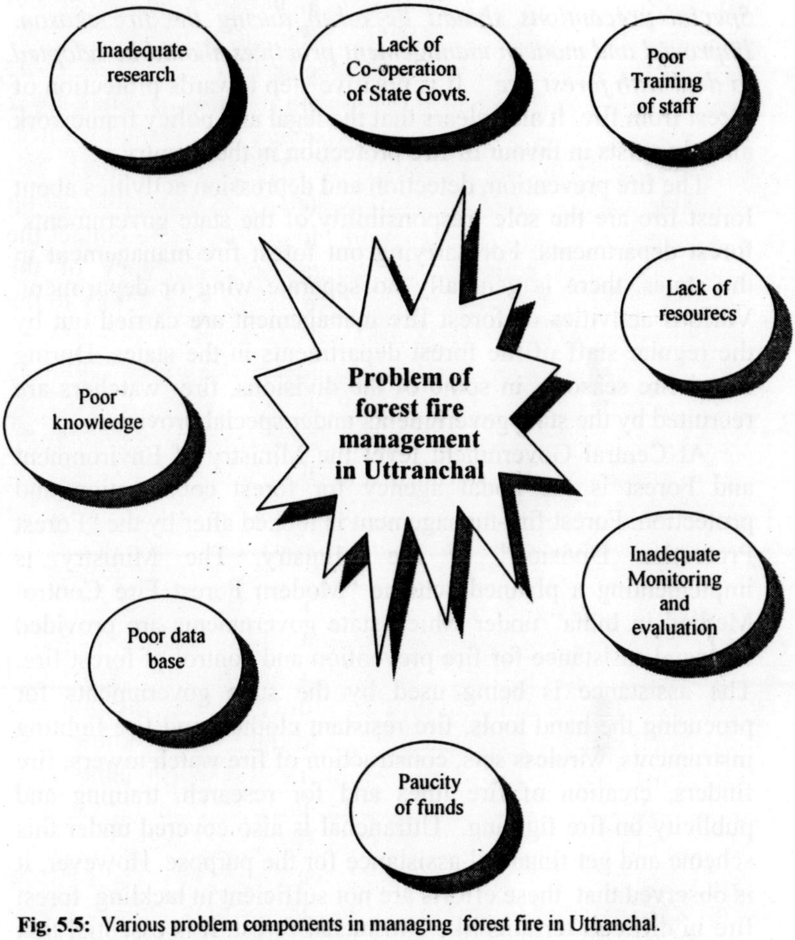

Fig. 5.5: Various problem components in managing forest fire in Uttranchal.

Operational Fire Management Systems and Organizations Present in the Country

Public policies concerning fire

India's National Forest Policy (1988), presents a visionary strategy for forest conservation and management and lays emphasis on protection of forest against encroachment, fire and grazing. It *interalia* states *"The incidences of forest fire in the country is high. Standing trees and fodder are destroyed on a large scale and natural regeneration annihilated by such fires. Special precautions should be taken during the fire season. Improved and modern management practices should be adopted to deal with forest fire"*. It is positive step towards protection of forest from fire. It also clears that the legal and policy framework already exists in favour of fire protection in the country.

The fire prevention, detection and depression activities about forest fire are the sole responsibility of the state governments' forest departments. For carrying out forest fire management in the states, there is generally no separate wing or department. Various activities of forest fire management are carried out by the regular staff of the forest departments in the states. During forest fire seasons, in some of the divisions, fire- watchers are recruited by the state governments under special provision.

At Central Government level the Ministry of Environment and Forest is the nodal agency for forest conservation and protection. Forest fire-management is looked after by the "Forest Protection Division" of the Ministry. The Ministry is implementing a planned scheme "Modern Forest Fire Control Method in India" under which state governments are provided financial assistance for fire prevention and control of forest fire. The assistance is being used by the state governments for procuring the hand tools, fire resistant clothes, and fire fighting instruments, wireless sets, construction of fire watch towers, fire finders, creation of fire lines and for research, training and publicity on fire fighting. Uttranchal is also covered under this scheme and get financial assistance for the purpose. However, it is observed that these efforts are not sufficient in tackling forest fire in difficult terrains like Uttranchal forest. It is essential that area-specific programmes are evolved to manage this disaster in the region.

Community Involvement

Conservation and protection of the forest is not possible without people's participation and involvement. In India, Joint Forest Management (JFM) Committees have been set up at village level for the purpose. These JFM committees have also been given responsibilities to protect the forest from forest fires. Help of NGOs for the purpose is also being taken by the state forest department to ensure the local peoples' involvement in the programme for better results.

Research Issues

In India for better management of forest fire, there is an urgent need to make research in the field of fire detection and suppression of forest fire. The research and technology developed in western countries is not suitable for the Indian environment, therefore, it is required that original research fit for Indian condition is carried out for fire management. The Government is considering, setting up a National Institute of Forest Fire Management with satellite centres in different parts of the country to bring the latest forest fire fighting technologies to India through proper research, training of personnel and technology transfer on a long term basis.

National Master Plan for Forest Fire Control

The incidence of the forest fire in the country are on the increase and more and more area is burnt year after year. Important forest fire management elements, i.e. strategic fire plans, coordination among departments, funding, human resource development, fire research, fire management and extension programmes are urgently required.

Taking into consideration the grim situation of the problem, it is the need of the hour that some serious efforts are made for evolving appropriate forest fire management strategy in the area. Recently, the Ministry of Environment and Forest, Government of India has prepared a National Master Plan for Forest Fire Control. Under this plan, it is proposed to introduce a well-coordinated and integrated fire management including many new components –

(i) Prevention of fire caused by man through education and environmental modification – including silvicultural activities, engineering works, peoples participation, education and enforcement. More emphasis is to be given on the people participation through Joint Forest Fire Management preventing forest fires.

(ii) Detection of forest fire in time through a well coordinated network of observation points, efficient ground patrolling, communication network etc. is of strategic importance. Use of modern techniques, i.e. Remote sensing etc. are also to be given due importance in the fire detection. For successful fire management and administration, National Fire Danger Rating System (NFDRS) is also to be developed in the country.

(iii) Vigorous follow-up action; and forest fuel modification system at strategic points.

(iv) Special emphasis is to be given on the research, training and development.

AVALANCHES

Avalanches are river like speedy flow of snow or ice descending from the mountain tops. Avalanches are very damaging and cause huge loss to life and property. In Himalayas, avalanches are common in Drass, Pir Panijat, Lahaul-Spiti and Badrinath areas. As per Snow and Avalanche Study Establishment (SASE), of Defence Research and Development Organisation (DRDO), on an average around 30 people are killed every year due to this disaster in various zones of the Himalayas. Beside killing people, avalanches also damage the roads and others properties and settlements falling in its way. The loss from various major avalanche disasters in Himalayas are as follows :

Time	Area	Loss
1. March 1979	Lahul and Spiti (H.P)	237 people killed
2. Winter of 1982	Ladakh (J&K)	100 people killed
3. Winter of 1982	Ladakh (J&K)	27 people killed
4. March of 1988.	(J&K)	70 people killed
5. March of 1991	H. P.	Road blockage for 40 days
6. September, 1995	H.P.	Flood caused by melting of snow brought by avalanche.

In Uttranchal avalanches are very common in the holy shrine of Hemkund, Badrinath, Kedarnath, Yamunotri and Gangotri. The pilgrims to these places very frequently face the danger of snow avalanche. Near Rupkund glacial valley, around 200 pilgrims were killed by one such avalanche.

Area Prone to Avalanches

- Avalanches are common in Himalayan region above 3500m elevation.
- Very frequent on slopes of 30-45°.
- Convex slopes more prone to this disaster.
- North facing slope have avalanches in winter and south facing slopes during spring.
- Slopes covered with grass more prone to this hazard.

Type of Avalanches

Based on the nature of the snow / ice movement, avalanches may be classified into three groups :

1. *Loose Snow Avalanches :* These avalanches are caused by movement of loose snow crystals with air. They usually occur during snowfall or when atmospheric temperature is low. These avalanches are small in size and are not very harmful.
2. *Slab Avalanches :* Due to continuous piling up of snow, the lower layers of snow become compact and hardened. These hardened layers may break into slabs or blocks for various reasons, i.e. presence of unfrozen ice, earthquakes, explosions etc. These avalanches are often dangerous as they flow rapidly moving upto miles down the slope.
3. *Hoar air borne Avalanche :* These avalanches are very common on northern fringe of High Himalayan Ranges. In this type of avalanche due to very low temperature conditions, large hollow crystals of ice are formed, which crumble due to over weight of more snow fall. This results into full depth hoar avalanche. Besides, during cold night on the snow surface, vertical ice crystals are formed which

collapse due to further snowfall. This also leads to surface hoar air-borne avalanche.

Causes of Avalanches

Topographic feature, temperature and wind velocity are three main factors that affect the triggering of avalanches.

1. Topography is the most important factor in deciding the initiation and nature of the avalanche. The shape of the slope also affect the avalanche to a large extent. The slope with elevated curvature is more prone to avalanche in comparison to other slopes. Vegetation helps in retaining the avalanche. Vegetation cover, its thickness and height of trees etc. affect the nature of an avalanche. The barren mountains without vegetation cover are more prone to avalanche. In Uttranchal the barren areas near Badrinath contribute to accelerate the avalanche movement.
2. The temperature variation also affects the avalanche movement upto an extent. The rain water percolating through the cracks of snow or ice also causes temperature variation which ultimately results into large avalanche. In Himalayas, on southern slopes, which face the sun, there is much variation in day and night temperature, resulting in the increased vulnerability of the region to the avalanches.
3. The fresh snow deposit is likely to be blown specially by wind. The wind which blows with high velocity can result in snow avalanche.

Beside these three factors, earthquakes may also shatter and trigger snow avalanches. The traffic noise and explosion created waves are the other causes of avalanche in the mountainous region.

Mitigating Avalanches

Snow and Avalanche Study Establishment (SASE) of Defence Research and Development Organisation, under the Defence Ministry, Government of India, is the nodal agency responsible for mitigating snow avalanches. The organisation carried out intensive research in the field of prevention and protection from this hazard in Himalayan region.

The methods to control or minimize the impacts of the hazard may be enlisted as:

Preventive Measures

1. *Artificial triggering :* The waves created by explosions may result into avalanche. This idea has been used to create small size avalanches by repeated and controlled explosions. These explosions are carried out under strictly controlled conditions. These artificial small avalanches upto an extent prevent the possibility of large scale avalanche.

2. *Preventive Structures:* To prevent avalanches, various structures have been found to be very helpful.

(i) *Retaining structures:* In the upper part of the slope these structures are built to prevent stress accumulation. These structures actually check snow deposition on the top (leeward side) of slope and minimize the load, resulting into prevention of snow/ice movement.

(ii) *Building terraces:* Building of terraces on the slope of mountain reduce the gliding force of snow/ice.

(iii) *Control fence :* Erection of control fence on mountain slopes may also help in preventing snow avalanches.

(iv) *Snow bridges:* Snow bridges made of steel or timber or aluminum are very effective snow direction control device. Snow nets of strong nylon ropes also serve the similar purpose in preventing avalanches.

(v) *Plantation:* Growing forest in path of snow movement also prevents large avalanche.

Protection/Diversion Structures

These structures are made to divert the flow direction of avalanche and thus protecting buildings, roads etc. from damage.

(i) *Avalanche ramps*: These structure are erected to allow snow passages over installations and buildings.

(ii) *Wedges:* Construction of concrete wedges in the snow flow path checks the speed of movement and also divert its direction, thus protecting buildings from damage.

(iii) *Underground structure*: Construction of underground structures, i.e. canals, roads, etc. protect them from adverse impact of avalanches.

(iv) *Resisting structures*: Earth mounds, piles etc. also help in reducing the velocity of the flow of snow.

FLOODS

Floods are very common geological hazards that affect the individuals and their property. Most of the floods are result of excessive rain fall or snowmelt, i.e. due to excessive run off. One another type of flood, i.e. flash floods are short lived extreme events, which usually occur under slowly moving or stationary thunderstorm, lasting for less than 24 hours. Such floods common through out Himalayas, including Uttranchal are quite damaging due to the high velocity of water with much energetic capacity to carry away all obstacles in its way.

Causes for Floods

The basic cause for all floods is excessive run off beyond the carrying capacity of the river channels. This excessive runoff may be a result of heavy rain fall, including cloud bursts, snow melting (due to change in climatic conditions), bursting of dams (human made and created due to landslides), excess release of water from dams etc. The another factor responsible for this excessive run off is reduction in infiltration capacity of the soil, mainly due to deforestation. The reduction in carrying capacity of the river channel as a result of sedimentation is also responsible for causing excessive runoff which ultimately results into flood. The main factors responsible for floods in Uttranchal are :

Heavy rainfall

Heavy rainfall in a region generates excess of water than the infiltration capacity of the land and river channels. This excess water flows beyond the river channels and causes flood. A rainfall of 5 centimetre over an area of one square kilometre generates around 15 million gallons of water. When such huge quantity of water accumulates and flows down the slope without infiltration, it may create heavy flood.

Cloud Bursts

Cloud bursts are very excessive rain within a short span. Cloud bursts cause many deteriorating impacts on the land. Landslides, debris flow, slope failure, gully erosion and debris deposition are common features involved with the cloud burst. They also cause huge damage to human life, cultivated land, banks of the rivers, roads, canals etc. Huge landslides and unconsolidated debris avalanches may also occur due to cloud bursting.

Causes of cloud bursts

Cloud burst usually occurs as a result of combination of different factors. In deep valleys of Himalayas, sometimes temperature increases suddenly, which creates air uplifting, resulting into low pressure in the valley region. To fill up this pressure gap the air from all sides move towards the valley, creating eddy conditions. In this situation two fronts of cold and warm air move towards each other and the cold air from high mountain comes in conflict with the warm moist air of the valley. Cold front is associated with strong atmospheric disturbances. The warm air then lifted, opens breaking out in violent thunder storms. Here again the cold air renders in contact with the ground warm air and is forced to rise as it ascending a long ramp. In such conditions the warm air becomes unstable and develops convection cells resulting into heavy shower and thunder storms.

Factors affecting Cloud Bursts

(i) Steep gradient and geological factors

Gradient of the valley and the terrain is also an important factor which affects the impacts of cloud burst. If the gradient is very high, the rain water is not allowed to percolate the soil and resulting run off becomes suddenly high causing rapid flood in the area.

The chemical composition and the structural features of soil or rock bodies are also upto an extent responsible in deciding the run off during cloud burst. If the rocks or soil are more porous and with sufficient fractures, shears etc. it will allow more water to percolate and reduce run off. On the contrary, if the rain water due to cloud burst suddenly accumulates in the valley and runs down the slope, it causes heavy damage to the human population and environment.

(ii) Vegetative factor

Dense vegetation cover in restricted area also helps in changing the micro climatic condition in hilly areas. In Himalayas the top of the hills are usually covered with dense forest whereas the area just above the valley are barren. With the change of temperature, there is very little change in temperature in forest covered areas, while the barren land experience sudden change in the temperature. This change in temperature in lower zones results into temperature differences and thunder storm/heavy shower is resulted as described earlier.

Other Causes of Floods

Snow melting

High peaks and valleys of Himalaya are abundant with many glaciers, from where many rivulets start with the melting of snow. This snow melting in general is within a limited range. In certain circumstances, due to change in climatic conditions there is increase in the temperature. This temperature increase leads to more snow melting causing more water flow from the glaciers to the river channels.

For this excessive snow melting besides local factors, the main reason is the "Green House Effect". Due to excessive burning of fuels (coal, petrol, diesel etc.) and large scale deforestation, the carbon dioxide content in the atmosphere is increasing at an steady rate. The carbon dioxide gas prevents the heat rays returning back to the atmosphere. Thus a part of the heat energy, absorbed by the earth and its objects, partially remains in the atmosphere, resulting into increase of overall global temperature or global warming. This effect, known as Green House Effect is responsible for increase in the temperature and consequently the snow melting in glaciers.

GLOBAL WARMING

Global warming had very adverse impact on the Himalayan Glaciers. According to United Nations Environment Programme (UNEP), the mean global temperature has risen 0.7 degree centigrade during the last century (highest level since first temperature readings were first initiated about 50 years ago. Due to this increase in temperature glaciers are the most adversely affected. Geological Survey of India and DRDO recently studied the behaviour of many Major Glaciers. The results of these studies are very disturbing. The studies show that the Glaciers of Uttranchal i.e. Gangotri, pindari and Milam have been receding at an alarming rate. The receding rates of these glaciers are 24.6, 23.4 and 12.5 meters respectively every year. Between 1842 and 1935 and 1935 the snout of Gnagotri has receded around 680 meters (@ around 7.3 meters per year). The receding rate of this large glacier increased tremendously and between 1935 and 1966 the receding rate was calculated 17 meters per year. Due to global warming the glacier starting receding at very fast rate and after 1977 and between 1977 and 1990 the receding rate has been estimated around 28 meters annually. The receding rates of other famous Himalayan Glaciers are as follows :

S. No.	Name of Glacier	State	Receding rate (m/year)
1	Barashingri	Himachal Pradesh	44.3
2	Gangotri	Uttranchal	17.5
3	Milam	Uttranchal	13.3
4	Pindar	Uttranchal	23.5
5	Dokriani	Uttranchal	17.0
6	Zemu	Sikkim	13.2

The main adverse impact of Global Warming on Glaciers and the consequent result on environment may be summarized as :

1. Scarcity of water in rivers – The Himalayan Glaciers are the perennial source of water to the main North Indian rivers i.e. Ganga, Indus and Brahmputra. The adverse impact on the health of glaciers will certainly result into shortage of water in the rivers originating from Himalayas. This is going to cause many problems in the Indian subcontinent, particularly in northern parts, where every thing like agriculture production, power generation, forests, human and wild life etc. is solely dependent on water from these rivers. The scarcity of water, caused by uneven rain fall also results into desertification of land.
2. Landslide and rock fall – The receding glaciers are leaving huge amount of debris on the steep slopes. The debris and mud is very prone to flow along the slope, causing landslides and rock falls in the areas near glaciers.
3. Floods due to bursting of glacial lakes – The huge amount of water being accumulating in the lakes due to global warming may lead to bursting of lake and consequent huge floods in the area.
4. Increase in siltation in Reservoirs – The glacial melting is resulting into huge amount siltation in the reservoirs of dams, which decreases their life and safety problems
5. Another important impact of Global Warming is on the Ocean surface. The snow melting of glaciers contributes to rise in sea level, which endangers the existence of low-lying areas near the oceans. Bangladesh and other

island in Indian and Pacific Ocean are at maximum risk. Low lying coastal areas and other island union territories of India i.e. Andman and Nicobar, Laksha-dweep etc. may disappear in near future under the ocean due to this increasing water level.

6. Global warming is responsible for increase in ocean surface temperature also, resulting into torrential rain, tropical cyclones etc. The land surface may be affected by increased windstorm and hailstorm due to climate change.
7. The Ozone layer depletion due to green house gases may result into increase in tropical diseases. An extreme change in fauna and flora may also be caused due to this natural phenomenon.

References

Jain, Sonu : 2002, Bad News : Ice is Breaking, *The Sunday Express* dated April, 28,2002.

Topics 2000 : Natural Catastrophes – The Current Position. Special Millenium Issue, Pub. By Munchener Ruck, Munich Re Group.

Bursting of Dams

Failure of man-made or landslide formed obstructions in the river channels cause catastrophic floods, resulting into heavy loss of life and property. Bursting of natural dams formed due to obstruction of landslides is major cause of floods in Uttranchal. Alaknanda, a major tributary of Ganga has generated numerous devastating floods during historical times. As per the available records, during 1857, river Mandakini flow was blocked by building of temporary natural dam as a result of heavy landslide in its valley. The breaching of the dam after three days caused large scale flood in the river valley. Just after eleven years of this catastrophe, Birehi river valley also experienced a similar havoc due to devastating flood resulting to extensive property loss.

On August 26, 1894 again Birehi river was blocked by massive landslide (3 kilometre long and 500 metre breadth). The blocked water after one year succeeded in making its way through the natural dam and the huge energetic flow of this stored water caused unprecedented damage in Alaknanda valley.

Again in 1930, near Badrinath the damming of Alaknanda created flood destroying many villages in its valley.

Plate 6 : Construction of dam at improper site may be very damaging

The most devastating flood in Alaknanda occurred on July 20, 1970, killing 55 people and massive damage to other properties, viz. roads, bridges, houses, agriculture etc.

During August, 1978 a natural dam was formed in the way of Kanodia river in Uttranchal due to heavy landslide in the river valley. This landslide was an outcome of cloud burst causing excessive rain in the area. Due to obstruction in the river channel a three kilometre long lake was formed in the river channel. Slowly the landslide flown material moved down stream and blocked the flow of river Bhagirathi. With increasing water pressure this huge blockage of debris burst away and massive quantity of water with massive energy flew and swept away, whatever came in its way.

Reduced infiltration

The infiltration capacity of a soil directly depends on texture of soil, gradient or slope of the land and after all the type and nature of vegetation in the area. All these three factors are interdependent and interrelated, i.e. it is the nature or texture of the soil that determines the type of vegetation and *vice versa.* Same is true for the gradient also. Among the three factors mentioned above nature and extent of the vegetation is the most important, in determining the infiltration capacity of the soil. The roots of the vegetation, the litter etc. make soil porous that permit more rain water infiltration into the soil depth and consequently reducing the run off. Deforestation in Uttranchal due to various human induced activities (developmental plans, illicit felling, burning, agriculture and grazing etc.) have reduced the infiltration capacity of soil tremendously, resulting into high rate of run off during rainy season.

Sedimentation/siltation in river channels

The deforestation in hilly terrains has converted a large portion barren making it prone and vulnerable to soil erosion. This eroded material is swept away by the flowing water and is deposited in the stream channels, making channels shallower (reducing its water carrying capacity). In Uttranchal region also the erosion rate of rivers has increased many times during the last two three decades. This large quantity of eroded sediments have made the river channels of the region rapidly shallow and consequently reducing their water carrying capacity. As a result, the region has become vulnerable and prone to flood disaster, not only in down stream plains but also in hilly terrain.

Plate 7 : Damaged checkdams during flood in Yamuna river near Dehradun

Managing Floods

Management of floods in hilly terrain like Uttranchal is slightly different from the plain areas. The structural methods like construction of dams and reservoirs, embankment along the river, channel improvement or diversion of flood waters are neither practical nor of much use in such terrain. On the other hand, the non-structural methods, i.e. treatment of watershed, implementation of land use regulation, flood forecasting and warning etc. may be very helpful for flood management in the region.

The basic principle behind flood control is reducing the excess and sudden run off and water flow and intensely in the drainage system. This can effectively be carried out by giving scientific treatment to the watershed (the total area from where the water accumulates in the main river system of a region). By proper watershed treatment the problem of flood may be solved very effectively and eradicated in the long run. The watershed management actually results into reduction of run off by inducing and increasing infiltration capacity of the catchment area. The afforestation in the catchment area with appropriate species is the best approach for making the soil quite porous, so that it can infilter more and more water.

The vegetation cover also decreases erosion of the soil and thus reduces he sediment flow in the river channel, which prevents it from shallowing.

Treating the natural drainage pattern of the catchment area is another very useful procedure to induce or increase the soil permeability. In this practice the shallowed small drainage channels like gadhera, gads etc. are deepened by removing the siltation.

To increase the infiltration, small check dams may be formed in small stream channels. Such check dams prevent the speedy water run off on steeper slopes and check the soil erosion. The cleaning and removal of silt from the ponds and lakes is also an important step in Watershed management. This increase the water retaining capacity of these bodies and also helps in infiltration of water.

Implementation of Land use Regulations

Land use pattern of an area is decisive factor for water flow, especially in the hilly terrain. Unscientific land use accelerates both the flood frequency and intensity. To formulate appropriate and effective land use pattern regulations for an area, hazard zonation mapping is to be carried out. This exercise includes mapping in the area that have recently been flooded, where construction is to be prohibited and where ground water recharge is taking place. After demarking these areas regulations are to be formulated to restrict construction, develop industrial or economic activities, which adversely affect the eco-system of the area. Such areas are to be developed into green belts by government or NGOs or the local inhabitants.

An appropriate land use regeneration regulation should maintain an adequate flood-plan and to regulate land use development. By hazard zone mapping of flood prone areas, various types of flood hazard zones may be recognized which need different land use regulation.

Forecasting and Warning

The success of a flood warning system basically depends on the hydrological character of a river system. Whereas for rivers with large catchment areas, it is usually sufficient time to make exact forecast about flood, for small river channels with steep gradient it is usually very difficult to predict flood quite early. As most of the Uttranchal rivers fall in the second category, it is required that more scientific researches are carried out to evolve new methods for forecasting floods in hilly areas. For this, it is required that a detail study is carried out about the various watersheds of the area covering the following aspects

- The amount of the rain falling in the watershed.
- The volume of discharge from various tributaries and rivers.
- Flood height and depth of flood in the area.
- Duration of infiltration and the areas likely to be inundated.

To carry out these investigations modern techniques like remote sensing, GIS etc. are also to be applied for forecasting. Flood warning systems in the flood prone areas can use rain gauges and stream sensors, equipped with self-activating radio transmitters to convey data to a central computer for analysis. For efficient flood management, it is required that new sophisticated techniques are used for forecasting flood in Uttranchal flood prone areas, particularly near reservoir sites where floods may cause havoc.

6

DISASTER MANAGEMENT
Present Approaches

Disasters have multi-dimensional impacts on various sectors, namely, personal, socio-cultural and economic. Beside undermining developmental efforts, they also put back development by destroying initiatives and infrastructures. Though disasters are inevitable, yet their adverse impact can be reduced to a large extent by undertaking various mitigation programmes and better management practices. Taking into consideration great loss to life, property and other resources due to frequent disasters, the Government of India and various other sectors have started taking initiatives for preventive measures in this regard. Now-a-days, disaster management is a burning issue, which is getting attention from each and every sector of the society in India.

India, with a total area of 32,87,283 sq. kms. comprises of four regions, namely, the Great Mountain Zone, Plains of Indus, Ganga and Brahmaputra, the Desert region and the Southern Peninsula. Beside geographical diversity, these regions vary in culture, traditions, language, fauna-flora and so on. Geographical, social and cultural diversities of the country gives it a status of subcontinent. The country is a union of 28 States and 7 Union Territories. The States are autonomous in relation to the sphere of activities under the Constitution. The States are further divided into districts totalling to 536.

The vast territory of India accomodates more than one billion population, 198 million housing units, unique geoclimatic conditions including very long coastal line and one of the youngest mountain range in the world. All this make the country vulnerable to natural catastrophe. Traditionally various types of disasters like floods, earthquakes, cyclones, droughts, landslides etc. are very common in the country. According to 1991 census, the literacy ratio in the country is 52.2%. To protect such a large population living in one of the most vulnerable zone to natural catastrophes, with its diversity and very low education level from the fury of natural hazards is not an easy task. However, the government efforts at Central and State level, along with local initiatives have tried to reduce the impacts of natural hazards.

EXISTING GOVERNMENT POLICIES FOR DISASTER MANAGEMENT

Central Level Efforts

The Disaster management in India dates back to 1878, when a Scarcity Relief Division was set up in the Agriculture Ministry to deal with the problem of food scarcity in the country. This Division, later started looking after other types of disasters also and was termed as "Natural Disaster Management (NDM) Division."

Under Indian Constitution, disaster management is a state subject and the responsibility for undertaking rescue, relief and rehabilitation measures in the event of disasters, is that of the concerned State Government. The role of the Central Government is supportive in terms of physical and financial resources. At central level the 'Department of Agriculture and Cooperation' in the Ministry of Agriculture[#], Government of India is the nodal Department for disaster relief. "The Natural Disaster Management Division" in Ministry of Agriculture and the "National Centre for Disaster Management" (NCDM), in the Indian Institute of Public Administration, New Delhi are the nodal agencies for Natural Disaster Management in India. The response of Central Government to a natural disaster depends on

- the gravity of the calamity,
- the scale of the relief operation necessary, and
- the requirement of central assistance for augmenting the state governments.

[#] The subject has recently been transferred to Ministry of Home Affairs.

The Central Government responses are basically of two types, i.e. policy and administrative responsibility as mentioned below :

Central Response

Policy level	Administrative level
Visit of the calamity affected areas by President, Prime Minister and other dignitaries; Activating the administrative machinery for assisting in relief measures; and Setting up a machinery for implementing reviewing and monitoring of relief measures.	Operational requirements; and provision of Centre assistance as per existing policy.

The operational aspects of Central Governments are as

(i) Forecasting and operation of warning systems.
(ii) Maintenance of uninterrupted communication.
(iii) Wide publicity to warnings of impending calamity, disaster preparedness and relief measures through TV, AIR, and news papers.
(iv) Transport with particular reference to evacuation and movement of essential commodities and petroleum products.
(v) Ensuring availability of essential commodities at reasonable prices particularly the commodities through the Public Distribution System.
(vi) Ensuring availability of medicines, vaccine and drugs.
(vii) Preservation and restoration of physical communication links.
(viii) Investments in infrastructure.
(ix) Mobilization of financial resources.

(x) Flood/inflow forecasts from the Central Water Commission.

(xi) Relief, rehabilitation and restoration through military aid to civil authorities.

(xii) Contingency plans for crops, cattle preservation, nutrition and health measures

(xiii) Technical and technological inputs for provision of drinking water

(xiv) Technical assistance in the water budgeting and water management for various uses.

(xv) Coordination of the activities of the State agencies and voluntary agencies.

Along with the Ministry of Agriculture, the responsibility for management of different disasters is shared among various Ministries also at Central level as shown :

Disaster	Nodal Ministry
Air accidents	Ministry of Civil Aviation
Civil strike	Ministry of Home Affairs
Railway accidents	Ministry of Railways
Chemical disasters	Ministry of Environment and Forests
Biological disasters	Ministry of Health
Nuclear disasters	Atomic Energy Department
Natural Disasters	Ministry of Agriculture

A National Crisis Management Committee (NCMC) headed by Cabinet Secretary and other Ministry in-charge, as member looks after the major aspects of disaster management at central level. The Central Relief Commissioner, working as Coordinator at central level functions to coordinate at central level and liaise with the State Governments. The Central Relief Commission after receiving information regarding forecasting/ warning about a natural calamity keeps the Secretary (Agriculture and Cooperation), Minister (Agriculture), Cabinet Secretary and Secretary through them to Prime Minister, the Cabinet and the National Crisis Management Committee (NCMC) informed. He also monitor the developments of the situation on a continuous basis and keeps on informing higher authorities about it (Figs. 6.1 and 6.2).

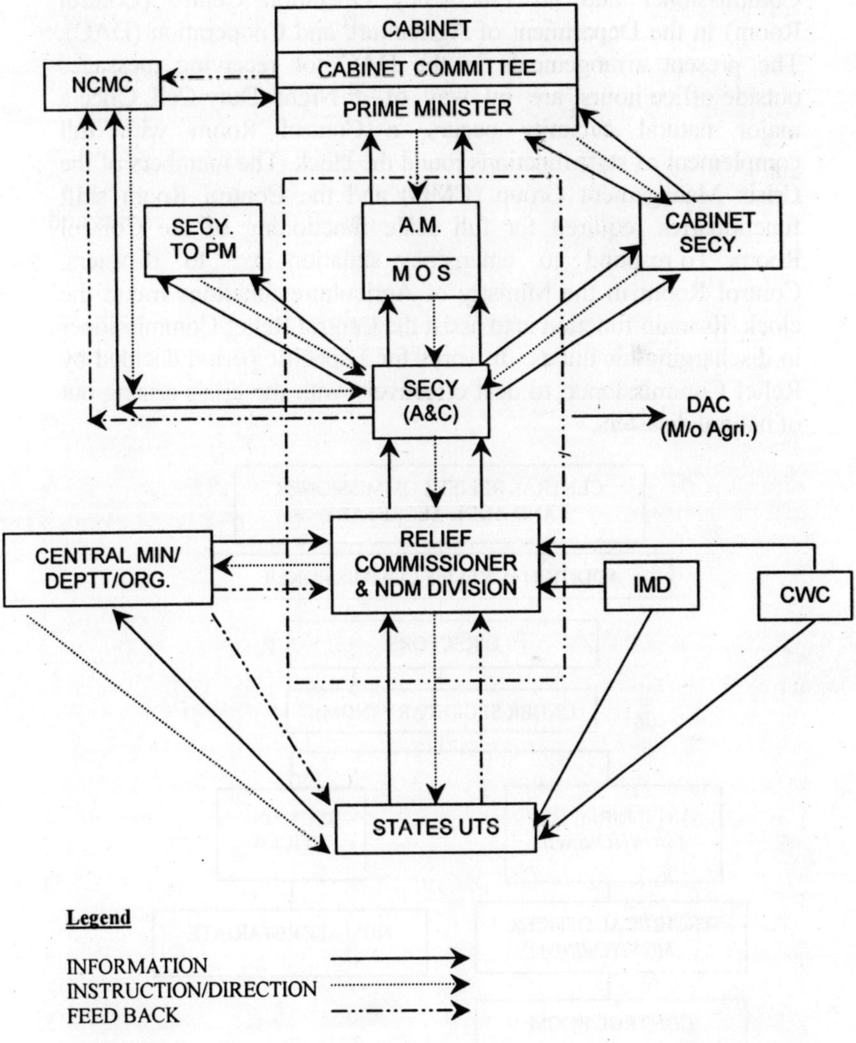

Fig. 6.1 : Management of Disasters in India – Interaction pattern
Source : Report (Part-I) of Expert Group set up by Ministry of Urban Development, 1998

Emergency Operation Centres (Control Rooms)

The Relief Commissioner is assisted by the Additional Relief Commissioner and an Emergency Operation Centre (Control Room) in the Department of Agriculture and Cooperation (DAC). The present arrangements in the DAC for receiving messages outside office hours are by way of a Night Duty Cell. Once a major natural calamity occurs, a Control Room with full complement of staff functions round the clock. The members of the Crisis Management Group (CMG) and the Control Room shift functionaries required for full scale functioning of the Control Room. To respond to emergency situation due to disasters, Control Room in the Ministry of Agriculture functions round the clock. Its main function is to assist the Central Relief Commissioner in discharging his duties. It works for a specific period decided by Relief Commissioner, to deal effectively with the crisis arising out of natural disasters.

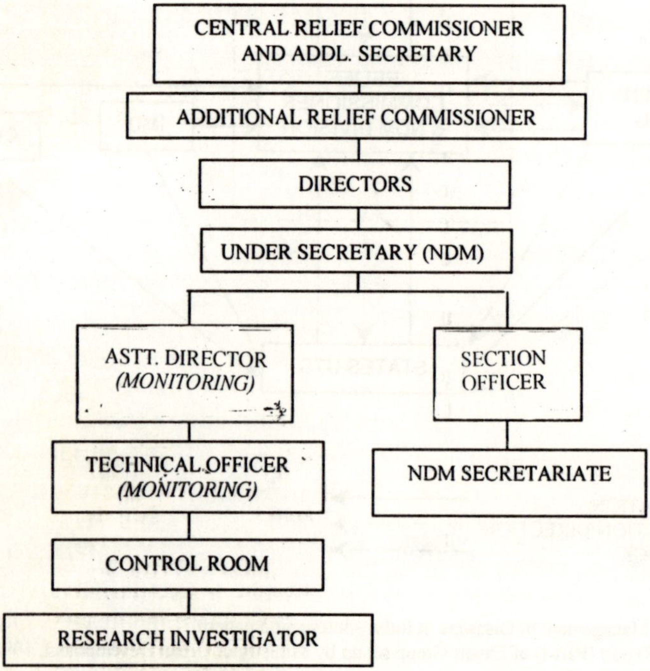

Fig. 6.2 : Organisational set-up of Natural Disaster Management Division in the Ministry of Agriculture, Department of Agriculture and Cooperation

Source : Ministry of Agriculture

The main objectives of the Control Room are:

(i) Collection and transmission of information concerning natural calamity and relief;

(ii) Keeping close contact with the Governments of the States affected by a calamity;

(iii) Interaction with other Central Ministries/Departments in connection with natural calamities and relief;

(iv) Maintaining records containing all relevant information relating to action points and contact points in Central Ministries/Departments/State Governments; and

(v) Performing such other functions and duties as may be entrusted by Relief Commissioner.

Cabinet Committee

For effective implementation of relief measures in the wake of a natural calamity, the cabinet sets up a Committee. On the constitution of such committee of the Cabinet, the Agriculture Secretary provides all necessary information to and seek directions, if any, of the Cabinet Committee in all matters concerning relief in the wake of natural calamity and takes steps for effective implementation of its directions. In the absence of such a Cabinet Committee, all matters relating to relief are reported to the Cabinet Secretary.

National Crisis Management Committee (NCMC)

A National Crisis Management Committee (NCMC) has been constituted in the Cabinet Secretariat. The composition of the Committee is as under :

(1) Cabinet Secretary	Chairman
(2) Secretary to Prime Minister	Member
(3) Secretary (MHA)	Member
(4) Secretary (MCD)	Member
(5) Secretary (IB)	Member
(6) Secretary (R & AW)	Member
(7) Secretary (Agri. & Coopn.)	Co-opted Member
(8) An officer of Cabinet Secretariat	Convenor

When a situation is to be handled also by the NCMC, it gives such directions to the Crisis Management Group (CMG) of the Ministry as deemed necessary. The Secretary (A & C) is responsible for ensuring that all developments are brought to the notice of the NCMC promptly.

Crisis Management Group (CMG)

There is a Crisis Management Group (CMG) for dealing with matters relating to relief in the wake of major natural calamities, consisting of the following :

(i)	Relief Commissioner	Chairman
(ii)	OSD, Cabinet Sectt. Or a representative of the Cabinet Sectt.	
(iii)	A representative of P.M.O.	
(iv) to (xiii)	Joint Secretaries in the Ministries / Departments of Finance, Food, Civil Supplies, Power, Urban Development, Rural Development, Health, Petroleum, Planning Commission ınd Deptt. of Women and Child Development.	
(xiv)	Director General, Indian Meteorological Department.	
(xv)	Senior officers of the Ministry of Railways.	
(xvi)	Railway Board and Ministry of Water Resources.	
(xvii)	A senior officer from the Ministry of Communications.	
(xviii)	A senior officer from the Ministry of Transport dealing with road communication.	
(xix)	Director General, Civil Defence.	
(xx)	Joint Secretary (SR) & Addl. Relief Commissioner.	

The Resident Commissioners of the States affected by major natural calamity may be cooped on the CMG during the period of crisis.

The main objectives of committing this CMG are:

- Review each year the contingency plan formulated by the Central Ministry/Department.
- Review measures required in dealing with a disaster

– Coordinate activities of the central ministries and state government in relation to disaster preparedness.

State Level

At State level relief measures are observed and supervised by Relief Commissioner or Chief Secretary of the State. He or she controls the relief operations through District Collectors. State Governments have their Contingency Plans which are updated from time to time, based on the experience.. This Contingency Plan is basically to follow a framework as laid down nationally, comprising of type of preparedness, the relief material required, need to work together and provide an efficient feedback and monitoring system. A contingency plan for the district for different disasters shall be drawn up by the Collector/Deputy Commissioner and get approved by the State Government. The Collector/Deputy Commissioner also coordinate and secure the input from the local defense forces unit in preparation of the contingency plans. These contingency plans lay down specific action points, key personnel and contact points in relation to all aspects (Fig. 6.3).

The relief measures are review by the district level relief committee consisting of official and non-official members including the local legislators and the Members of Parliament.

In the wake of natural calamities a Control Room is set up in the district for day to day monitoring of the rescue and relief operations on a continuing basis.

The collector maintains close liaison with the Central Government authorities in the districts, namely, Army, Air Force and Navy, Ministry of Water Resources etc., who could supplement the efforts of the district administration in the rescue and relief operations.

He takes all steps for enlisting of voluntary efforts and channeling the non-governmental organization response to natural calamities and interact with different implementation agencies and furnish information on a regular basis to the State Relief Commissioner on the implementation of rescue and relief measures.

The district level contingency plans and the State Action Plans are reviewed annually and updated in the light of lesson learnt in dealing with natural calamities from time to time.

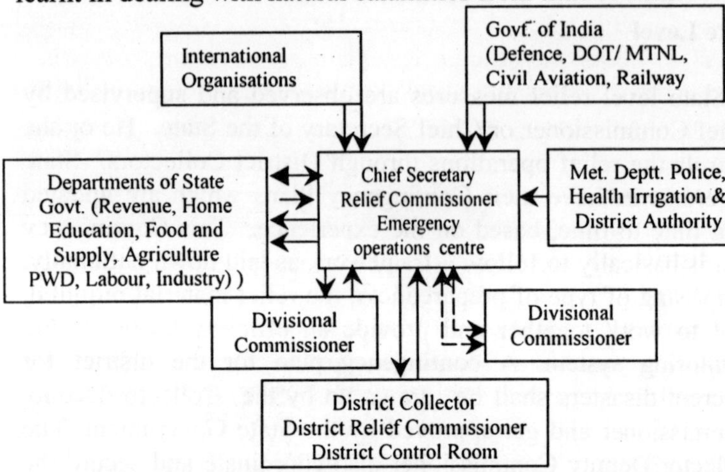

Fig. 6.3: Disaster Management at state level.

The other departments at district level, i.e. Revenue, Home, Civil Supplies, Power, Irrigation, Water Supply, Gram and Zila Panchayat (Local self-government), Agriculture, Forest, Rural Development, Health, Planning, Public Works and Finance are also required to provide all types of technical and physical support during a disaster. Whenever there is a disaster, a control room is set up at State level also. This control room is responsible for:

(i) Updating the Central Relief Commissioner on the progress and development of crisis management on an ongoing basis;

(ii) Receiving instructions and communicating it to appropriate agencies for immediate action;

(iii) Collection and submission of information relating to implementation of relief measures to the Central Relief Commissioner; and

(iv) Keeping the State level authorities apprised of the development on a continued basis.

In the State, at district level, the Collector heads the "Coordination and Reviewing Committee." He is responsible for presentation of district level plans and directing, supervising and monitoring relief measures. He also coordinates with Central Government Authorities, channelizes efforts of Non-Government Organisation and keeps close interaction with different implementing agencies.

District Level

The district administration is the focal point for directing, supervising and monitoring field level contingency plans and relief measures. The powers of the collector are considerably enhanced during the actual operations for disaster mitigation. The District Collector works together with the Sub-division Officers/Tehsildars of various sub-division/*Tehsils* and *'Patwaris'* of villages along with the entire machinery of the district, which includes the technical officers of other departments also.

Sub-district Level

A district is sub-divided into sub-division, i.e. *Tehsils* or *Talukas* and *Tehsil* into blocks and blocks into village. The head of the sub-division is called the Sub-Division Officer (SDO), head of the *Tehsil* is generally known as *Tehsildar* or *Talukadar* or *Mamlotdar*, while the head of a block is called Block Development Officer (BDO), the head of the village or Panchayat is recognised as *Gram Pradhan* or *Sarpanch* . Contact with the individual village is through the village officer or *Patwari* who has one or more villages in his charge. When a disaster is apprehended, the entire machinery of the District including officers of Technical and other departments, gear-up into action and maintain almost continuous contact with each village in the disaster threatened area. The sub-district level officer, i.e. Sub Divisional Officer (SDO), *Tehsildar* and *Patwari* (the village officer) are in continuous touch with District Collector for relief and other operations during a disaster. Thus the entire hierarchy from the Central Government Ministry up to village level is involved in disaster management.

Financial Aspects

Under the Constitution of India, State Government is responsible for providing assistance and relief to the people affected by natural calamities. The Central Government supplements the efforts of the State Government by providing additional resources on the recommendation of the Finance Commission.

Till 1989-90 there was no clear cut guidelines for financing of relief expenditure and an amount known as *"Margin Money"* was provided to each state government for immediate relief measure. In case of a large scale calamity, state government was required to present a memorandum for additional central assistance. On receipt of the memorandum giving details of damage and requirement, a central team was deputed to assess the same. A high level committee on relief chaired by Secretary Planning Commission use to consider it and recommend additional assistance. This procedure usually caused the delays in extending help to the people affected by natural calamities. It was felt by the ninth Finance Commission that the system did not provide for any ready availability of adequate fund with the state government to react to natural calamities expeditiously. Keeping this in view the ninth Finance Commission recommended the constitution of a Calamity Relief Fund (CRF) for the financial years 1990-91 to 1994-95. This fund was made readily available with the state governments to take immediate relief measures in the wake of natural calamities. The CRF was continued on the recommendations of 10th Finance Commission.

The 10th Finance Commission also recommended constitution of a National Fund for Calamity Relief (NFCR) to deal with calamities of rare severity only. The NFCR initiated at an initial allocation of Rs. 700 crores for the period of 1995 to 2000. A total amount of Rs. 2555.28 crores was released to the states from the NFCR during this period.

On the recommendation of 10th Finance Commission a committee of experts and representatives of state governments finalized a list of items which alone to be chargeable from the CRF. The State level committee headed by the Chief Secretary has to decide the norms for the amount that can be given for the approved items. Based on the recommendation of the committee, a list of the recommended items for expenditure from CRF was communicated to the state governments for fixing the norms for each item.

For financing the relief and rehabilitation activities under the existing system, each State has a corpus of funds, i.e. Calamity Relief Fund (CRF). This fund is allocated every year to state governments from Centre. The state governments are free to utilise this fund in the case of disaster. Following the constitution of CRF, the entire expenditure on management of natural disaster becomes the State Government's responsibility. The total allocations for the CRF for the year 1995-2000 is shown in Fig. 6.4

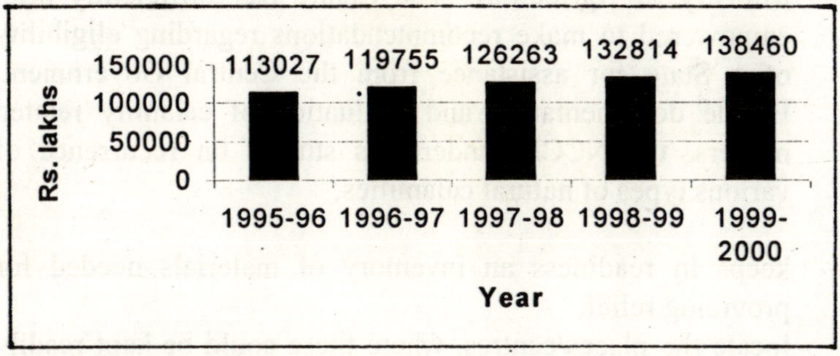

Fig 6.4: Allocation of CRF.

The 11th Finance Commission while recommending continuation of CRF approved that NFCR should be abolished. The Eleventh Finance Commission (applicable 200-2005) has suggested the creation of National Calamity Contingency Fund (NCCF) with an initial contribution of Rs. 500 crore by the Government of India and further augmentation by way of surcharge on central taxes. The Government of India has in fact imposed a surcharge of 1 per cent on corporate tax for meeting, the additional expenditure on recent calamities. A provision has been made for establishing a National Center for Calamity Management (NCCM) under the Ministry of Agriculture to monitor all types of calamities.

The Eleventh Finance Commission has provided Rs. 11007.59 crore for the period of 2000-2005, Rs. 8255.69 crore (75%) out of which is the central share and Rs. 2751.90 crore is the state share. The yearwise CRF (central plus state share) is as follows:

Year	**Rs. in Crore**
2000-2001	1992.10
2001-2002	2091.70
2002-2003	2196.29
2003-2004	2306.10
2004-2005	2421.41
Total	**11007.60**

National Centre for Calamity Management (NCCM) has also been recommended by Finance Commission under the Ministry of Agriculture. The Centre has sufficiently been empowered to make recommendations regarding eligibility of a State for assistance from the Central Government. Beside documentation and evaluation of calamity related matters, the NCCM undertakes studies on recurrence of various types of natural calamities,

- keeps in readiness an inventory of materials needed for providing relief,
- locate the places/centres, where these could be kept readily available, and
- provide training to the State cadres, identified for deployment of calamity relief duties.

NEW DEVELOPMENTS IN THE FIELD OF DISASTER MANAGEMENT

The experiences during the last decade revealed that despite its best efforts in handling the situations, created due to various natural catastrophes, the country still lacks efficiency in many strategic issues in the field of disaster management and there is a great need to review and modify the existing policies and *modus operandi* of its implementation. It was strongly felt that disaster management in the country needs an effective disaster management strategy to lessen disaster impact and also to strengthen its organizational structure. Along with this, regular updating of codes/manuals/disaster plans of the states on the basis of experience gained and technological development is essential.

Taking this important issue into consideration, recently a High Powered Committee on disaster management plan has been constituted at national level. The main objectives of this committee are –

(i) To review existing arrangements for preparedness and mitigation of natural and man-made disasters including industrial, nuclear, biological and chemical disasters.

(ii) Recommend measures for strengthening organizational structures.

(iii) Recommend a comprehensive model plan for management of these disasters at the National, State and District levels.

The committee has identified 30 types of hazards and further categorized them into five subgroups:

Sub-Group 1 : ***Water and Climate Related Hazards*** – Flood and Drainage Management/Droughts/Cyclones/Tornadoes/Hurricanes/Hailstorm/Cloud burst/Snow avalanches/Heat and cold waves/Sea erosion/Thunder and lightning.

Sub-Group 2 : ***Geologically Related Hazards*** – Earthquakes/Landslides/Mudflows/Sea erosion/Dam bursts and dam failures/Mine fires.

Sub-Group 3 : ***Chemical, Industrial and Nuclear related Disasters*** – Chemical, industrial and nuclear disasters.

Sub-Group 4 : ***Accident Related Disasters*** – Road, rail and other transportation accidents including water ways (Boat capsizing)/mine flooding/major building collapse/serial bomb blasts/festival related disasters/electrical disasters and fires/forest fires/urban fires/oil spill/village fires.

Sub-Group 5 : ***Biologically Related Disasters*** – Biological disasters/Epidemics/Cattle epidemics/Pest attacks/Food poisoning.

The HPC taking into consideration the necessity of quick response in the case of a disaster, has developed the concept of **Trigger Mechanism** and incorporated as an emergency quick response mechanism. This is envisaged as a preparedness plan whereby the receipt of a signal of an impending disaster would simultaneously energize and activate the mechanism for response and mitigation without loss of crucial time. Beside this, the HPC has emphasized on preparing on state level and district level disaster management plans.

Keeping in view the crucial role of voluntary organizations in democratic set up like India, the committee has formed a nationwide network of the NGOs i.e., VASUDEVA – Voluntary Agencies for Sustainable Universal Development and Emergency Voluntary Action with the intention of creating a bridge between the NGOs and the Government Sector, as also within the NGOs working in the field of disaster management. In this regard the Committee has also identified six nodal NGOs. A committee has also been setup to deliberate upon mapping of vulnerable zones for different types of disasters for disaster preparedness. Dissemination of knowledge and actual information is very crucial in the case of a disaster. In this respect the role of media becomes very important during disaster. The Committee has emphasized this issue very strongly in its recommendations.

For effective dealing of a disaster the networking of knowledge is very essential. A committee has been setup for networking of knowledge-based institutions classified into three types of disasters, viz. natural, man-made and biological. Giving due consideration to awareness in handling a disaster effectively, the Committee has recommended inclusion of disaster management in the school syllabus. In this regard a committee has been constituted under the chairmanship of Secretary, Council of Boards of School Education, Delhi.

A committee has also been constituted to prepare a Model District Management Plan to be adopted through out the country. A source book on Disaster Management has been prepared to provide a framework for the disaster managers and the district administration in its efforts to mitigate the impacts of disasters. A National Act for Calamity Management was drafted by a Committee constituted by the HPC and circulated to the states and concerned ministries and departments for their comments.

In nutshell the major recommendations of the HPC are –

1. Each State and Union Territory to constitute the sub-groups.
2. Various Ministries, Departments and NGOs to be involved and appropriate steps for legislation may be taken.
3. The Source Book on District Disaster Management Plan be widely circulated and discussed.
4. The decade for National Decade for Disaster Reduction be utilized for community awareness, preparedness and mitigation efforts.
5. Building Community leadership and a chain of trained community cadres through participatory approach can help to harness the resilience and resourcefulness of the community to cope together with disaster and mitigate their efforts.
6. A network of the training institutes led by a national level disaster management institute with symbolic linkage with other National and State level institutions will need to be forged with and developed.
7. A National Fund for Disaster Mitigation can be created for human resource development.
8. A National Act for Calamity Management was drafted.
9. The structure of National Disaster Management System and the National Centre for Calamity Management (NCCM) as suggested by the Eleventh Finance Commission evolved by the HPC.
10. A district level CRF raised locally by the District Magistrate needs to be institutionalised.
11. A National Fund for Disaster Mitigation of Rs.500 crore has been suggested by the HPC for human resource development.
12. Apart from National, State and District plans, HPC has suggested village level plans for all vulnerable areas. More emphasis has been given on community participation in disaster management.
13. HPC has also recommended annual updating and rehearsal of the plans.

SUPPORT ORGANISATIONS

Thus we see that in India, at Central and State Level the disaster management is being given a serious thought. Beside the governments at Central and State level, various other national and international bodies also cooperate and provide all types of support to fight against natural calamities of various origins. Some of these organisations are: -

A. United Nations Organisation (UNO)

The UNO proclaimed 1990-2000 decade as the "International Decade for Natural Disaster Reduction" (IDNDR). The framework of action of IDNDR provided the vulnerable countries all types of support for preparedness, mitigation and rehabilitation process during natural disasters.

In the conference of the IDNDR programme held in Yokohama in May 1994 a plan of action for disaster reduction – **"the Yokohama Strategy"** was evolved. The Yokohama strategy gave guidelines for Natural Disaster Prevention, Preparedness and Mitigation, shifting the focus and emphasis from disaster management to disaster prevention and preparedness.

The UN agencies provide a support system with increased information database, a forum for communication, a format for co-ordination and increased efficacy through pooled resources.

The UN General Assembly has ensued in the setting up of a standing **"United Nations – Disaster Management Team (UN - DMT)"** in each disaster prone country. The composition of the UN - DMT is determined by taking into account the types of disasters to which a country is prone and the organizations present and working towards disaster relief and mitigation.

The primary purpose of UN – DMT is to ensure a prompt, effective and concerted response at country level in the event of a disaster. Coordination of UN assistance to the Government in post disaster rehabilitation and reconstruction, long term disaster mitigation measures are some other functions of the UN – DMT.

The various agencies of UNO involved in the field of Disaster Management are UNDP, UNDRO, FAO, WFP, WHO, UNHCR, UNESCO, UNCHS, UNICEF, ADRC, ADPC.

B. National Centre for Disaster Management (NCDM)

The body working in "Indian Institute of Public Administration" (IIPA), is the nodal agency for research, training and advocacy in the field of natural disaster management in India. The Centre is engaged in preparing the national, state and district level plan to tackle natural hazards and coordinating various research and training programmes in the field of disaster management. It is also building a data base on natural hazards with several case studies. The main objectives of the Centre are –

- To prepare an exhaustive information base on damage caused and resource spent on mitigation practices and relief work for various types of natural disasters.
- To establish links between the nodal ministry for natural disasters and various state training institutes involved in the field of disaster.
- To provide technical assistance and services to programmes on natural disaster management and assist the South- East Asian and SAARC countries in formulating the policies and developing their capabilities in all aspects of disaster management.

The Centre conducts research regarding various aspects of disaster management, i.e. preparedness, mitigation, cost-benefit analysis of the preparedness plan etc. It also carries out research and surveys about the impacts (socio-economic and environmental both) of various natural hazards. The NCDM is deeply involved in collecting various information about the effects of disaster preparedness on impacts of disasters, economics of preparedness plan, rehabilitation and resettlement issues, effective relief programmes, impact of environmental degradation on disasters, community involvement in various phases of disaster management, role of NGOs in disaster mitigation etc.

C. Indian Meteorological Department (IMD)

This government department provides information about various types of disasters in the country and thus helps administration in making arrangements and to take precautions in handling the disasters. The main objectives and functions of the department are –

- To provide cyclone warning from the Area Cyclone Warning Centres (ACWCs) at Kolkata, Chennai and Mumbai and Cyclone Warning Centres (CWCs) at Bhubaneshwar, Vishakhapatnam and Ahmedabad.
- To develop necessary infrastructure to formulate and disseminate cyclone warning at appropriate levels. The department has made operational a satellite base communication system called Cyclone Warning Dissemination System (CWDS) for direct dissemination of cyclone warning to cyclone prone areas.
- It operates Limited Area Analysis and Forecasting System (LAFS) based on an Optimal Interpretation (OI) analysis and limited area Primitive Equation Model to provide numerical guidance. It also seeks international cooperation in the field of forecasting and warning cyclones/floods etc. The Department receives numerical guidance operational from models being prepared in the United States and the European Centre for Medium Range Weather Forecasting (ECMWF).
- The Department operates national network of 36 seismic stations to record seismological observations.
- The Department has set up Cyclone Warning Division (CWD) at New Delhi to co-ordinate and supervise the totality of the cyclone warning programmes.
- By monitoring the rain fall it also makes long range rainfall forecasts based on mathematical model. The forecasts are very useful in flood and drought forecasting in the country.

D. Central Water Commission (CWC)

This government organisation has established a network of "Flood Forecasting Stations" in the country, which issue daily reports on flood forecasts and manages the flood season effectively. There are in all 157 flood forecasting stations in the country located at various strategic locations spread over twelve states and union territories. These stations issues daily forecasts and warning through out the flood season. The CWC has recently established a procedure of carrying out a self-analysis and appraisal of the forecasting network at the end of monsoon season, which helps in making forecast more accurate. The commission also maintains consolidated data bank about the loss due to floods in various states, which is used for further planning and mitigation of floods in the country.

E. Housing and Urban Development Corporation (HUDCO)

The body helps in reducing disaster impacts by developing and disseminating disaster resistant building technologies, particularly in earthquake prone areas. It also organises awareness drives and training camps in the disaster prone areas. The organisation has setup many centres which provide training to local masons in using local material for construction of earthquake resistant houses. These centres also carry out research in this field. The role of HUDCO in providing training, organising awareness camps and other related aspects has been very appreciable during the last many years.

F. Building Material and Technology Promotion Council (BMTPC)

The Government of India established the Building Material and Technology Promotion Council (BMTPC) in 1990 to bridge the gap between research and development and large scale application of new building material technologies. The Council has carried out very innovative and effective work in the field of disaster management. Recently it has published a "*Vulnerability*

Atlas of India", which along with giving vulnerability of various parts of the country to natural hazards also provides construction guidelines in these areas. This effort of the Council has strengthened the capacity of State Governments in tackling various types of disasters more effectively.

G. Various Research and Educational Institutes

Various research and educational institutes like Universities, Indian Institutes of Technology (IITs) and engineering colleges contribute in the field of research, training, collection of data etc. and thus help in the field of disaster preparedness and disaster management efforts. Roorkee University; Indira Gandhi National Open University; Central Building Research Institute, Council for Scientific and Industrial Research, Civil Defense College, National Institute of Rural Development, National Institute of Communicable Diseases etc. are major institutes are playing very active role in the field of Disaster Management.

H. Non-Government Organisations

Beside all these government, public sector and educational institutes, many NGOs also play very important role in the area of disaster preparedness and mitigation. They are emerging one of the most effective means of achieving an effective communication link between the Disaster Management Agencies and the affected community. At present many are working at advocacy level as well as at the grassroot level. They can be of help not only in preparedness but also in relief, rescue and rehabilitation measures. The fields in which NGOs can play a crucial role are :

- Collection and transmission of information concerning natural calamity and relief.
- Keeping in contact with Government of the states affected by the causality.
- Interaction with various other Central Ministries and Departments
- Maintaining records with regard to action points and contact points in the Central Ministries and the State governments.

7

DISASTER MANAGEMENT IN UTTARANCHAL
A Case Study

Uttaranchal happens to be one of the very active seismic zones of the country. Beside earthquakes the area is equally prone to landslides, avalanches, floods, excessive soil erosion and lastly forest fires. Except for earthquake the causative factors for all other disasters are primary due to unplanned development and ruthless exploitation of the natural resources. Even to a large extent, the frequency, intensity and magnitude of earthquakes increased in the recent past due to human interference.

To overcome the impacts of these natural calamities, traditionally the local people adopted various techniques and approaches. However, it was only after independence that organised and planned attempts were initiated to counter the situation. Beside the efforts of the government, some well meaning NGOs are actively engaged in managing the scenario. In spite of the best efforts of the government, still lot needs to be achieved. Due to the ever increasing population pressure, abject poverty and unemployment, the situation is turning out to be worst. The over-exploiting of the natural resources is more or less responsible for this worsening situation over time. To overcome the situation, this area needs organised attempts to strengthen all the 3 phases of disaster management i.e., Pre-disaster, Emergency and Post-disaster phases. For this, the adoption of appropriate management tools has become increasingly important.

METHODOLOGY

The author with this express intent extensively travelled in this area and documented the factual data. The author also participated in the operations during disasters as member of the 'Central Relief Team'. As an insider, he got the opportunity to critically analyze the situation and identify the gaps and reasons for the failure/partial failure of the system and the approach. The basic intent was to critically analyze the disaster management programme as adopted by the local administration, state government and the Central Government, the steps taken immediately to combat the situation and the long term measures adopted to ratify the same.

The scientific temperament and knowledge base of the author helped him to critically analyze and evaluate the situation with reference to :

- Causes of the hazards (Natural/Man-made)
- Demarcate the zones prone to hazards.
- Impact of hazards on people.
- Disaster management practices being applied and their impact.
- Views and opinions of various sections of the society on the management practices adopted by the government.

Primary Data Review

Equipped with the knowledge and information base made available through secondary literature review and review of government policies about disaster management, the process of questionnaire/interview was initiated. The primary data was collected using a combination of research tools and techniques, namely, schedule, observation, group discussion and personal interviews. The basic work was carried out in Rudraprayag district of Garhwal Region. The district experienced landslides and earthquakes in 1998 and 1999 respectively.

Five categories of people were contacted for firming of the reality. Population affected, people's representatives, administration, NGOs and academicians were interviewed for primary data generation. These five categories represent almost all the groups which are directly or indirectly related to disaster and its management.

Secondary Data Review

Secondary data for the study was generated from the exhaustive literature available on the disaster management in the form of books, research papers, reports and articles and discussion with

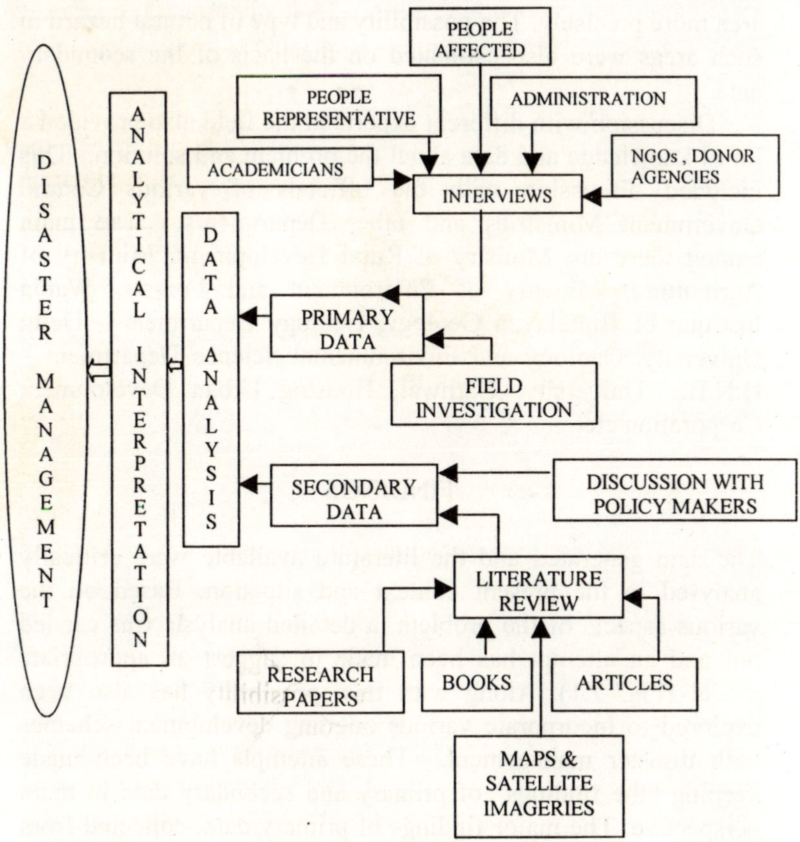

Fig. 7.1 : Methodology adopted.

experts and policy-makers. The material available on internet was also scanned for documenting the most recent and current trends. Various techniques of disaster management with special reference to rehabilitation and case studies in this regard were studied and analysed in detail. Methods and techniques suggested in literature were tried and applied to in the present context.

Beside literature, the help of other secondary data, i.e. maps, aerial photographs, satellite imageries, and various other sources were also referred alternatively, which helped in understanding the mechanism of hazards and demarcating the disaster prone area more precisely. The possibility and type of natural hazard in such areas were also estimated on the basis of the secondary data.

Discussion with different experts in the field also provided a lot of knowledge and data about the problem and solution. This included discussion with the officials of various Central Government Ministries and other Departments. The main among these are Ministry of Rural Development, Ministry of Agriculture, Ministry of Environment and Forests, Wadia Institute of Himalayan Geology, Geology Department – Delhi University, Geology and Environmental Science Department – H.N.B. University, Garhwal, Housing Urban Development Corporation etc.

FINDINGS

The data generated and the literature available were critically analysed in the present context and situation. Based on the various aspects of the problem, a detailed analysis was carried out and an attempt has been made to suggest an appropriate model (Fig. 7.1). Along with this, possibility has also been explored to incorporate various ongoing development schemes with disaster management. These attempts have been made keeping "the findings" of primary and secondary data in main perspective. The major findings of primary data, collected from five categories of stakeholders are briefed in the following text.

People Affected

In the process of disaster management, villagers affected by the disasters are the main stakeholders. The information provided by them is of prime significance in the process of modifying or improving various processes, involved in disaster management and to make them more appropriate and need based. To generate information from affected population, an in-depth study was conducted in 27 villages of three blocks and 2 refugee camps of Rudra Prayag district. The selection of the villages was purposive in nature keeping in mind the following selection criteria :

- Villages affected by disasters recently.
- Developed and relatively less developed villages.
- Villages, representative of the region.

The identified villages were affected by some disasters in the recent past and their first hand experiences has been documented systematically.

Immediate Relief

During survey of stakeholders, it was found that for immediate rescue and relief, the local administration was the first.to come to their rescue. The village officer (*Patwari*), who is a part of administration and looks after 2-3 villages, was first to reach the spot with his force for rescue operations and immediate relief. Along with rescue operations, transporting the wounded to hospitals, survey, restoration of blocked roads etc. were the work carried out by administration on priority basis. Temporary shelters, food etc. were also supplied by the administration to the affected population.

It is observed that in the second phase of relief, the compensation for deceased, cattle loss and house or property damaged was distributed based on the survey carried out by the administration. The compensation was mainly in the form of cash and tin sheets for temporary house construction. The house construction material was distributed irrespective of local needs or conditions, ignoring people's opinion and demand. Despite all these, it is considered that the most effective intervention was carried out by administration during such disasters.

Various public undertaking, NGOs etc. also came for relief during the disaster. Housing Urban Development Corporation Limited (HUDCO), U.P. Bridge Development Corporation,

National Social Service Core and Rotary Club are some of the prominent organisations, which involved themselves for relief and rehabilitation. It is notable here that these organisations worked in the villages which were badly affected by hazards irrespective of their location and accessibility access. Their assistance was mainly restricted to make shelters or houses for the affected population. In some cases, e.g. HUDCO provided some training also to the local people for constructing earthquake resistant houses. Regarding the time of relief, it is learnt that in most of the cases though rescue operation was immediate or within a day or two, the second phase of relief i.e. shelter or house construction was delayed. The most controversial aspect was about the fairness of the survey carried out by the local administration.

Rehabilitation

About rehabilitation of the sensitive villages, one thing emerged out clearly that no serious effort is made for the same. In few cases despite the willingness of the villagers to shift, only temporary assistance was provided by the administration. Some of the villagers lost their agriculture land, cattle etc., the only sources of their livelihood. To compensate their loss, only monetary assistance was provided and very less effort was made to restore their source of livelihood. In some villages, due to continuous threat from landslides and rock falls, some families have migrated to other villages and are living with their relatives or friends without any source of income or means for livelihood. The condition of such families is quite grave and pitiable. In the villages surveyed, few families migrated from some villages to other parts of the area.

It has to be mentioned here that though the political leaders and administrations made promises for rehabilitation of very sensitive areas, yet nothing concrete has been started. Many more assurances, given by the local leaders, administration have been either partially fulfilled or not attempted at all. A very non-significant group of the villagers are fully satisfied and contented with the interventions undertaken after the disaster. For other assurances also, in about 60% cases nothing has been done and only in 28% cases assurances were partially fulfilled. Out of 27 villages only one village is satisfied with fulfilment of the assurances.

About monitoring and evaluation of the various relief, rescue or rehabilitation activities, the response is not very enthusiastic. The villagers were very critical and negative about the monitoring and evaluation of the work being carried out by various agencies.

People's Representatives

In order to generate a realistic picture, the people's representatives were personally contacted. The people's representatives were village level panchayat members, sarpanch, block level representatives and Zilla level representatives besides the local MLAs and MPs.

The people representatives play very crucial role immediately during the disaster. Their role is equally important even after the rescue operations are over for organizing and implementing the post disaster rehabilitation interventions. Unbiased judgment for compensation both for life, livestock and property attains prime importance after the immediate rescue operation. People representation form the important link between the people and the administration in identifying the affected groups and delivering the requisite services and goods.

The Assistance

The people's representatives were more or less satisfied with the immediate assistance made available in terms of food, clothing and material for construction of houses etc. Mostly the material made available was for temporary housing structures, i.e. tin roof etc. In few cases some assistance was made available for reviving their means of livelihood and to re-equip their livestock. The village representatives gave idea about the assistance provided and the purpose. In most of the cases people representatives mentioned that assistance was provided for the purpose of house construction, food and clothing. The rest mentioned it was for livelihood and livestock.

Rehabilitation

The representatives equally stressed about rehabilitation scheme being considered by the administration for the people living in very sensitive areas. According to them some environment and soil conservation programmes, i.e. check dam construction, watershed schemes etc. were initiated in the area. But such types of schemes are very few and most of them accepted that no serious attempt was made for revival of situation. According to this category, road, water, electricity, health care and public distribution system damaged/disturbed due to disasters showed marginal improvement after disaster in the area. The major improvement has been in the drinking water supply, the roads and lastly, the supply of electricity to disaster affected areas. About the socio-economic changes in the severely affected areas, all people surveyed accepted that the overall condition of the people deteriorated after disaster in the area. About the training programme for the disaster affected population, the representatives felt in general that this part was almost neglected. Except few preliminary training about construction of earthquake resistant houses by HUDCO (a Government of India public sector undertaking) and few programmes by local administration about health care, nothing concrete was undertaken in this regard.

About the revival of livelihood resources, the people representatives mentioned that such schemes are under consideration, but nothing has materialized till date.

Adminisration

During the survey of people affected by disasters, the main feature that came out about immediate relief, was that the local administration was first to carry out this function. It was the local administration who performed their duties for rescue and relief operations immediately after the disaster. In most of the cases the assistance was provided within a day or two or at the most within one week. But due to resource constrains, in some villages this assistance was delayed also.

Working Mechanism

About the working mechanism of the administration, it was observed that Development Block, Health, Police, Revenue, Public Works Departments, Paramilitary forces were the departments which were involved directly or indirectly in the rescue or relief operations. At local level the Block Development Officer (BDO) worked as coordinator for other departments. The distribution of the work was mainly carried out on the basis of the expertise of the department concerned, e.g. the police mainly participated in the rescue operation, the PWD in road blockage removal, the health department in the treatment of wounded and preventing the spread of disease or epidemic, water department mainly for supply of drinking water to the people and so on.

Availability of Resources

About the availability of resources, this category felt that the resources available with them were very scarce and due to this limitation they could not do much, despite their will and capacity.

Departmental Coordination

It was felt that the coordination, among different departments of the district was poor. This hampered the work of restoring the situation to normalcy. It was also observed that there was no force, which could coordinate the work being carried at the grassroot level.

Cooperation from Local People

The main thing that was pointed out by this category was that the cooperation and coordination of the local population in the relief and rescue operation was not very enthusiastic. In some cases, the people totally boycotted the assistance provided by the administration. This indicated that the mutual trust and belief between the administration and the local people was totally absent or negligible.

Relief Distribution

The amount of assistance and relief was distributed depending upon the extent of damage in the area. To estimate the extent of damage, surveys were conducted by the administration independently and local assistance was rarely sought. The non-involvement of people or their representatives also created problem for the administration during the survey.

Monitoring

About the monitoring of the work for relief/rescue, the administration accepted that it was negligible due to scarcity of resources and lack of exposure/training and also manpower to handle the same. The work was carried out mostly as per guidelines/instructions issued by the district headquarters and other higher officials.

VIPs Visit

The other important aspect that emerged was the impact of VVIPs and VIPs visits on the progress of the work. In most of the cases the administration felt that the visit of VIPs increased the speed and progress of the work. Few felt opposite and mentioned that the visits of VIPs hampered the work progress. Some administration officials (specially at lower level) accepted that the whole administration's attention was diverted and there was unnecessary delay in the progress of work.

Rehabilitation

About the rehabilitation plan and policies, the response was not very enthusiastic. Most of the administrators had no clear-cut idea about the policies or planning for rehabilitation. Discussion with the Sub-Divisional Magistrate revealed that in the district, two villages are to be shifted to safer location, but was unable to clarify as to how this activity would be carried out. About the exact number of people to be rehabilitated, no clear picture was given by the administration.

About any long term planning for rehabilitation and revival of livelihood sources and resources, despite some schemes under consideration, nothing concrete was mentioned by the administration.

NGOs/Autonomous Bodies

The fourth category interviewed was NGOs/autonomous bodies. Some NGOs and HUDCO work was examined during investigation. It was found that these organisation mainly worked on regional basis. Their functions were restricted to extending assistance in the form of shelter, food and clothing. About the support of administration to these bodies· the expressions were mixed. In some cases the administrative support was quite restricted.

NGOs mainly complained that there was no coordination among different departments of the administration. The irregularities in assistance distribution and survey of damage were some of the main shortcomings, pointed out by the NGOs. The non-involvement of local NGOs in relief distribution and cooperation was one of the concerns of these bodies. NGOs also emphasised on long term planning for rehabilitation of the people affected by frequent disasters.

Academicians

Various academicians especially from the local universities -- H.N.B. University, Srinagar were interviewed for seeking their suggestions and views about the appropriate disaster management practices in Uttranchal Himalaya. Some of these academicians interviewed, have been working in the field of disaster management for long. Beside having knowledge of the local culture and tradition, they are well aware of technical aspects of disasters in the area and its management. They have carried out extensive study about Himalayan geology, environment, soil conservation, land use pattern, disaster etc. In the author's view this type of knowledge and experience can be very helpful for evolving appropriate disaster management plans, specially rehabilitation plans in the area.

Rehabilitation

According to these academicians, there is need for intensive research to be carried out in the area. These scientists have categorised some of the areas into very sensitive zones (by technique of hazard zonation mapping). In very sensitive areas there is need for proper strategy and planning while formulating rehabilitation plans. They emphasised that rehabilitation of very sensitive villages should be in stable zones, with the availability of water and communication facilities.

Houses are to be constructed with technical support from concerned institution and research bodies. These houses should be constructed using mostly the locally available material.

Environmental Aspect

The other important suggestion made is on the soil and water conservation. Proper land use pattern is yet another field, which certainly will help in disaster mitigation in the area.

Research and Training

The other area which was emphasised by this community was, training of the stake holders and proper implementation of the various activities for disaster management. The scientific research work carried out in the area is to be taken into consideration while making policies/plans in the disaster prone area.

Task Force

The community also emphasised that there should be a task force or a team consisting of technocrats and administrators, who can make detail investigation of the area and make suggestions about the various measures to be taken for mitigation and managing such disasters in future. This task force can also make suggestions about the rehabilitation plan of the endangered villages.

PROBLEMS AND SHORTCOMINGS

Detail analysis of the primary and secondary data regarding disaster management reveals that the results of disaster management operations are not satisfactory. The study highlighted the main problems, being faced during disaster management operations (Fig. 7.2) :

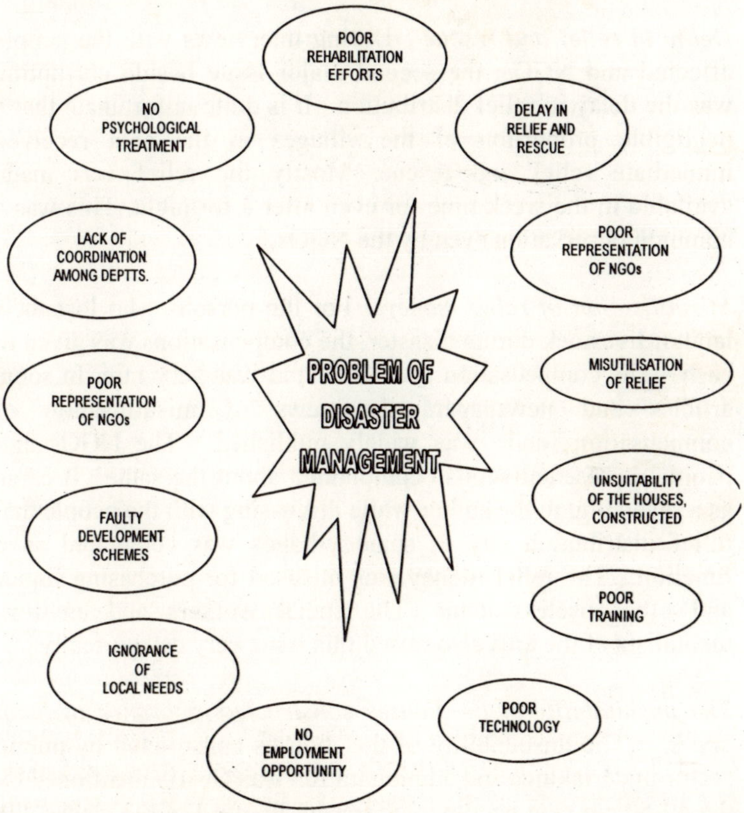

Fig. 7.2 : Various Components of Disaster Management Problem

Discrimination in survey : During field visits and personal interviews with people, it was a common complaint from most of the villagers that survey to assess the loss of property or livestock was not fair and there were lot of irregularities. The villagers were mostly dissatisfied with the survey norms and practices carried out in the area. Some people made allegations about corruption and bribe being asked by the surveyors to include their names in the list being prepared for compensation. This issue has been already raised and mentioned in many research papers and articles. Beside the affected population, the NGOs working in the area and village representatives also highlighted this aspect in their interviews.

Delay in relief and rescue : During interviews with the people affected and NGOs, the second major issue beside corruption was the delay in relief distribution. It is quite unfortunate that a negligible proportion of the villages in the area received immediate relief and rescue. Mostly the relief was made available in the week time or even after a fortnight. This was a common observation even by the NGOs.

Misutilisation of relief money : For the persons who lost their land or livestock during disaster, the compensations was given in cash. The compensation given for land was very rare. In some articles and newspapers the news of misutilisation of compensation fund was widely published. The NGOs and people representative also complained about the same. It came as a revelation to the author while discussing with the people that relief distribution day in some villages was celebrated as a function. The relief money was misused for purchasing liquor and other useless items. The social workers and environmentalists of the area also raised this issue very categorically.

The unsuitability of the houses constructed/Ignorance of local needs : The unsuitability of the houses constructed by public sector undertakings and administration was clearly mentioned by the 40-50 per cent people interviewed. In most of the places, the tin sheets supplied were seen lying unutilised. While constructing houses, the needs of local people were ignored and hence the houses were vacated after some time by the occupants, as they were not fulfiling their basic needs and were not getting with their local ethos.

Poor Training of locals : During implementation of the disaster management programmes, the training and awareness programme were either very few or mostly ignored. Most of the people interviewed had attended no training/awareness programme. Except one or two training camps by HUDCO and medical department, no serious effort was made in this direction. While discussing with H.N.B. University experts, it was mentioned that university has expertise in the field and was eager to organise training camps for the people and other functionaries involved in the disaster management activities. There are other departments endowed with knowledgeable people, who have extensive knowledge about local problems. These resources have been totally ignored. Revenue, medical, university and other staff can also handle training programmes very effectively. The most unfortunate aspect is that the university or other institute of the area do not run any course or training programme on disaster management for any category of the society, despite having adequate infrastructure and local expertise, be it the resource constraint or will to do the same.

Lack of technology : It was observed during field visits that the house construction or reconstruction of damaged houses by various organisations was not technically suitable or earthquake resistant. Except HUDCO, the administration and other agencies involved in the construction activities, were not even having simple technical know-how about the construction of disaster resistant houses. It was simply due to lack of the proper awareness and training about such technology to the functionaries.

No provision for creating employment : In effective disaster management strategy, the agenda for generating employment opportunity is very critical and important. During the field survey, it was observed that some of the villagers have lost their productive land, shops or other livelihood resources. In such cases, the generation of employment for such population is very essential and crucial. But in the region, this aspect of disaster management was almost missing or negligible. No serious effort was seen to be made in this regard either by Government or other agencies involved in relief operations.

Rehabilitation or shifting of people from very sensitive areas : The experts from various fields, especially from Earth-Sciences have carried out extensive research work about the hazard sensitivity of the area. Hazard zonation maps have been prepared for some parts of the area. Selected villages, falling in these areas have been declared very sensitive and are under continuous threat from one or another type of natural calamities.

The experts have submitted the report to Government, suggesting to shift these villages to safer locations. But no sincere effort seems to have been made in this regard by the administration. Thus the people residing here are under continuous threat from calamity, which can strike anyday.

Faulty development schemes : Along with relief and rescue operations, assistance is being provided from central and state governments and other agencies for employment generation and other developmental activities. The common practice is to use this fund without giving any consideration to scientific aspect. It was observed that in most of the cases, this fund is used for developmental activities, which are very hazardous to environment and stability of this fragile zone. The improper construction of roads and buildings etc. is a common example for such activities. These activities generate stress in the rocks of sensitive areas, which further accelerate disasters.

Poor monitoring and evaluation : In the interviews of people affected, the NGOs and the local peoples representative; almost every group denied awareness of any monitoring and evaluation for the programmes being run for the relief, rescue or rehabilitation. The lack of proper monitoring lead to corruption, inferior construction and many other irregularities.

False promises and assurances by politician and administration: During interviews and discussion with the people, it was felt that their expectations from the administration were very high. The reason for this was that the politicians and senior bureaucrats made promises, which were not feasible with the limited resources. In some villages the administration announced that they would ensure safety of the relocated sites, which required detailed sensitive study of the area. But this could not be undertaken as per schedule and the effect of the government announcement was that no NGO or other agencies made any effort to undertake the task. This created a disbelief and unrest among the people and they were not ready to cooperate with the administration.

Poor representation of NGOs : The representation of NGOs and other public and private sectors was not very encouraging. As per the expectations, their representation and contribution in the operation was bit poor. It was also learnt that some NGOs marked their presence only for the sake of name and no concrete work was carried out by them. Some articles have cited that some of the NGOs made their presence to take political mileage and monetary benefits. On the contrary some good NGOs, who really wanted to work sincerely, could not do so, due to non-cooperation of the local administration.

Lack of co-ordination among various departments : Proper co-ordination among various departments is absolutely essential in handling emergency situation like disasters, which was seen lacking in the present situation. This hampered the rescue, relief and rehabilitation work badly. The lack of cooperation also caused delay in relief and rescue operation and also resulted in overlapping or duplication in some of the activities.

VIP visits : Though some sections of the society accepted that the VIP visits accelerated the relief and rescue operation yet few cited that the visits of ministers and other VIPs created problems for the administration. One NGO – "Himalayan Research and Development Society" has quoted "*Disaster situation in our country is usually encashed by politicians for deriving political mileage. Political parties wait for days together with their relief in store, waiting for arrival of their top leaders and the TV camera team and media, which obviously delays relief operations.*"

Medical facilities : Though during the survey and interview this aspect was not highlighted, yet during the visit to affected area at the time of landslides, the author observed that medical facilities provided were not very satisfactory to the wounded. It was reported that in some cases, plaster bandage was not fixed to people with broken or displaced bones even after a week time.

No efforts for psychological recovery : During disasters psychological or emotional injuries are very significant and causes various disorders. In the region no mechanism was applied to handle this widespread malaise.

No link between need and relief : The relief material that came in from various agencies was not based on any feedback from the area affected. Most of the material supplied was of no use for the affected population. The material, which needed most, was not supplied on time. Thus, this communication gap between the donor agencies and the administration caused a lot of confusion and wastage of energy and resources.

8

SITUATIONAL ANALYSIS

A detailed analysis of the data collected, field investigations and experiences gathered in the preceding chapters, reveal that the disaster management practices being implemented do not meet the local needs effectively. As discussed earlier, there are many shortcomings and drawbacks in the existing disaster management policy and its implementation. Hence even after spending million of rupees and energy, the condition of people in disaster prone area has not improved drastically. People inhibiting these areas are insecure about their future. Unemployment, diseases, poverty, illiteracy and scarcity for basic needs, i.e. food, house, water etc. along with continuous threat to their lives are the main problems that are still prevalent and rampant.

Plate 8 : Discussion with affected villagers about the Problems and Issues related to Disaster Management

From interpretation of the data collected, it is clear that though the country has developed administrative machinery to combat and minimise the disaster impacts, yet the results are far from being satisfactory. The results of the present study show that the country is still lacking full proficiency in matters of preparedness, mitigation, rescue, relief and rehabilitation. While going into the depth of the problem, we find that the root cause of the problem lies in lack of any long term strategic planning for disaster management in the country. It is not true that the government is not aware of this fact but due to one or the other reasons unknown, nothing much concrete has been done in this regard. It is observed that as long as the memories of recent disasters are fresh, government seems to be willing to develop long term strategies. However, long term orientation is forgotten as memory fades while other priorities supersede under the pretext of scarcity of resources.

SWOT ANALYSIS

The views of various experts cited in literature, the discussion with various experts (technocrats, people's representatives, NGOs and others) and author's owns field observation and experience depict that the result of implementation of existing policies in the field of disaster management are not satisfactory. The primary and secondary data mentioned identify many opportunities, which if explored properly may bring revolutionary change in the field of disaster management. A SWOT analysis of the existing policies of disaster management and their implementation in light of the data available gives a brief idea about the various aspects of the problem and identifies the fields, which need more attention.

Conceptual Model

The major set back in the current disaster management process is that the main issues of disaster management are not clearly conceptualized at the national level. Consequently, little emphasis is placed on constitutional strengthening and more focus is on studying and developing emergency responses and processes. Thus, disaster mitigation is still seen as a civil defense activity in our country.

SWOT analysis of existing policies and other secondary data reveal that disaster management in the region has many shortcomings and various important areas are untouched or unexplored (Fig. 8.1). The data clearly indicate that the existing policies and their implementation are more concerned about the immediate relief and rescue operations. The other important aspects of disaster management, i.e. preparedness, mitigation and rehabilitation are not given due importance. Some of the important aspects are totally ignored. A critical review of disaster management in area indicates that mainly two aspects, i.e. economic and politico-administrative and partially social aspect are broadly addressed in the existing disaster management policy and its implementation (Fig. 8.2).

The politico-administration aspect covers the political will and administration capabilities to prepare and implement disaster management policies. The economic aspect includes the assistance to revive the economic losses during disaster viz. life, house, agriculture, livestock etc. The social aspect, which at present is given less attention, includes consideration of social set up and conditions of the society, which reflects their needs and requirements during rescue, relief and rehabilitation processes.

The most important aspect, which is totally neglected during disaster management, in the area is the environmental aspect. This aspect which includes the eco-friendly development and other related activities to check the deteriorating environmental conditions, ultimately leads to disaster mitigation. This aspect attains crucial importance in the unstable and fragile areas like Uttranchal.

BASIC ASPECTS OF DISASTER MANAGEMENT

The outcome of the present study reveals that the problem of disaster management in the area is multi-dimensional. Various issues raised in the preceding chapters reveal that this problem basically has four aspects, i.e. politico-administrative, social, economic and environmental aspect.

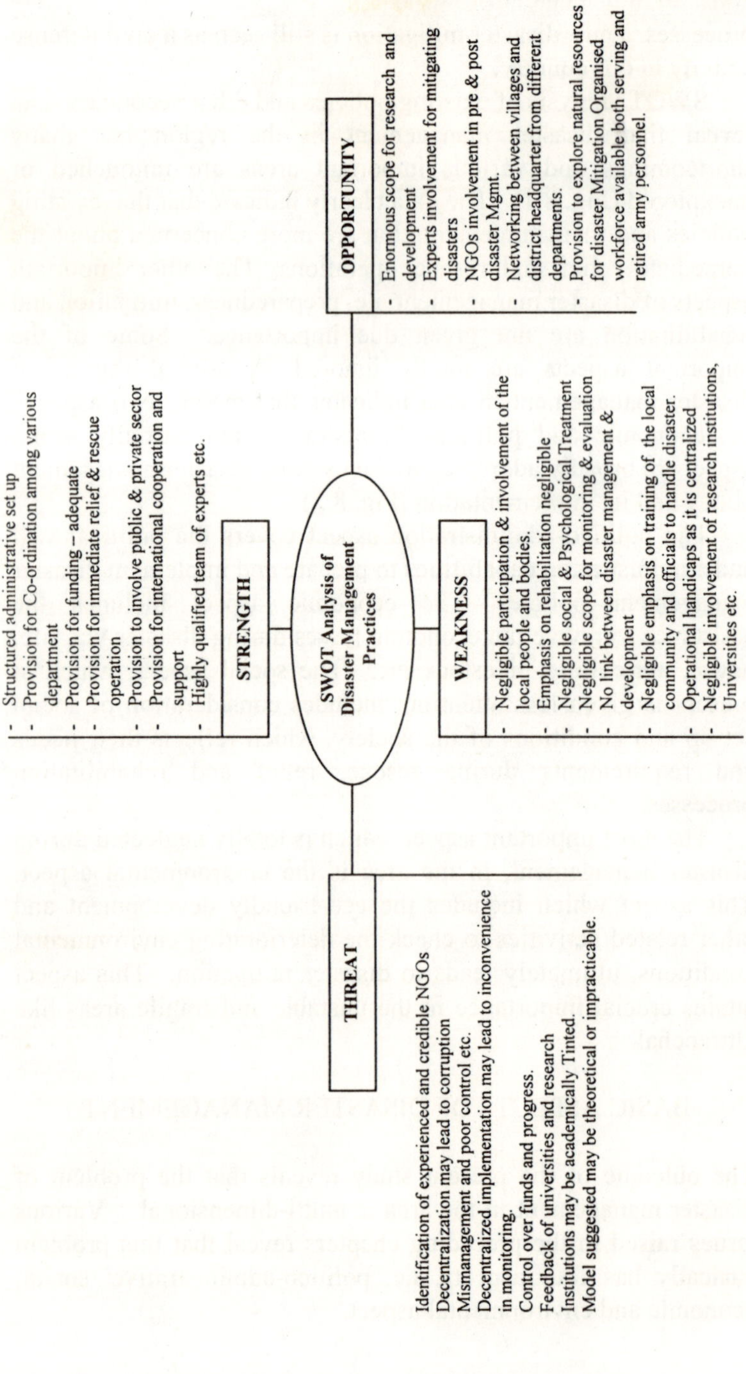

Fig. 8.1 : SWOT Analysis of Disaster Management Practices

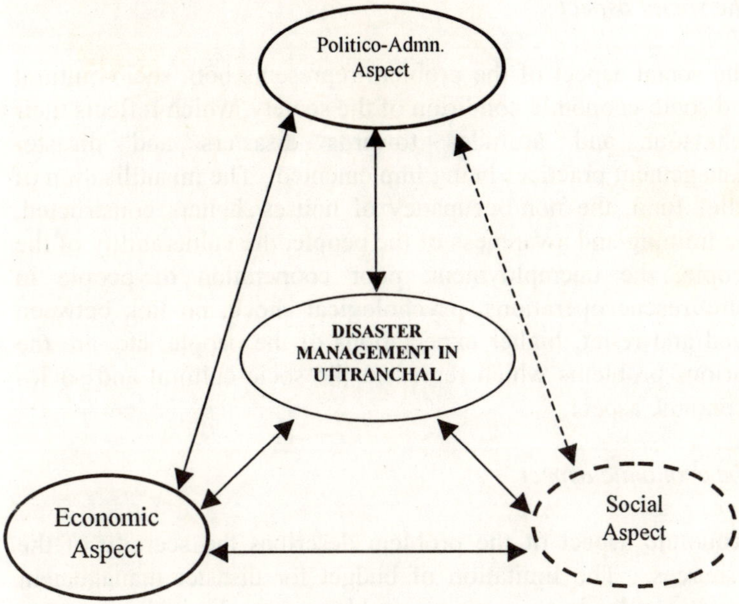

Fig. 8.2 : The Conceptual Model for Disaster Management in Uttranchal.

All the four aspects mentioned are of strategic importance in disaster management in disaster prone areas. It is to be further mentioned that these four aspects of the problem are interdependent and alteration in one will certainly effect the other aspect of the problem.

The politico-administrative aspect

As mentioned above, this aspect covers the political will and the administration capability to prepare and implement an appropriate disaster management policies. The discrimination in survey, delay in relief, poor monitoring and evaluation, false promises by politician and bureaucrats, poor representation of NGOs, lack of coordination among various departments etc. are the main problems which are due to the prevailing politico-administrative set-up and the mutual trust endowed on each other.

The social aspect

The social aspect of the problem represents both socio-cultural and socio-economic condition of the society, which reflects their behaviour and attitudes towards disasters and disaster management practices being implemented. The misutilisation of relief fund, the non-occupancy of houses/shelters constructed, the training and awareness of the people, the vulnerability of the people, the unemployment, poor cooperation of people in relief/rescue operations, psychological shock, no link between need and relief, higher expectations of the people, etc. are the various problems which represent the socio-cultural and socio-economic aspect.

The economic aspect

Economic aspect of the problem describes the scarcity of the resources. The limitation of budget for disaster management operations leads to various problems, viz. limited resources, delay in relief/rescue operations, inability of generating employment, rehabilitation or shifting of people residing in very sensitive zones, improper medical care and educational facilities, poor training and lack of awareness etc. Beside these, the economic aspect affects other problems also, mentioned under social and politico-administrative aspects.

The increasing frequency of disasters put pressure on the already poor economy of the country. A major portion of the resources of the country are to be diverted for various disaster management activities, i.e. relief, rescue and rehabilitation. In such circumstances, it is of utmost importance that while formulating policies and its implementation, emphasis should be on optimum use of available funds so that with limited resources, maximum results can be obtained in the field of disaster management.

The environmental aspect

In sensitive and fragile zones like Uttranchal, the environmental aspect plays very crucial and critical role. The faulty development policies/schemes lead to environmental degradation and disturb the area ecology. The faulty employment opportunities generation and other development schemes in sensitive areas etc. are the direct results of ignorance of this important aspect, which causes further deterioration of the situation and accelerates disaster frequency and its severity in the area.

Thus we see that the essence of the problem of disaster management in Uttranchal region lies in not giving due importance and weightage to these aspects. Keeping this in view, it becomes imperative that while suggesting an appropriate strategy for disaster management with long term perspective, all these aspects are given due consideration and importance.

9

EMERGING APPROACHES IN DISASTER MANAGEMENT

Various forms of natural disasters are basically natural forces, what are seen afterwards is the result of the impact of these forces on human beings. The quantum of loss due to a disaster, natural or man-made is the result of vulnerability of a society/region to disaster. The capacity of a society to resist the impact of these forces finally decides the degree of loss by these hazards and it depends on the precautions, the society has taken during various stages of development. The disasters is are inextricably linked to the development and it is the development pattern of the society, which decides its susceptibility/vulnerability to disasters.

Disaster management in a region basically companies of three stages i.e. pre-disaster, emergency and post-disaster. For an effective disaster management, it is a pre-requisite that balance is maintained among all the three stages. But mostly it is not like that and it is observed that the common practice adopted for disaster management is that it is treated like a fire fighting process, giving more emphasis on emergency and post-disaster stages. The pre-disaster stage, including mitigation and preparedness, is either totally neglected or given less importance. This imbalance leads to increased vulnerability of a society, resulting into huge quantum of loss due to the impact of natural hazards.

In general Disaster Management activity basically comprises of three stages, i.e.

- Pre-disaster stage.
- Emergency stage.
- Long term post-disaster stage (Fig. 9.1).

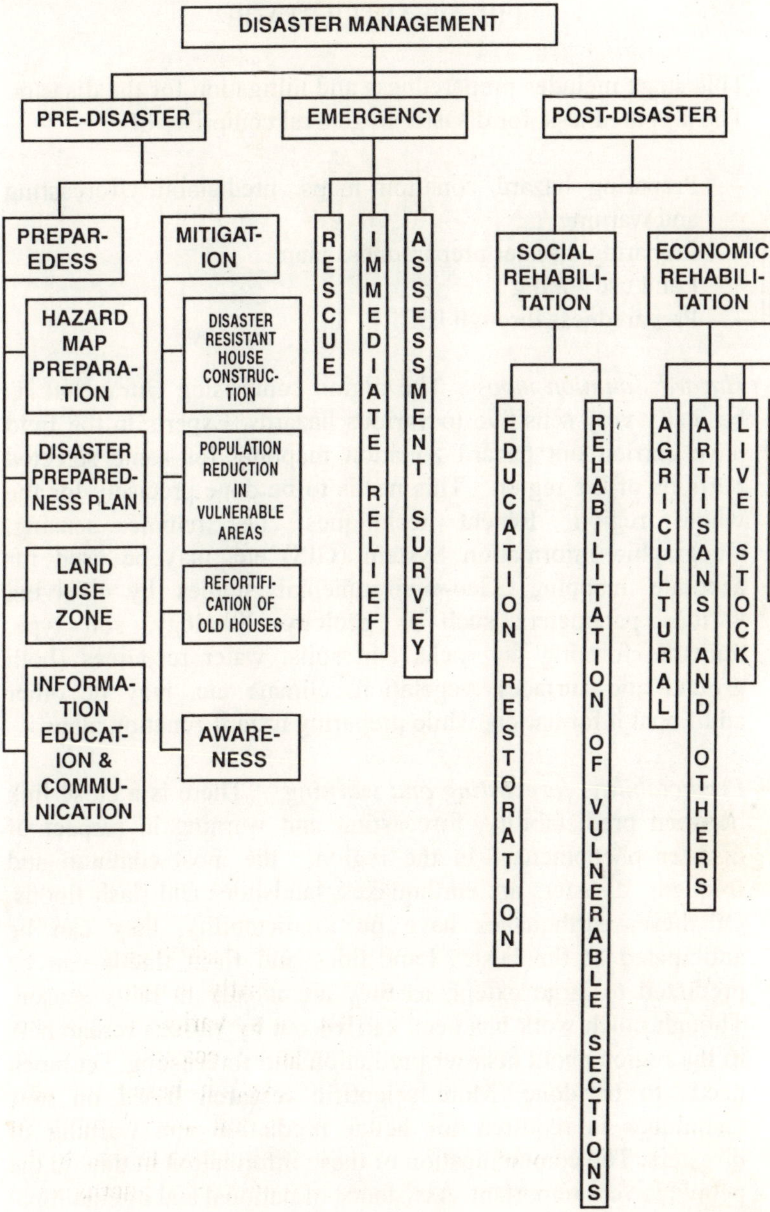

Fig. 9.1 : Three Stages of Disaster Management

PRE-DISASTER STAGE

This stage includes preparedness and mitigation for the disaster. The preparedness for disaster in general comprises of :

- Preparing hazard zonation maps, predictability/forcasting and warning
- Preparing disaster preparedness plan
- Land use zoning
- Preparedness through IEC

Hazard Zonation maps : The region comprising Uttranchal is basically very sensitive to various hazards. Experts in the field have carried out hazard zonation mapping for some selected portions of the region. This needs to be done precisely for the whole region. Recent techniques, i.e. remote sensing, Geographic Information System (GIS) etc. may be used for accurate mapping. Geo-environmental studies by evolving various parameters such as geology, lithology, soil type, minerals forming the rocks and soils, water resources (both ground and surface), vegetation, climate etc. may be other additional information, while preparing hazard zonation maps.

Predictability, forecasting and warning : There is a close link between predictability, forecasting and warning in respect of disaster phenomena. In the region, the most common and frequent disasters are earthquakes, landslides and flash floods. Of these, earthquakes have no predictability, they can be anticipated at the best. Landslides and flash floods can be predicted to large extent, as they are mostly in rainy season. Though much work has been carried out by various researchers in the region about disaster prediction and forecasting, yet much needs to be done. More scientific research based on new techniques is required for better prediction and warning of disasters. The communication of these information in time to the people is very important. Assistance of national and international satellite network may be sought for this purpose. It will certainly help in making the forecast and warning system more efficient and effective.

Disaster preparedness plan : In disaster prone areas like Uttranchal, a well coordinated comprehensive preparedness plan is very essential for disaster mitigation. This plan can be prepared by different departments separately, clearly depicting its preparedness for the emergency situation.

Land-use zoning : In the region, rapid growth of population is a matter of great concern. This has forced the people to reside and do agriculture in very fragile zones. The Madhyamaheshwar valley (where landslides caused more than 50 deaths in 1998) is one such area, where people have developed agriculture fields on very steep slopes making it unstable and fragile.

To avoid such situations, it is of utmost importance that for whole of the Uttranchal region, a land use plan is prepared. Geographical Information System and remote sensing data may also be invoked for this task. Based on this plan, the activities in sensitive areas may be redesigned. The satellite data may be used to produce various land use information data base at micro and macro level. Other associated data about the geo-environment, viz., barren land, water resources, saline land, water logged areas, erosional features, and extent of eroded land, forest fire etc. may also be collected and compiled using satellite imageries and GIS information.

Preparedness through IEC : Information, Education and Communication are means for creating awareness, wisdom and knowledge among people in order to prepare them for disaster mitigation. In the region these three components can play an important role in disaster mitigation. Various tools, i.e. rapid appraisal, action plan, awareness campaign etc. can be used to make people aware and knowledgeable about natural disasters management in Uttranchal.

A museum for better and ideal communication to the general public about various disasters and their management in Uttranchal can be developed at a centrally located city/town.

This planned museum shall be more than an a amusement park and can cater to the educational needs of engineers, scientists, social workers, rescue workers, disaster-management students, children and common people.

Items to be displayed in the Museum :

- Some of the typical structures damaged by the earthquake or other disaster could be preserved for display and study, along with the other models of typical structural failures.
- Models showing the geological phenomenon responsible for tectonic movements in Himalayan belt can be displayed to make people understand the causes of geological hazards in Uttaranchal.
- The social aspects after a tremendous loss of life and property, the rescue operations, the relief operations, the contribution of volunteers, the medical teams and of the entire national and international efforts can be depicted in the museum to give idea about the disaster and its management.
- Videographic user friendly interactive computer shows to make the visitors experience about disaster events.
- Facilities to study and demonstrate the effect of disasters on buildings and structures by structural models.
- Geological and seismographic models to give idea about the natural causes of earthquake and other disasters and to make people understand their mechanism.
- Models can be displayed showing the impact of environment degradation on disaster frequency and intensity.

The second aspect of Pre-Disaster stage, i.e. Mitigation covers different aspects which reduce the impact of disaster, that can be undertaken prior to its occurrence. In Uttranchal region for earthquakes and landslides (the common types of disasters), following mitigation measures are essential for effective disaster mitigation measures.

- Construct disaster resistant houses.
- Reduce population pressure in very sensitive zones.
- Refortification (strengthening) of existing houses in sensitive areas.
- Make people aware of do's and don'ts at the time of disaster.

Development and Disaster Mitigation

Development is an inextricable component of disaster management. Though this aspect is universally applicable, it is more relevant in the areas with continuous threat and frequencies of disasters like Uttranchal.

In general development is treated as the causative factor for disasters. But it is true for unplanned and non-scientific development. A planned and systematic development in a region certainly helps in reducing the susceptibility of a region and society to losses and thus mitigating disaster. Keeping this in view, in disaster prone areas disaster management activities are to be considered as developmental activities and *vice versa*. The approach of the developmental programmes in such areas should be positive, with stress on building strong and resistant socio-economic and physical structures, capable to resist the impact of natural hazards. It is also necessary to view disaster management activities as developmental activities while revitalizing structural as well as non-structural vulnerability reduction strategies and recognize and integrate the positive elements of indigenous technology.

Thus, the main emphasis of a disaster management system should be on reducing the vulnerability which will automatically take care of other two stages, i.e. emergency and post disaster up to large extent. As development pattern and vulnerability are two aspects of a single problem and are inter-dependent, the approach of an appropriate disaster management should be tailor made development of the region in such a manner that the susceptibility of a society to disaster is minimized. This is applicable not only for pre-disaster but for the post disaster stage also. Conventional development is not able to take care of vulnerability and hence the areas with high disaster frequency need specialized development planning. For effective results, appropriate and sustainable development is to be designed to meet the basic needs for vulnerability reduction, survival and recovery. For this the best approach is that the development and disaster management should be inter-linked and managed by the same authority. But in most of the cases it is not like this and disaster management is separated from the development, leading to increased vulnerability. Generally these two aspects are handled separately in different sectors, similar to a bicycle, cycled by two riders in two deferent directions, leading nowhere.

The risk of a society to disasters is dependent on its vulnerability and type of natural hazards.

Risk = Vulnerability × Nature and intensity of disaster

As the type and intensity of the natural hazards is beyond human control, the emphasis of an appropriate disaster management should be to reduce the vulnerability of the society, so that the risk is minimised and this can be achieved by moulding the developmental processes. Separation of disaster management from development will certainly increase vulnerability of the society and subsequently the risk to natural hazards. But the question arises is what type of development makes things worse and what type of developmental interventions make them better? The appropriate response is that the development should take due care of four essential aspects of socio-economic and physical system of a society, i.e. politico-administrative, economic, social and environmental aspects.

- There should be politico-administrative will for such type of development. The development should be acceptable to political/administrative bosses and all other sections of the society. For this the involvement of the people right from the planning is essential.
- While considering the social aspect, the development should be acceptable to the people and in tune to their local needs. It should cover all the social obligations, i.e. education, health facilities, taking necessary care of the vulnerable groups of the society etc.
- To take care of the economic aspects, the development should take care of all the economic requirements of each and every section of the society and should not be heterogeneous. The uneven or heterogeneous development leads to increase the vulnerability of all the sections of the society to natural hazards.
- The most important aspect for appropriate development, specially in disaster prone area is the environmental strategies to combat the vulnerability. This means the

development should be eco-friendly and in such a way so that environment is least disturbed.

Proper attention and consideration to these four aspects during development in disaster prone areas will certainly help in reducing vulnerability of a society and region to disasters and thus minimize the loss.

EMERGENCY STAGE

This stage of disaster management comprises of rescue and evacuations, shelters for victims, relief for livestock, disposal of dead and finally damage assessment survey. The stage requires literally a 'Rapid Action Task Force', that is aware of the contextual social norms and conditions and is psychologically attuned to face the abnormal human conditions. The team should have the concern and technical knowledge and skills to conduct such operations.

The contextual findings of the region of disaster reveal that during emergency stage the major role is played by administration alone. With limited resources, the administration can hardly perform these operations effectively. To deal with this, it is required that local people are trained to handle emergency situation. The formulation of disaster management committees at local level may be another alternative. If various NGOs, local bodies (panchayats), National Social Service Core, and other voluntary organisations are given adequate responsibility and resources to tackle emergency situation, the results will be better and satisfactory. For assessment of damages, there is no scientific method used for this process. For actual assessment and successful reconstruction planning, the assessment process must be transparent. This will help in reducing corruption and irregularities in assessment survey.

Training for search and rescue operation (At National and Regional Level)

It is very strongly felt that during rescue and relief at the time of disaster, there is an urgent need for a specialized national facility to provide professional training in Search and Rescue. It is proposed that a centre for training in search and rescue operation be immediately created. Organisation like Army, Para Military Forces, BSF, CISF, scouts, NCC cadets, teachers, postmen, village panchayat, NGOs, community leaders need to be trained for this purpose.

The centre may be developed at centrally located areas so that trained people can move quickly to the affected areas. The facility should be able to provide professional training in and also handle situations arising out of any and all of the following happenings.

- Earthquakes
- Landslides
- Avalanches
- Floods
- Fire

The proposed centres needs be networked and equipped with:

- Instant mobility in air, land, hills etc.
- Instant communication systems.
- Inventory of rescue equipment and trained manpower available.
- Life detecting devices like dog squads etc. and other advance equipments.
- Portable generators, pumps and lights.
- Drills, RCC cutters, winches, hoists, cranes etc. Special light weight equipments will be of much use in hilly terrains.
- Life saving and survival kits.

The facility, apart from being a training centre shall have trained manpower to manage rescue and relief operations. The trainees may be mobilized from defence forces, para-military organisations, police, voluntary organisations, NCC and NGOs from all over the country and other source of such trained persons be maintained in the centre. In Uttaranchal there is a good number of Ex-army personnel in each district. Some of the selected may be trained for the purpose.

REHABILITATION

The most important phase of disaster management starts with the passing of emergency phase. In the disaster prone areas, rehabilitation should not be simply viewed as only shifting of people from one place to another and resettling them. The past experiences (as in the case of Tehri Dam construction) have shown that such type of practice is a partial failure and had left the majority of people as refugees in the new area. The study of socio-cultural aspect of the Uttranchal region shows that the inhabitants of the region are sentimentally attached to their land. At a new place, particularly in plains, they find themselves totally unfit. Hence, the rehabilitation of the disaster affected population needs a revised approach different from the other rehabilitation processes. The rehabilitation here does not merely means providing financial support or rebuilding/repairing/retreating the damaged houses etc., instead it is to be focused on overall development of the region.

To be specific the people to be rehabilitated in Uttranchal region can be divided into 2 categories, i.e.

(i) People whose villages and livelihood resources are lost due to disasters, and

(ii) People who are residing in very sensitive areas and are under continuous threat from disasters like landslides, earthquakes etc.

The successful rehabilitation policy or planning for these two categories need to analyse all the four aspects (Fig. 9.2), i.e. politico-administrative, social, economic and environmental, which means that there should be –

- politico-administrative will for rehabilitation.
- The rehabilitation should be acceptable to the community, i.e. to be formulated considering the local needs of the people, their culture and traditions. This aspect of rehabilitation also covers the revival/strengthening of educational system and health facilities and rehabilitation of vulnerable groups of the society.

- The rehabilitation plan is required to consider various economic aspects related to the livelihood of the people affected by the disasters.
- For successful and sustainable rehabilitation plan in hilly regions like Uttranchal, the environmental aspect is of very crucial and strategic importance. A rehabilitation plan devoid of the environmental aspect is bound to fail in such fragile and unstable zones.

Politico-Administrative Aspect

The long-term rehabilitation of the people affected by disasters and from sensitive areas in the region necessarily requires a strong political and administrative will as it includes many issues which cannot be taken care without political and administrative support. The allocation of land, availability of funds, engagement of planners and other experts etc. are such issues which cannot be undertaken without proper consent and willingness from these quarters.

To ensure long term socio-economic and psycho-cultural rehabilitation, political and administrative support is to be considered essential. This requires a rehabilitation plan, which can convince the political leaders at local and at national level. The viability of the plan/project is necessary which will clearly visualise the benefits and expenses to be incurred.

Social Aspect

Social aspect of rehabilitation covers the traditional and cultural values of the community, strengthening the educational system and health facilities and rehabilitation of vulnerable group, i.e. women, children and old persons affected by the disaster.

Traditional and cultural values of community: The people of Uttranchal region are very much attached to their land, culture and traditions. Keeping this in view, it is a must that the rehabilitation is to be planned in such a way, so that their traditional and cultural values are preserved. In this area the housing patterns in most of the villages is based on some old traditions. The construction of houses without taking this aspect into consideration, leaves these units unoccupied. To solve such problems, the involvement of people at the planning stage is essential.

Restoration and strengthening of education system : Restoration of education system is also an important aspect in the rehabilitation process. After disaster, i.e. earthquakes or landslides, the educational buildings are damaged and it is seen that schools are closed almost for months and even for years in some cases. For proper restoration of the education activities, the teachers and the children of the disaster affected areas require constant counselling. These people require someone with them to share their sorrow and grief. They also require encouragement and motivation to start their life once again. Hence, the role of local NGOs may be very effective in this aspect. The responsibilities assigned to these local groups may include:

(i) Counselling and encouraging the children to attend the schools regularly.
(ii) Helping the school administration for ensuring participation and cooperation of the children in all activities of the school.
(iii) Developing an atmosphere for students to seek knowledge and information.
(iv) Inculcating conducive attitudes among the students enabling them to develop a positive role in self-development.
(v) Establishing the village level education committees for proper monitoring of schools within the village.
(vi) Restoration of confidence among the people.

For achieving good results in the disaster affected areas, orientation programmes can be conducted for NGOs involved, with clear objectives to train the group members and identification of target groups, methodology to be adopted, typology and timings etc. to carry-out the various educational activities in the affected villages/areas.

Rehabilitation of vulnerable sections of society : Aged people, women and children are the most vulnerable groups of the society at the time of disaster. In Uttranchal, the ratio of this population is relatively higher in comparison to other parts of the country due to the fact that a large number of young people are in army or other government services and do not reside locally. In such circumstances, the rehabilitation of this group becomes the first priority under any rehabilitation scheme or plan.

For this region the rehabilitation programme for these groups should include :

(i) An attempt must be made to attach the widows and orphans within their extended family or through a foster family in case of orphans.
(ii) The mental health of such affected groups must be strengthened through programmes of regular counseling and psychological treatment.
(iii) The proper health, nutrition and hygiene aspects must be taken care of within the long-term rehabilitation of the women and children group.
(iv) The economic independence of widows must be ensured with the help of various programmes, i.e. small scale industries, formation of self-help groups etc.
(v) The groups should be rehabilitated in familiar environment.

Economic Aspect

The economy of Uttranchal is mixed. As agriculture land is very limited due to geographic reasons, the people are dependent on other sources of income. Most of the young people are in army or other services. Small shops and petty businesses are other source of income for some of the people. Thus the overall economic condition of the people is not very good in this region. Frequency of disasters in the region has further deteriorated the situation and a large number of population have lost their petty source of income and people are forced to migrate from their villages to cities or towns to earn livelihood. Keeping this in view, it is important that rehabilitation plan is formulated giving the economic aspects due consideration. To consider the economic rehabilitation in the region, the following components are essential :

- Agricultural rehabilitation.
- Rehabilitation of artisans, petty shop owners etc.
- Rehabilitation of livestock.
- Employment generation based on local resources.
- Shelter/Housing.

Agricultural rehabilitation

Agricultural land is limited and usually unproductive in this area. The agricultural fields are mostly on slopes, and thus more prone to degradation. In brief, the agricultural practices in the region are not economically and environmentally viable. The agriculture practices make the area vulnerable to erosion and degradation. The 1998 landslides near Madhyamaserwar river was primarily due to the unscientific land use for agriculture purpose. It is observed that the people in the area are forced to survive on agriculture due to scarcity of other livelihood sources. Thus, there is urgent need to discourage that unscientific agriculture practices and use this agriculture land for more eco-friendly activities like horticulture, social forestry etc. All necessary support and cooperation should be extended for achieving the same.

Rehabilitation of Artisans and Petty business/shop owners

The economic status of artisans and other small business persons is also not at all satisfactory in this region. These groups survive on a day to day basis and during disaster the financial condition of such groups become really miserable. In case of a large number of people under this category, the disaster results in loss of a market place for their finished products or raw material. It is advised that they should be provided small work sheds, necessary tool-kits and soft loans to enable them to secure raw materials and to market the unfinished/finished products. Another way is to rehabilitate the affected people, by initiating rural industrial units at block level within the disaster affected areas. In these units, various artisans like carpenters, black-smiths, gold-smiths, tailors, potters, mechanics etc. may be provided with basic infrastructural facilities like working sheds, internal roads, electricity, water supply, raw material, etc. for rehabilitation The assistance of rural development schemes of Ministry of Rural Development, may specially be provided for such groups as discussed under heading "Sustainable Rural Development – A Remedy to Disasters".

Livestock Rehabilitation

In Uttranchal cattle are an integral part of rural economy. These cattle are used for milk, wool, meat, agriculture labour and transportation. The death of cattle during disasters causes adverse impact on the economic conditions of the area.

Precautionary measures for rehabilitation of livestock may be :

- Scientifically developed superior breeds of cattle are to be made available to villagers.
- Establishment of Research Centres for breed improvement.
- Development of pasture land.
- Establishment of small milk based industries.
- Distribution of cattle feed in the initial stage.
- Preventive medication for entire livestock to check the spread of any disease or epidemic.

Housing

During recent disasters in Uttranchal, maximum damage was caused to houses and household properties. The collapse of houses was also responsible for most of the casualties in the area. During field investigations, it was observed that the traditional housing pattern in rural Uttranchal is no more existing. The traditional houses constructed with local materials and techniques have survived the onslaught of the recent earthquakes, while the newly constructed houses were severely damaged. The place of traditional houses constructed of mud, wood, and slates has been taken by brick and stone houses with

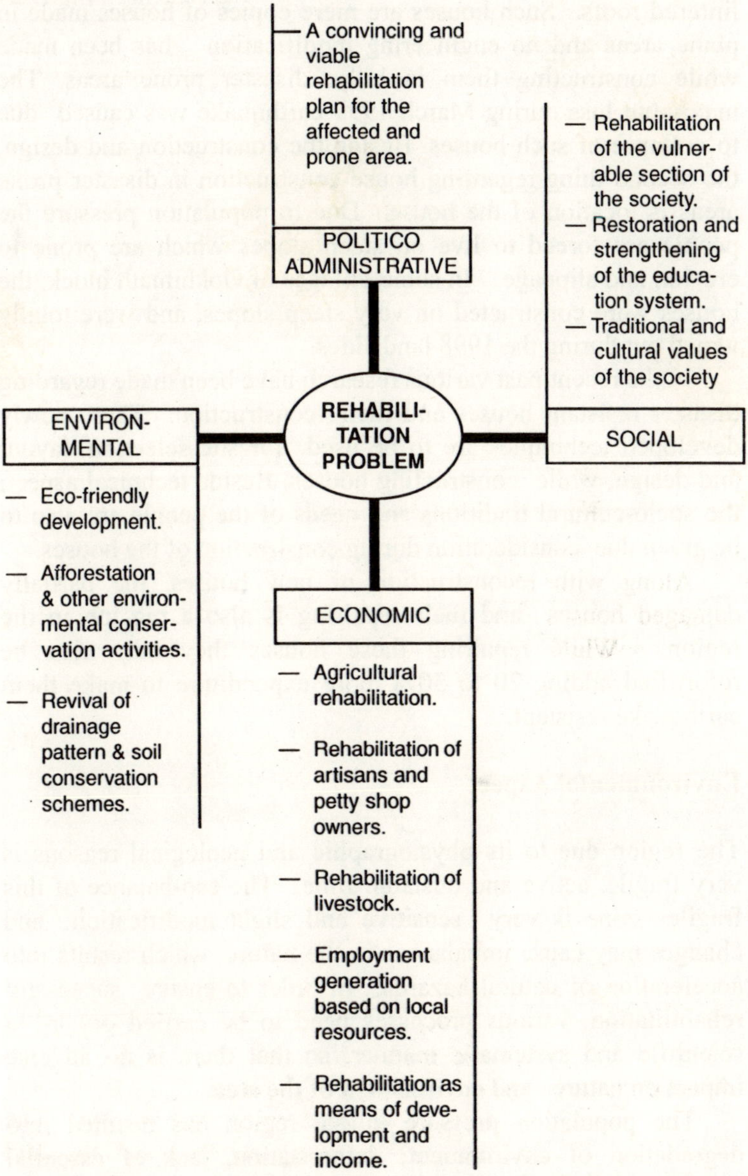

Fig. 9.2 : Four Aspects of Rehabilitation for Disaster Affected Population.

lintered roofs. Such houses are mere copies of houses made in plane areas and no engineering modification has been made while constructing them in hilly, disaster prone areas. The maximum loss during March 1999 earthquake was caused due to collapse of such houses. Beside the construction and design, the second thing regarding house construction in disaster prone areas is location of the house. Due to population pressure the people are forced to live on steep slopes which are prone to erosion and slippage. In some villages of Ookhimath block, the houses were constructed on very steep slopes, and were totally wiped out during the 1998 landslides.

In the recent past various research have been made regarding disaster resistant houses and their construction. These newly developed techniques are to be used for site selection, layout and design, while constructing houses. Beside technical aspect, the socio-cultural traditions and needs of the people are also to be given due consideration during construction of the houses.

Along with reconstruction of new houses, the partially damaged houses and their repairing is also a big job in the region. While repairing these houses they may also be refortified adding 20 to 30% more expenditure to make them earthquake resistant.

Environmental Aspect

The region due to its physiographic and geological reasons is very fragile, active and unstable zone. The eco-balance of this fragile zone is very sensitive and slight modification and changes may cause imbalances in the nature, which results into acceleration of natural hazards. In order to ensure successful rehabilitation, various processes need to be carried out in a scientific and systematic manner, so that there is no adverse impact on nature and environment of the area.

The population pressure in the region has resulted into degradation of environment; deforestation, lack of essential services like water and sanitation, economic backwardness etc. and the occurrence of natural disaster has further weakened the carrying capacity of the area. In such situation, it is imperative that the relationship between sustainable environment planning for such areas and natural disaster reduction be recognised. Risks in such areas can be reduced only if they are systematically analysed and policies are designed to reduce them through the planning process. During field investigations, it is observed that the local planning authorities are competent enough to deal with these issues within their jurisdiction. But the environmental protection is nobody's agenda. Therefore, there is a need for developing an institute which can address the issue of environmental conservation in such areas.

The hilly region of the State has been recognised as backward and underdeveloped since independence. However very few efforts have been made to carry out a distinct and area specific development policy for the region. Instead both plain and the hilly region of erstwhile Uttar Pradesh were treated in the similar way as far as the development was concerned. Hence the lack of perception on the part of the policy makers and as well as implementers caused a lot suffering to the State and inspite of sufficient funding both from the central and state, the region could not achieve any thing significant in the field of development and there is not much visual change in the economic pattern of the society. Agriculture, which is very less productive, unscientific and damaging to the already fragile environment is still the predominant sector in terms of employment and income generation. Due to intensive growth in population and lack of other livelihood resources the dependency of the people on agriculture is increasing day by day and cultivation is being extended to the marginal and forest land leading to destabilisation of the ecological balance of the hilly terrain of the region. According to G.S. Mehta, fellow, Giri Institute of Development Studies, Lucknow, "*the real challenge in planning for development of Uttrakhand has been recognised in terms of creating employment and income opportunities by introducing a comprehensive planning approach for developing various identified economic sectors through which development would have greater intensity of providing increasing level of opportunities with larger income generation potentials without having any adverse impact on the local environment and the ecological system.*" Surprisingly this aspect has been ignored in the past while preparing development policies for the region.

The environmental aspect has been given very less or negligible importance and an integrated approach to development planning has not been given due consideration. Environment is an integrated part for the otherwise fragile regions like Uttranchal, therefore the development approach for such regions should give due consideration and importance to this aspect and appropriate approach should be to focus on development without adversely affecting the environment and the ecology of the region. For this it is must that the development in such fragile and sensitive zones should be more selective and with much more precaution.

Taking this issue into consideration, it is essential that the developmental activities in the region are carried out giving due importance to the environmental aspect. Along with development the resulting factors, i.e. deforestation, forest fire, degradation of drainage pattern etc. are also to be taken care. All these issues are of major concern in the region as they have adversely affected the environment. Afforestation, control of forest fire and revival of drainage pattern should be given due importance along with development of the area. One important observation in the region is that the accelerating factor for landslides is the gradual damage of the drainage system. To deal with this problem and the physical features of the mountains, it is advised that integrated land use and treatment plans are implemented. For the protection of physical features of the land, all the district departments, i.e. soil conservation, irrigation, forests, agriculture etc. should prepare an integrated land treatment plan. This will help in making special arrangements for developing a proper drainage system, special soil conservation measures, water harvesting techniques and promotion of local shrubs and herbs before going in for any tree plantation activities on the vulnerable degraded slopes.

Over and above, forestry with an integrated approach and, watershed management with proper land use may really be helpful to check the deteriorating environmental conditions of the area. More emphasis is to be given on forestry related activities with sustainable development and scientific technologies, which will certainly lessen the intensity and incidences of disasters in the region. For soil and water conservation and to reduce run off, afforestation along with minor engineering treatment is being prescribed with appropriate technology and by adopting suitable forest species (Fig. 9.3).

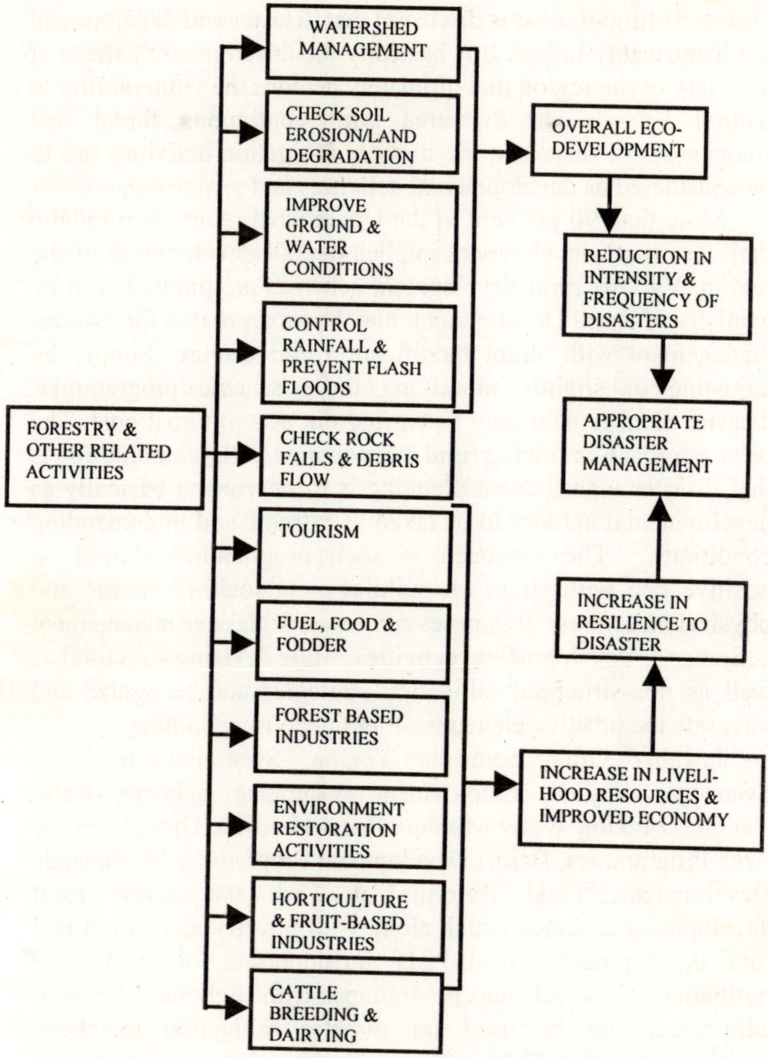

Fig. 9.3 : Role of Forestry in Disaster Management

SUSTAINABLE RURAL DEVELOPMENT – A REMEDY TO DISASTERS

In the preceding section under the subtitle "Development and Disaster Mitigation" it is discussed that disaster and development are inextricably linked. It is basically the development pattern of a society or the region that ultimately decides the vulnerability to natural hazards. In the area with continuous threat and frequencies of disasters, the disaster mitigation activities are to be considered as developmental activities and *vice versa.*

More than 90 per cent of the Uttaranchal region is rural and therefore rural development implies overall development of the region. Various rural development schemes/programmes run by Ministry of Rural Development, may be incorporated for disaster management with slight modification and change. Simply by adjusting or slightly modifying these schemes/programmes, disaster management may be carried out at a minimal cost. The basic approach in linking rural development with rehabilitation is that disaster management planning is to be viewed basically as developmental activity to be taken in extreme and in demanding conditions. The approach to such programmes should be positive one with stress on building new socio-economic and physical structures. It is necessary to view disaster management activities as developmental activities, while devising structural as well as non-structural mitigation strategies and recognize and integrate the positive elements of indigenous technology.

Jawahar Gram Samridhi Yojana, Swaranjayanti Gram Swarojgar Yojana, Employment Assurance Scheme, Rajiv Gandhi Drinking Water Mission, Rural Housing, Drought Prone Area Programmes, Desert Development Programme, Wastelands Development, Land Reforms etc. are the major rural development schemes which along with poverty alleviation and rural development, can also play an important role in disaster mitigation. These schemes/programmes with slight modification/ adjustment can be used for disaster mitigation to check environmental degradation (responsible for man made disasters) and rehabilitation in the disaster prone areas. This integrated approach of combining rural development with disaster management will help in reducing vulnerability of the people to disasters in sensitive areas and thus strengthen them against temporary disruption of economic activities caused by natural calamities (Fig. 9.4). How these schemes can be managed for disaster mitigation is elaborated below :

Jawahar Gram Samridhi Yojana (JGSY)

The basic objective of the scheme is the creation of demand driven village infrastructure including durable assets to enable the rural poor to increase the opportunities for employment. The second objective is generation of supplementary employment for the unemployed poor in the rural areas. In the disaster prone/affected areas, the scheme may be slightly modified, keeping its broad objectives intact. The development works, which are to be carried out in such areas should be oriented in such a way so that they help in mitigation of disaster in the region. Revival of drainage pattern, afforestation, plantation in landslide prone areas to check further erosion and degradation, construction of check-dams, mechanical work to check soil erosion and landslides etc. are the major works, that can be carried out under the scheme. These types of works in disaster prone areas along with generating employment opportunities for the disaster affected population, will also help in reducing the environmental degradation and thus reduce the chances of disasters.

Swaranjayanti Gram Swarozgar Yojana (SGSY)

The scheme aims at establishing a large number of micro enterprises in the rural areas, building upon the potential of rural poor. It is rooted in the belief that the rural poor in India have competencies and if given the right support, can be successful producer of valuable goods and services. It is conceived as a holistic programme of micro enterprises covering all aspects of self-employment, viz. organisation of rural poor into self-help groups and their capacity building, planning of cluster, activities infrastructure building, technology, credit and marketing.

In the disaster prone areas like Uttranchal, the scheme may be slightly modified, so that along with overall development of

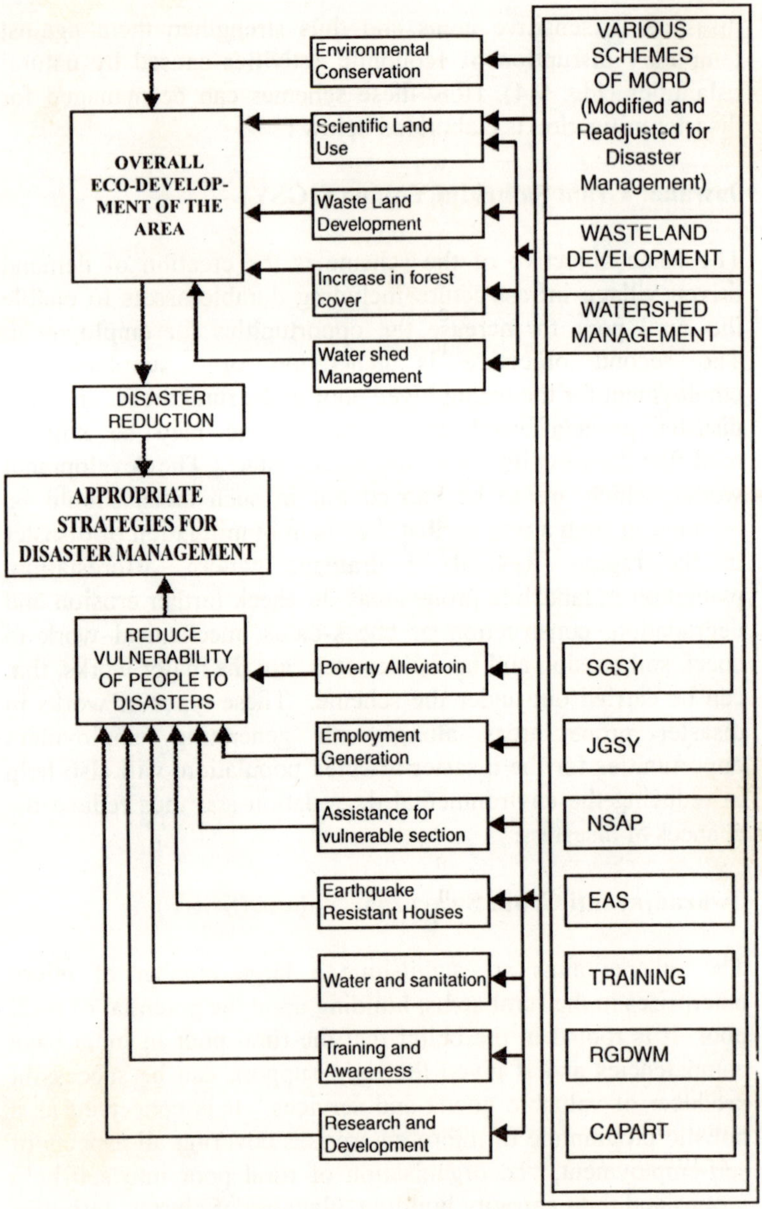

Fig. 9.4 : Four Aspects of Rehabilitation for Disaster affected Population.

rural poor, it may help in environmental conservation and disaster mitigation. Under the modified scheme, various eco-friendly activities listed below may be carried out:

- Plantation of fast growing species which have market value.
- Installation of small forest based industries, which will create interest of people in afforestation.
- Horticulture activities, which along with giving livelihood to the disaster affected population, will also check soil erosion and environmental degradation.
- Installation of small horticulture based industries, i.e. fruit juice, jam, pickles etc.

These types of activities under the scheme will certainly help in poverty alleviation and employment generation in the disaster prone areas along with disaster mitigation.

Employment Assurance Scheme (EAS)

The scheme is to provide gainful employment during the lean agricultural season by way of manual work to all able bodied adults in rural areas, who are in need and desirous of work, but are unable to find the same. The secondary objective is the creation of community, social and economic assets for sustained employment and development.

In Uttranchal region, the agriculture land is a scarce resource. This limited land resource is unable to provide livelihood to the rural poor. In such areas Employment Assurance Scheme can be a good source of employment generation for the people residing in disaster prone areas. Works to be carried out under the scheme are to be selected in such a way so that they are as per the requirement of the land and the people. Afforestation, soil conservation, revival of drainage pattern, construction of check-dams, watershed management etc. should be the major works, which can be carried out under the scheme. These types of works will definitely help in disaster mitigation in the area.

Rajiv Gandhi Drinking Water Mission (RGDWM)

The objective of the scheme is to supplement the efforts of the State Government by providing central assistance under the Accelerated Rural Water Supply Programme. The broad objectives of the scheme is to :

- Cover the residual, Not Covered (NC), Partially Covered (PC) and quality affected rural habitations.
- Evolve appropriate technology mix.
- Improve performance and cost effectiveness of ongoing programmes.
- Create awareness on the use of safe drinking water.
- Take conservation measures for sustained supply of drinking water.

In disaster affected areas the scarcity of water becomes a major problem. The scheme can help in providing water to the affected population. In rural Uttaranchal, people are dependent on natural resources like springs, ponds, lakes etc. for drinking water. During disaster, these resources are damaged and the people have to face the problem of water scarcity. Under the scheme, these natural sources of water may be revived and thus the problem of water scarcity may be solved upto a large extent.

Rural Housing (RH)

The Rural Housing scheme of Ministry of Rural Development aims at providing houses to the rural poor along with improving the quality of life as well as overall habitat in the rural areas. For disaster prone areas, necessary amendments may be made to suit the local needs and environment. In such areas, the houses to be constructed may be made earthquake resistant with slight modifications and changes. These houses should be constructed in such a way so that they fulfil the local needs of the people and the material used for these houses is locally available. In such areas, the scheme may be implemented with these amendments and.modifications to solve the problem of housing.

National Social Assistance Programme (NSAP)

The objective of the programme is to extend financial assistance to old persons having little or no regular means of subsistence or households living below the poverty line in case of death of the primary breadwinner and to pregnant women of households below the poverty line up to the first two live births.

In Uttranchal this scheme may be very useful to give relief to the affected population. As the old persons, women and children are most vulnerable to disasters, provisions can be made under the scheme to give financial support to such persons under the scheme. Special funds may be created for these relief activities in disaster affected areas of the region.

Training

Ministry of Rural Development, Government of India has good networking of various training institutes throughout the country. The basic aim of these institutes is to give training to the rural development functionaries about the various schemes of the Ministry. In Uttranchal, new centres may be opened under the scheme, which along with giving training about the rural development schemes may also include disaster management as special subject in its syllabus. The institutes may provide training to various departmental officials, the village representatives and the villagers about the disaster management. These institutes may also organise off campus training programmes in disaster prone areas. This will certainly increase the knowledge base and awareness of the people about disasters and thus help in reducing their vulnerability to natural/manmade hazards.

Council for Advancement of People's Action and Rural Technology (CAPART)

The voluntary sector plays an important role in development, particularly with reference to the programmes aimed at rural poor and for improving the quality of life in rural areas. The main objectives of the CAPART are to :

- Encourage, promote and assist voluntary action for the implementation of projects intending enhancement of rural prosperity.

- Strengthen and promote voluntary efforts in rural development with focus on injecting new technological inputs.
- Act as a catalyst for the development of technology appropriate for rural areas.
- Promote, plan, undertake, develop, maintain and support projects/schemes aimed at all-round development, creation of employment opportunities, promotion of self-reliance, generation of awareness, organisation and improvement in the quality of life of the people in rural areas through voluntary action.

Under this scheme, financial assistance is provided to the Non-Government Organisations (NGOs) for the works mentioned above. In disaster prone areas, the scheme can play a very important role. In Uttranchal, there are many NGOs who are really working in good capacity for various developmental activities in the area. Such NGOs may be encouraged to do work in the field of disaster management and mitigation. The Ministry may decide about the fields in which these NGOs may be given financial support. It is also advised that a new cell be created in CAPART which exclusively may look after the disaster management projects in the country.

Wastelands Development (WD) :

Under this programme various sub-schemes being implemented are as follows :

- Integrated Wasteland Development Project (IWDP) Scheme.
- Technology Development Extension and Training Schemes.
- Support to NGOs (Grant-in-Aid) Scheme.
- Investment Promotional Scheme (IPS).
- Wasteland Development Task Force (WDTF).

The basic objective of all these schemes, is to develop wastelands, check land degradation, increase bio-mass availability and thus put such wastelands into sustainable use.

In Uttranchal region, where the bio-mass is decreasing due to increasing biotic pressure, the scheme may be very appropriate and useful. Special amendments may be made in the scheme to suit the local needs. In disaster affected areas, where the land is turned into wasteland, the implementation of these schemes may be of immense utility. A special Task Force may be formed recruiting retired army personnel (who are in a good number in this region). This Task Force may work for soil and moisture conservation, plantation and its protection, revival of drainage pattern, checking soil erosion etc.

Beside the above mentioned schemes, the Ministry of Rural Development is running few schemes for drought prone and desert areas. Drought Prone Area Programmes (DPAP) and Desert Development Programme (DDP) are the examples of such sustainable rural development schemes. It is advised that a new programme, i.e. Disaster Prone Areas Programme may also be included in the schemes of Ministry of Rural Development, which may target the fragile areas like Uttranchal, which are under continuous threat of severe natural hazards.

Thus we see that various rural developmental schemes mentioned above with slight modification and amendments may prove very useful in disaster affected/prone areas. If these integrated rural development programmes are adopted with area specific modifications, they will certainly revitalise the rural life of the region. Along with directly influencing the factors responsible for the disasters in the hilly terrain they will help in making the society strong enough to resist the adverse impact of natural and manmade hazards. These ongoing schemes, with suggested modifications will certainly help in disaster mitigation with minimal expenditure. The suggestions may be given a serious thought by the planners and policy makers and after thorough research and study of the disaster prone areas, various amendments along with the suggested one may also be made in these schemes to get the maximum output of the expenditure incurred on such programmes.

DISASTER MANAGEMENT THROUGH PANCHAYAT

Majority of Uttranchal population lives in villages and is dependent primarily on agriculture and other petty livelihood resources. If visualized in term of economy, the overall condition of rural population in the state is not good and still large portion of the population is forced to live below poverty line. Beside poverty, there are other factors also which worsens the condition of this rural population. Among such factors natural disasters come on the top. Due to its increased vulnerability, rural population is much more affected by the adverse impact of natural disasters in comparison to its urban counterpart. Despite many sincere attempts at governmental and non-governmental levels, very less progress has been made in the field of disaster management, particularly in rural areas. The main reason for this is the absence of a local efficient organization, which can manage this job sincerely. The existing Panchayat Raj Institute may be the best alternative for this. The 29 subjects mentioned in the XI Schedule to the 73rd Amendment of the Indian Constitution, if dealt keeping the issue of disaster management in mind, may solve the problem up to an extent. If slightly reoriented and given proper facilities and strength, panchayats may work very effectively in managing the disasters in rural areas. The vital strength of PRIs is their working at grass-root level and providing ideal form of decentralized planning and implementation of programmes in accordance with the people's need and aspirations and this is what is in reality required for long term sustainable disaster management in the rural areas.

The basic objectives of the Panchayati Raj System are :

(i) Ensuring people participation in local level administration.
(ii) Innovative methods for enhancing the people involvement in the local development issues.
(iii) Create sense of responsibility among the rural population of the country so that they become more responsible and give more concentration to the development activities in the village.
(iv) To ensure that the development reach to all components of rural society and more to the persons for whom the benefits of these programmes are intended.

The Government of India aims to decentralize the power right up to village level. Devolution of responsibilities and powers upon PRIs has to be carried out by the State Govenrments in term of –

- transfer the function,
- transfer the functionaries, and
- transfer the funds.

ROLE OF PANCHAYATS IN DISASTER MITIGATION

The Constitution recommends for an important role to the PRIs in respect of 29 important subjects such as education, health, agriculture, housing, land reform, social and farm forestry, drinking water, poverty alleviation programmes, social welfare etc. which play very important and strategic role in the field of disaster management. These subjects if dealt effectively at local level taking into consideration the local needs and conditions (physical and social both), may be very effective in reducing the vulnerability of the land and the people and make the society resilient to the adverse impact of the natural hazards.

If viewed broadly the PRI system in the country has two important points, i.e. it encompasses the development needs of the micro unit and is based on the local felt needs of the people. The need is that while implementing the developmental programmes in a region, the socio-economic, socio-cultural, politico-administrative and environmental aspects are given due weightage and consideration.

The important factors that make the PRIs role more effective in dealing disasters in Uttranchal are :

- Disaster management through PRIs may be an economic way because it is able to devolve greater autonomy and resources very conveniently.
- PRIs may be very effective in using local tradition and wisdom supported with scientific application.
- May effectively deal the programmes which need large scale people participation, i.e. land reforms, revival of drainage pattern, sanitation etc.
- NGOs and other grassroot of organizations may be more comfortable while working with PRIs.

- More effective for better resource allocation and more public service in rural areas and effective in mobilising local resources.
- Can help poor more effectively to organize them through grassroot organizations.
- PRIs being a local body will be liable and responsible for long term impacts of development or other activity being carried out in disaster prone areas. PRIs may more effectively do environmental impact assessment in comparison to other outside agencies.
- New researches and investigations in the field of disaster management may be more effectively propagated through panchayats.
- While preparing disaster management plan for the village or the community, local factors may be given more importance and nothing important or strategic will be left without giving due consideration. This will certainly increase the quality of the plan and its practicability.
- The vulnerable group of the society will be given more importance during the disaster management.
- The relief may be more appropriate and as per the need and the chances of mis-utilisation will certainly decline.
- May be more effective in organizing the training programmes for the people as per their need and requirement.
- May be helpful in formulating a task force of the able-bodied persons of the village, who can be trained for rescue and relief during disaster.
- Panchayats could create their own relief fund by imposing taxes, rents etc. This fund can be used for emergency and long term disaster management practices.
- The most advantageous thing with the panchayat working for disaster mitigation is that it can provide services without delay and wasting time and waiting out side help. The immediate initial time after a disaster is very precious for rescue and saving life. But it is observed that this time is wasted in waiting outside help, which multiplies the life loss during disaster. If this help is locally available from the panchayat, many precious lives may be saved.

- The panchayats are more efficient to check the environment degradation, the most prominent cause for increasing the intensity and frequency of natural disasters. They can make the people aware about the adverse impact of environmental degradation in more effective manner. The Joint Forest Management Committees (JFMs) may be formed by Panchayats to look after the natural forest near the villages. It can also persuade people to grow more trees under the social and agro-forestry programmes The awareness programmes by panchayat may be very helpful in reducing the forest fire incidences also.
- Panchayats could persuade people residing in dangerous and sensitive zones to shift from. Panchayats, by providing alternative livelihood resources to such people may make them agreed to shift from such locations to safer positions and thus reducing their vulnerability to disasters.
- Taking assistance of various development programmes like Employment Assurance Schem (EAS), Jawahar Gram Samridhi Yojana (JGSY) etc. of Ministry of Rural Development, the Panchayats may develop good projects which may provide sufficient employment opportunities to the local people and thus make them economically more strong. Panchayats may develop and implement such projects without adversely affecting the environment. The local employment generation may also make a check on the migration of rural population to urban areas in search of livelihood.
- One basic drawback with the existing disaster management practices is the lack of any effective monitoring and evaluation system to make the appropriate check and modify the programmes. Social audit by the Gram Sabha may fill this gap. The Panchayati Raj act has given power to Gram Sabha to perform a watch dog function to supervise and monitor the functioning of the Panchayat and other organizations. This check may be more effective in the case of disaster management programmes, as being a local body the Gram Sabha may monitor and Supervise the programmes at micro and macro level both, which is not possible for an outside agency.

– The psychological injuries due to disasters may be very harmful causing various disorders. Mutual support of the community in the form of panchayat may be very consoling to the affected people.

As mentioned earlier also, the 29 developmental activities enlisted in the XI Schedule to the Indian Constitution may be successfully utilized for disaster mitigation in the rural areas of the country. Broadly these activities can be grouped into seven categories taking care for almost all types of vulnerabilities (both social and physical) as shown here.

S. No.	Category of Developmental Activities (under XI Schedule)	Type of Vulnerability that is taken care
1	Conservation and development of natural resources such as forest, land, soil and water resources and take steps to check the environmental degradation.	Ecological vulnerability
2	Necessary steps to increase the production of agriculture, horticulture, livestock, fuel, food, fodder and raw material for small cottage industries	Economical vunerability
3	Development of physical structures such as rural housing, roads, school buildings, place of weekly market or hats, school and dispensary buildings etc.	Physical and Economic vulnerability
4	Programmes for Poverty Alleviation and Social Justice covering weaker and vulnerable section of the society like Below Poverty Line (BPL), families, scheduled castes and tribes, women, children and old persons of the society.	Economic and Social vulnerability
5	Providing education, awareness and training for the human resource of the rural society	Educational, motivational and cultural vulnerability
6	Providing various social services like power supply, drinking water and medical facilities	Social vulnerability
7	Providing strong leadership to the rural people specially the rural poor	Organisational vulnerability

Thus it is clear from the table that if the developmental activities to be handled by the PRIs are slightly modified and tailored as per the need of the society, in which they are to be implemented, it may be an effective tool to reduce various types of vulnerabilities. The reduction in vulnerability will automatically take care of the risk or loss due to adverse impacts of the natural disasters – the ultimate aim of the disaster management.

10

MODELLING AS AN APPROACH

Modelling as a technique has been found to be very effective in resolving issue which are of multi-pronged origin and options and when more than one agency is involved to mitigate the same. One of the primary requirement for management of disasters is to prepare a comprehensive Disaster Management Plan. As per the Indian Constitution, the primary responsibility of disaster management falls on the state and the centre only supplements the same. As a basic requirement, every state should have their own elaborate disaster management plan for effective implementation of the disaster management policies and schemes. In certain specific areas, such as Uttranchal, where the incidence of natural disasters is relatively high, specific district level management plans should be readily available for appropriate action in time.

Uttranchal is prone to recurrent disasters primarily due to its locational disadvantage, i.e. Himalayan region, where tectonic movements are active and secondly, due to man-made developmental interventions – planned and unplanned. Modelling technique may be quite appropriate for effective management of the disasters in near future in this area.

Modelling techniques help in improving the performance of the implementing agencies be it government agencies, public sector organisations or NGOs. It also helps in assessing the performance level and enables the administrators to identify the gaps and shortcomings in the approach towards mitigating the same. While preparing disaster management plan either for state or district, the main aim should be to get the maximum output from the functioning of these organisations by improving their performance. In an organisation the performance improvement is basically measured in term of timeliness and quality of service and by reducing the cost of providing such services. Although the government or non-government organisations engaged in the field of disaster management do not operate with a motive to generate profit which is true for business development units, the techniques used for profit seeking organisations may be successfully utilised by them to improve their performance. This technique may also be of the utmost use while preparing a district or state level disaster management plan.

THE MODELLING TECHNIQUE

Modelling techniques may be used for better planning of an organization. In the present case, functionaries involved in disaster management, i.e. various Ministries and Departments of State Government dealing in the field, and the district and other junior level administration units can apply the same. The modelling technique basically has four steps, i.e. recognition and analysis of the problem, identification of the variables, collection of data and lastly, the model building.

The Problem and its Analysis

The first step in modelling is recognition of the problem.It is observed that disaster management in most of the cases is just like fire-fighting and no conscious attempt is made in term of long term strategies. Partial failure of the administration and other agencies to counter the situation results in further deterioration of the condition. Unemployment, diseases, scarcity of livelihood sources, food and water shortage, shelter/housing problem, failure of communication and other infrastructure facilities, environmental degradation etc. are some major problems which are being faced due to one or the other form of disasters in the area. In the recent past, mainly due to increasing population pressure and various other man-made/natural factors, the intensity and severity of disasters have increased many times and subsequently the problem of managing them has become more serious, particularly in disaster prone areas of the country.

SWOT analysis of existing policies, their implementation and other secondary data reveals that disaster management in the State has many shortcomings and various important areas are untouched and unexplored. The data clearly indicate that the existing policies are more concerned about the immediate relief and rescue operations. The other important aspects of disaster management, i.e. preparedness, mitigation and rehabilitation are not given due importance. Some important aspects are totally ignored. The analysis and the interpretation of the primary and secondary data collected conclude that the problem of the disaster management in the Uttranchal region is multifarious. The disaster management in the area is suffering mainly from poor rehabilitation efforts, delay in relief and rescue, unscientific assessment survey, misutilisation of relief, unsuitability of the relief (mainly houses constructed), poor technology and training of the people and the officials engaged in disaster management, ignorance of local needs, faulty developmental schemes, poor representation of local bodies, lack of coordination among various departments, poor monitoring and evaluation of the programmes and most significantly the total negligence of the environmental aspect and so on.

The Variables

After analysing the problem, the next step in formulating a model is the recognition of various variables affecting the problem. In the case of disasters in Uttranchal, the different variables recognised are – geological structure, topography, climate of the area, type of vegetation/forest of the region, population density, land use and development pattern, environmental conservation measures, the training level of the people and officials, the education level and knowledge of the local population about disasters, the resources available to detect and suppress the impacts of disasters. These variables may further be classified under three heads, namely, outcome, controllable and uncontrollable variables.

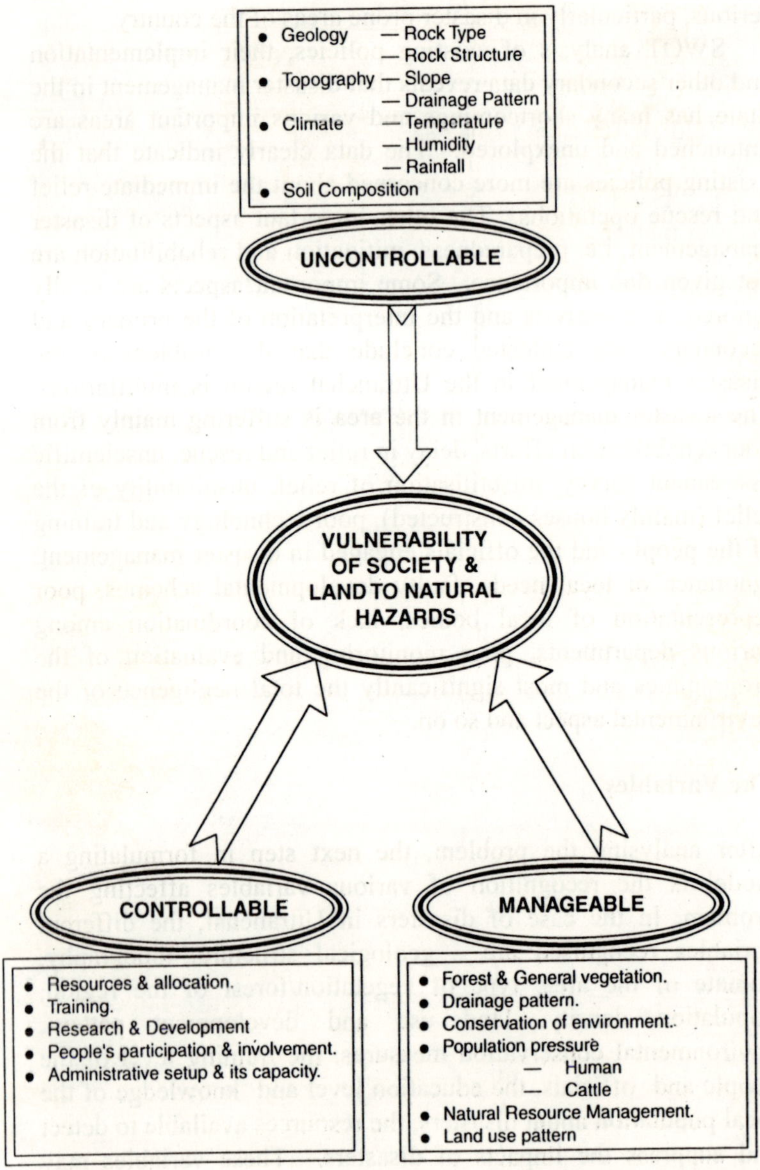

Fig. 10.1 : Disaster Variables deciding vulnerability to natural hazards

Outcome variables : The impacts of disasters, indicated by the loss of property and lives and deterioration of the environment.

Decision/Controllable variables : Research and development in the field of disaster management, training of the people and officials involved, land-use and development pattern of the region, people's participation, the budgetary provision for disaster management etc.

Uncontrollable variables : The geological and topographic structures, climate, drainage pattern, vegetation and forest cover of the area, which decide susceptibility of the region to disasters.

The objective of the appropriate disaster management policy should be to reduce the impacts of natural hazards. Thus the modelling for this problem is result oriented. The controllable and uncontrollable variables influence the impact of natural hazards and the performance of the disaster management authorities. The variables mentioned are the outcome of various other variables, e.g. the climate is influenced by the temperature the rainfall, the humidity, the wind, etc. Similarly the topography or slope of the area also influences the intensity of landslides Thus the variables in the case of disasters are closely linked interrelated or dependent.

Collection of the Data

The next steps after identification of the variables is the collection of data. Data collection is very important task and necessary care is to be taken while undertaking this job. In the present case the most important data to be collected will include vulnerability of the area and the society to disasters. These will be decided by various variables, i.e. geology, climate, topography, peoples' awareness about disasters, environmental conservation and after all the development pattern of the region and society. This data will be helpful for planning an appropriate disaster management project for an area. Based on these data a rough picture may be drawn about the susceptibility of the area to natural hazards. Further planning and modelling will basically be determined by this data.

The data about the disaster incidences and their intensity and impacts in the area for the past few years will also be required for the purpose. These data may be collected from various sources. Instead of relying on the official data, it will be better to verify such data from the local people and other sources also by carrying out intensive and detailed field survey. The knowledge about the cultural traditions, education standard, traditions, the livelihood resources etc. will also be of immense utility for formulating the project.

Beside this, the other data required for the project formulation will include –

(i) Data about the availability of the staff,
(ii) Data about the equipment available for forecasting and resisting the disasters.
(iii) Funds/resource available for disaster management activities.

Model Building

Based on the data collected and the other informations mentioned above, the model is prepared for the disaster management. In the disaster management there are basically three steps, i.e. pre-disaster, emergency, and post-disaster. The disaster management activity can be divided into pre-disaster, emergency and long term post-disaster phases, which are interconnected and inter-dependent. The pre-disaster stage activities include the preparedness and mitigation aspect in a better and planned manner. The next phase involves rescue and relief operations. The third stage, post-disaster refers to rehabilitation.

Disasters are the direct consequence of the vulnerability and, therefore, the main objective of an appropriate disaster management model should be to reduce the same. Vulnerability of a region or society is decided by its developmental pattern. Therefore, the basic aim of an appropriate disaster management model should be to control and monitor the developmental pattern in a disaster prone area in such a way that it ultimately leads to vulnerability reduction. Along with the developmental pattern, while formulating a project for disaster management in such areas, equal importance is to be given to other variables also. Research and development, information and education of the society, availability of the resources, environmental conservation, population control and improving socio-economic condition of the society also play an important role in deciding the vulnerability. On a whole these variables are given due importance in the project formulation so that the society of disaster prone areas will have sufficient capacity and strength to resist the impacts of natural hazards. Prevention is better than cure, this is true in the context of disaster management also and for effective and long term strategy, priority is to be given to the preventive measures, which will automatically reduce the vulnerability and increase resistance of people against the impacts of natural hazards.

The ultimate aim of the model is two-dimensional, i.e. (i) to increase the performance of the disaster management functionaries and (ii) decrease the vulnerability of the region and the society to disasters that is controlled by different variables. The chances of controlling uncontrollable variables are negligible hence the modelling technique and approach in the present case must aim to manage the controllable variables, so that the outcome variable, i.e. the impact of the disasters is minimised. In the present case among the controllable variable, i.e. research and training, awareness of the people and the functionaries, resources to mitigate and manage disasters, environmental conservation, people participation, land use and development pattern etc. are to be managed in such a way so that the vulnerability of the society and the region is reduced. As is clear from the influence diagram these variables may be controlled by using the best technique of monitoring and evaluation (Fig. 10.2).

For better results of the functionaries involved in disaster management, there is urgent need for their review on the basis of modern principles of accounting and budgeting. Rather than reviewing the investment adjustments of previous years, level of funding and expenditure, the budget should be analyzed in its totality. Beside this, unit cost measurement may also be used as a tool for performance analysis and progress indicator for the disaster mitigating programmes. This indicator measures all the expenses of programme's implementation.

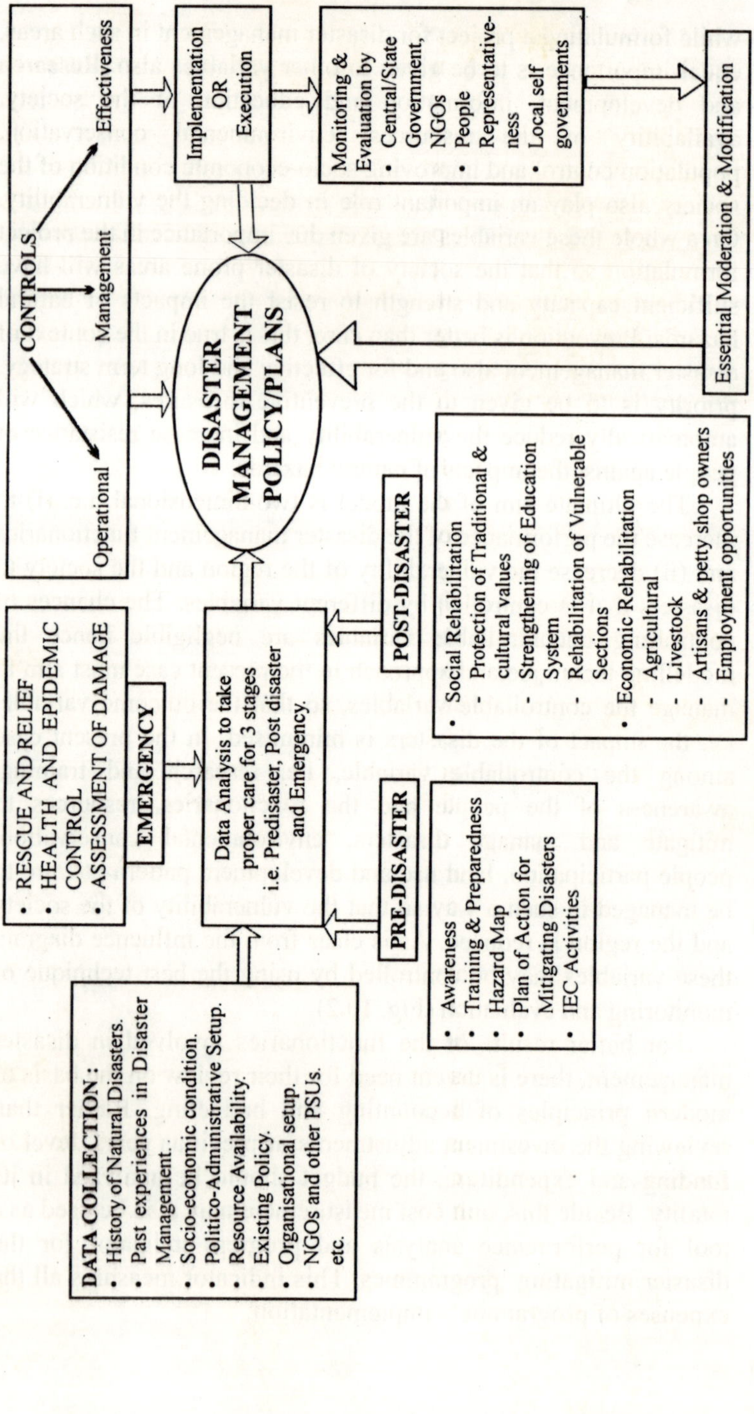

Fig. 10.2 : Appropriate model for disaster management.

The other modern accounting techniques, which can be used for performance measurement, are – appropriate supervisory and management techniques and performance auditing. Both these techniques can be successfully used for the performance analysis of the implementing agencies, i.e. the state government and the district administration. The supervisory and the management techniques that apply to operating more efficiently, economically and effectively include planning, executing and controlling. Controls are developed at each stage of planning to ensure that the action at the executing stage is accomplished with the results contemplated from the agreed upon plans. Operational controls are needed to measure the accomplishment of the plans at the operational stage. Management controls are needed to measure the accomplishment of various plans developed at the organizational stage. And effectiveness controls are needed to assure the development of appropriate goals and timing for the accomplishment of these goals.

For the disaster mitigation programmes, the implementing agencies, i.e. various state government departments, district and lower level administration and other agencies (government and non-government both) are to be made accountable for :

- Setting appropriate goals.
- The developing standard needed to accomplish these goals.
- Effectively carrying out those standards.
- Developing those organisational and operational standards for economical and cost efficient operations.

In the present model as there is no direct profit concept, the various benefits direct and indirect are to be estimated/ calculated. The return here may be estimated by calculating the losses, which would have been avoided by using the disaster mitigation methods, indicated in the project. However, it will not be so easy and various assumptions are to be made for this purpose. In the present case the return from the project will be in the form of direct and indirect benefits.

Viability of the Model

Before implementation, it is wise to know the viability of the model. The viability of the model may be found out using various modern techniques. The Accounting Rate of Return, Net Present Value (NPV), the Decision Tree etc. are such famous and quite frequently used techniques.

Accounting Rate of Return : A long-term project may be assessed by calculating its estimated accounting rate of return (ARR) and comparing it with the predetermined target. The ARR may be calculated by using the following formula –

$$ARR = \frac{\text{Estimated total profit}}{\text{Estimated initial investment}} \times 100$$

(Berry, J. and Jarvis, R.,1997)

The estimated ARR is to be compared with the target ARR, if the estimate exceeds the target, the project is acceptable.

Though the ARR gives some idea of the viability of the project, yet it has many drawbacks. The main drawback of ARR is that it does not take into account the timing of the profits generated from the investment and thus ignores the inflation factor. Keeping this in view the other more reliable technique for finding out the viability of the project, i.e. the NPV calculation may also be carried out for the project.

Net Present Value (NPV) Calculation : The viability of a project may be found out by using the method of NPV calculation. The NPV is the value obtained by discounting all cash out flows of an investment opportunity by a chosen rate of interest. The rate of interest indicates the opportunity cost of a shareholder and generally referred as the "Cost of Capital". It is basically the present value of the cash in flows minus the cash out flows. If NPV is positive then the inflows from the investment will yield a return in excess of the cost of capital. This refers that investment in the project will yield a return in excess to the cost of the capital and the project is viable.

Decision Trees : The other famous technique for making decision is the Decision Tree method. The technique helps in taking the holistic approach of problem by recognizing the elements of certainties and uncertainties. It is very useful in deciding the course of action. In the case of the Project of Disaster Management, similar approach of Decision Tree may be applied to make decision about the implementation of the project.

The various control methods described earlier will have to be applied for ensuring proper implementation. While implementing, the project is to be monitored and evaluated closely and regularly. From the outcome of monitoring and evaluation the feed back is to be made to the policy makers, so that timely review of the operation and appropriate modification of the same may be done for better results.

ANNEXURES

ANNEXURE - I

QUESTIONNAIRE FOR VILLAGERS/ AFFECTED POPULATION

a) Name of the person -
Sex -
Age -
Educational Qualification -

b) Name of the village
- Block -
District -

c) Name of the Nearest Police Station -

d) Distance of the village to the nearest Hospital/Public Health Centre -

a) Distance of the village from district headquarter -

b) Village connected by Road - yes/no
If Yes, type of road -
If no, nearest road (approx. distance)

g) Village geographical profile/ terrain
- Plain land
- Undulated land
- Adjacent to Foot hill
- In a valley
- On a river Bank/nala
- Any other (specify)

h) Population of the village: (Now/before disaster)
- No. of households
- Total population - Male
  - Female
- Children (boys & girls)

Sl.No	Male/Female/Children	Now	Before

i) Total agricultural land (Now/before)
- Irrigated : Plane
  Terraced
- Non-irrigated:Plane
  Undulated
- Wasteland
- Panchayat land
- Grazing land
- Village panchayat forest land

Sl.No.	Type of land	Now	Before

j) Basic Infrastructural Facilities (Please mark ✓ at the facilities available)
- Water
- Electricity
- Educational Institutions : Primary
  Middle
  High School
- Doctors/PHC
- Connected by Transport
- Weekly Market - Exact location from village
- Local Market - Distance from village

k) Basic occupation of the villagers
- Agriculture
- Skilled/Traditional Occupation

- Labour - agriculture or wage earners
- Employed (Government/Private)
- Forest based activities
- Petty traders etc.
- Employed outside of the village

1) Do you know about the types of Land Hazards (name)

- Earthquake
- Landslide
- Flash flood

2) Can you recollect the recent disaster

- when
- where
- how

3) What were the major casualties

- Land and habitation related
- Livestock related
- Population related

4) Who came for rescue immediately?

5) What was the relief extended and volume/tone?

6) When did you get the immediate relief
(Please mark ✔ at appropriate option)

- within 1-2 days
- within a week
- within a fortnight
- Any other (specify)

7) Did the local administration intervene – if yes, then when and how? Please describe. (Maximum in 5 lines)

8) Any organised efforts made by the local administration for rehabilitation. If yes - specify. (Maximum in 5 lines)

9) Which are the other agencies who came forward for organised rehabilitation for ? If yes, name them and specify, their type of work.

10) How do you rate the intervention made by the local administration ?

S. No	Name the work	Good	Fair	Poor	Not appropriate	Useless

11) What should have been the role of the local administration - Nature of work/time/volume?

12) What was the intervention which was most effective, who initiated these interventions (specify in brief)?

13) What benefits the villagers received specifically the families of the deceased or the persons disabled and when they received the relief?

14) What benefits the villagers received who lost their livestock and when?

15) What benefits the villagers received whose houses have destroyed and when?

16) Can you name all the agencies/individuals involved in the relief operations in your village?

17) Did the villagers migrated to other areas after the disaster, if so, how many families?

18) How many families are still within the village?

19) How many families have moved out of the village?

20) How many families have lost their occupational source?

Occupation	No. of families
- Agriculture - Livestock - Farming etc. - Forest based - Any other (specify)	

21) How many families lost their agricultural land and tune?

S. No.	No. of families	Total land lost	
		Agriculture	Non-Agriculture

22) Did the Government implemented the schemes as per the proclaimed announcement by the Collector/Minister/ Member of Legislative Assemblies /Any other?

23) How many families have changed their occupation after the disaster ?

S. No.	No. of families	Occupation earlier	Average Income	Occupation now	Average income

24) Are you aware of any monitoring and preventive measures undertaken by the Government?

25) How effective is their surveillance and information?

26) Did they made any prior announcement before the last disaster?

27) Did the villagers take the information seriously and took necessary measures?

ANNEXURE - II

QUESTIONNAIRE FOR VILLAGE REPRESENTATIVE

1. Specific aid received for

Assistance for	Amount	Material
Reconstruction of house		
Rehabilitation of livelihood source		
Restoring livestock		
Basic survival & existence (food & clothing)		

2. Any scheme still operational after the disaster.

3. Any drastic improvement in the basic facilities damaged during disaster .

Roads	
Water	
Electricity	
Health Care Services	
Preventive Surveillance	
Public Distribution System	

4. Any major change in the village profile

- Water
- Agricultural land
- Adjoining forest
- Pasture land
- Communication system (basic approach)
- Bridges/Rope ways/Small Culverts etc.
- Other infrastructure in the village (connectivity level)

5. Has the disaster brought any major social-economic change in the village/area, specify? (maximum 5 lines)

6. Any awareness programme/training programme arranged for disaster affected villagers.

Sl. No.	Name of Agency	No. of families/ villagers involved	Type of awareness training

7. Any intervention for rehabilitation of livelihood source & average income/no. of families benefited.

Sl. No.	Type of Rehabilitation of livelihood source	No. of families benefited.	Average income

8. Any long term interventions undertaken for controlling land hazards.

- Forest
- Check Dams
- Any other specify

9. Any work undertaken by the villagers for improving the conditions after the disaster.

Sl. No.	Nature of work	No. of families involved	Financial contribution (if any)

ANNEXURE - III

QUESTIONNAIRE FOR ADMINISTRATION

1. Designation of the officer.

2. Since when posted in district?

3. How and when information about disaster was received?

4. What was the immediate action taken?

5. Whether resources were sufficient to take immediate necessary action?

6. If not, what were the drawbacks?

7. Whether there was proper co-ordination among different levels of beneficiary?

8. How many departments were involved?

9. What were the duties allocated to the departments?

S. No.	Name of Deptt.	Duties allocated	Duration	Performance

10. Assistance provided by :

a) Central Government
b) State Government
c) Other Agencies

11. Criteria adopted for damage assessment

12. Mode of utilization of fund :

i) Rescue

S.No.	Name of village	No. of families benefited	Money spent

ii) Relief

S.No.	Name of village	No. of families benefited	Money spent

iii) Rehabilitation

S.No.	Name of village	No. of families benefited	Money spent

13. How many VIPs visited the area?

14. The impact of their visit.

15. Criteria adopted for operation examination.

16. Whether there is any scheme for rehabilitation?

17. If yes, then its aims/objectives -

    a) When started/to be started?

    b) Agencies involved -

    c) If started, what is present status?

    d) The work remained -

18. No. of families rehabilitated

    i) Partially - (specify)

    ii) Completely - House
    - Occupation
    - Livelihood

19. Future rehabilitation plan -

20. Is there some long term policy of Government / Administration to minimise the damage by possible calamities? Please specify.

ANNEXURE - IV

QUESTIONNAIRE FOR NGOs/DONOR AGENCY

- Name of the Agency

  Type : Government ☐

  NGO ☐

  Address

  Activities in which involved:

  Experience : __________ years.

  No. of Members/strength in the Organisation :

- Source of Funding : Collection from public -
  Govt. funding -
  International funding -

- How the agency came to know about the disaster ?:

- What was the first reaction?:

- Type of the Assistance provided : monetary/articles/physical.

- What was the criteria for distributing the assistance?

- Way of distribution - Direct/Through District Admn. Any other agency.

- The role of the agency during rescue and relief.

- If involved directly, what was the criteria for selecting the beneficiaries?

- No. of families benefitted by your assistance:

S. No.	Village	No. of Families	Distributed Amount/goods

- Do you feel your assistance was relevant as per the requirement, if not, what should have been done in your opinion? (Please specify briefly).

- How you ensured that the assistance provided was utilized properly (what monitoring and evaluation criteria were involved)?

- Are you satisfied with it? If not, then what would have been done?

- How was the cooperation from
  - a) Administration/Department
  - b) Other agencies
  - c) Local population/representatives?

- Your opinion for better management of such calamities in future.

- Your experience during relief/rescue operation.

- Did the agency had any plans/scheme for rehabilitation of the victims, if yes, specify?

ANNEXURE - V

QUESTIONNAIRE FOR ACADEMICIANS

1. Field of study –

2. Summary of the work (100 words)

3. Outcome of the study

4. How study is recommended useful for the people and society?

5. Suggestion for rehabilitation.

6. Suggestion for management of future possible calamities

ANNEXURE - VI

SHOWING DETAIL OF LOSSES DURING RECENT EARTHQUAKES (MARCH, 1999) AND LANDSLIDES (AUGUST, 1998) IN 27 VILLAGES OF RUDRAPRAYAG DISTRICT (BASED ON INTERVIEWS OF PEOPLE AFFECTED)

S. No	Name of village	Block	Cate-gory	Type of Dis-aster	Major Causalties				How many families lost their livelihood		
					Population	Habitation	Live stock	Land	Agri-culture	Cattle	Any other
			1	2	3a	3b	3c	3d	4a	4b	4c
1.	Bandertoli	Jakholi	C	LS-EQ				Collapse			
2.	Tat	,,	C	EQ	10 wounded	Houses damaged		Agr. Land damaged	3		
3	Badh	,,	C	EQ	10 wounded	Houses damaged	2 Killed	Agr. Land damaged	4		
4	Taila	,,	B	EQ	1 killed, 10 wounded	Houses damaged	4 Killed	Agr. Land damaged	6		2 shops
5	Pandhrola	,,	B	EQ		Houses Damaged		-			
6	Bhimli	,,	C	EQ		-		-			
7	Mehargoan	,,	C	EQ		House Damaged		-			
8	Jaily	,,	C	EQ		House Damaged					
9	Shisho	,,	B	EQ+ LS	2 killed	All houses damaged	6 killed	Agr. Land damaged	5	6	1 shop
10	Kandali	,,	B	EQ		Houses damaged				6	
11	Sirsoliya	,,	B	EQ+ LS		Houses damaged					
12	Pali	,,	B	EQ		House damaged					
13	Gavnigoan	Agastya muni	A	EQ		House damaged					
14	Gugli	,,	C	EQ		Many houses					

S. No	Name of village	Block	Cate-gory	Type of Dis-aster	Major Causalties				How many families lost their livelihood		
					Population	Habitation	Live stock	Land	Agri-culture	Cattle	Any other
			1	2	3a	3b	3c	3d	4a	4b	4c
15	Kanasili	Agastya muni	C	EQ	1 boy killed	House damaged	2 Killed	Agr. Land damaged	All village	2	
16	Chandarpuri	,,	B	EQ+ LS	2 killed	Houses damaged		Agr. Land damaged	6		
17	Gair	,,	B	EQ+ LS		,,		-			
18	Jaikandi	,,	C	EQ		Houses damaged		-			
19	Mehargoan	,,	C	EQ		,,		-	3		
20	Sera	,,	C	EQ		,,		-			
21	Talsari	,,	C	EQ		,,		-			
22	Hat	,,	C	EQ		,,		-			
23	Ooring	,,	C	EQ		,,		-			
24	Naguri	Ookhi math	A	EQ		,,		Agr. land	7 families		
25	Pali	,,	C	LS		,,		,,	5 families		
26	Burva	,,	C	LS	2 killed	,,		,,	21 families	2	5 shops
27	Rodu	,,	A	LS	-	,,		None	10 families		

EQ = Earthquakes, L.S. = Landslides, Agr. = Agricultural

ANNEXURE - VII

SHOWING DETAIL RESCUE/RELIEF DURING RECENT EARTHQUAKES (MARCH, 1999) AND LANDSLIDES (AUGUST, 1998) IN 27 VILLAGES OF RUDRAPRAYAG DISTRICT (BASED ON INTERVIEWS OF PEOPLE AFFECTED)

Rescue/Relief

Rescue Operation (by whom)	Type of Rescue		When				Intervention of local administration and Type	Rating of intervention
	Monitory	Material	1-2 days	A week	A fort-night	Another		
5	6a	6b	7a	7b	7c	7d	8	9
Village Officer	Rs.1500/-	Tent & food		✓	—	—	Survey, Food Grains distribution	Not relevant
Village Officer	Rs.1500/-	Tent & food			✓		Immediate relief	Fair
Village Officer	Rs.1500/- per family	Tent & food			✓		Treatment	Not relevant
Village Officer	Rs.1500/- to selected families	Tent & food			✓		Death Compensation , free treatment and 2 shelters	Not relevant
Village Officer	Rs.1500/- for few families	Tent & food			✓		Survey and tin sheds to 10 families	Poor
Village Officer	Rs.1500/- per family	Tent & food			✓		-	Poor
None	Nil	Tent & food				✓	Construction of 2 tin shelters	Poor
Local Admn.	Rs.1500/- to very few families	Tent & food			✓		Only survey	Not relevant
Local Admn.	Rs.1500/- per family	Tent & food		✓			Cremation of dead and treatment to wounded	Fair

Rescue Operation (by whom)	Type of Rescue		When				Intervention of local administration and Type	Rating of intervention
	Monitory	Material	1-2 days	A week	A fort-night	Another		
5	6a	6b	7a	7b	7c	7d	8	9
Local Admn.	-	Tent & food					Only survey	Poor
Local Admn.	-	Tent & food					Only survey	Poor
Local Admn.	Rs.1500/- per family	Tent & food				✓	Survey and House compensation	Fair
Local Admn.	Nil	-		✓			Food, Tents	Fair
UP Bridge Corpn. Local Admn.	Rs.1500/-	-		✓			UP Bridge Corpn. Constructed houses	Poor
Police and Local Admn.	Rs.1500/-	Tent & food		✓			Immediate relief	Fair
Local Admn. (SDM)	Rs.1500/-	-	✓				Food grains and General relief	Fair
Local Admn.	Rs.1500/-	Tent & food		✓			Food grains and Gen. Relief, in one week	Poor
Local Admn.	Rs.1500/-	Food		✓			Gen Relief after EQ	Fair
Village Officer	Rs.1500/-	Tent		✓			Survey and General Relief	Fair
None	Rs.1500/-	Food grain + tent			✓		—	Fair
Village officer	Rs.1500/-	Food grain + tent		✓			Food grain +shelter	Fair
None	Nothing	Food grain + tent		✓			Survey, General relief, temporary shelter	Fair

Rescue Operation (by whom)	Type of Rescue		When				Intervention of local administration and Type	Rating of intervention
	Monitory	Material	1-2 days	A week	A fort-night	Another		
5	6a	6b	7a	7b	7c	7d	8	9
None	Rs.1500/- to 1 family only	Tin sheets tent					Tin shelters, but useless	Poor
Local Admn.	-	Food, tents				6 months	Late intervention, only survey	Poor
Local admn.	-	Food, tent				✓	Shifting to safer places,	Poor
Local Admn.	-	Food, tent	✓				Wounded shifting to hospital, removing of road blockage	Fair
Local Admn.	-	Tent	-			✓	Survey and shelters	Poor

ANNEXURE - VIII

SHOWING DETAIL OF REHABILITATION PROGRAMMES DURING RECENT EARTHQUAKES (MARCH, 1999) AND LANDSLIDES (AUGUST, 1998) IN 27 VILLAGES OF RUDRAPRAYAG DISTRICT (BASED ON INTERVIEWS OF PEOPLE AFFECTED)

Organised rehabilitation efforts by local administration and type	Any other agency which made organised intervention and how	Relief for Deceased	Relief for loss of live-stocks	Relief for Property Damaged		Expectations of people from administration	Name agencies involved in relief operation	Implemen-tation as per assurance	Monitoring and evaluation
				Monetory	Material				
11	12	13	14	15a	15b	16	17	18	20
Not Fair, only tin sheds distributed	—	—	—			Should have provided house construction fund immediately		No	
-	—	—	—	House Const. grant		People representative should have been included in survey and relief distribution. Immediate		No	
Only Survey	—	—	—			Immediate relief		No	
Nothing	promises by Rotary Club	Rs. 75000/- for dead	Nil	Nil	2 tin sheds	Priority for house construction and immediate relief	Rotary Club (only promises)	No	No
-	—	—	—			Survey should have been fair and immediate relief		No	No

Organised rehabilitation efforts by local administration and type	Any other agency which made organised intervention and how	Relief for Deceased	Relief for loss of live-stocks	Relief for Property Damaged		Expectations of people from administration	Name agencies involved in relief operation	Implemen-tation as per assurance	Monitoring and evaluation
				Monetory	Material				
11	12	13	14	15a	15b	16	17	18	20
-	—	—	—			Immediate relief and construction of EQ resistant houses.		No	No
Nothing	Nil	—	—			Immediate relief and compensation		No	No
Nothing	Nil	—	—		Tin sheds to few families after six months	Immediate relief		No	No
-	Tin sheds by HUDCO to each family	Rs. 75000/- for dead	Nil		Tin sheds by HUDCO	Immediate house compensation and rehabilitation	HUDCO	No	No
Tin sheds after six months	—	—	—			Priority for rehabilitation and house compensation and monitoring. Local representation in survey		No	No
Nothing	—	—				Immediate relief		No	No

Organised rehabilitation efforts by local administration and type	Any other agency which made organised intervention and how	Relief for Deceased	Relief for loss of live-stocks	Relief for Property Damaged		Expectations of people from administration	Name agencies involved in relief operation	Implemen-tation as per assurance	Monitoring and evaluation
				Monetory	Material				
11	12	13	14	15a	15b	16	17	18	20
—	—	—	—	Rs. 10000/-	10 Tin sheds (After six months)	Immediate relief and proper monitoring and evaluation. EQ resistant house construction.		No	No
—	UP Bridge Corpn. Constructed Tin sheds but of no use	—	—	Rs. 5000/-	10 Tin sheets	Relief to only suffered, transparency and proper supervision of works carried out, local representation.	—	No	No
—	—	—	—			Should have provided building material – should have made fair survey	—	Partial	No
Nothing serious	HUDCO constructed 29 houses. UP Bridge Corpn.- Tin shelters	Death–Rs. 70000/- Wounded – Rs. 2500/-	Rs. 4000/- per cattle	Rs.10000/-	House cons-truction	Should have used locally available material for house construction at proper site. Relief to only suffered	UP Bridge Corpn. & HUDCO	Partial	No

Organised rehabilitation efforts by local administration and type	Any other agency which made organised intervention and how	Relief for Deceased	Relief for loss of live-stocks	Relief for Property Damaged		Expectations of people from administration	Name agencies involved in relief operation	Implemen-tation as per assurance	Monitoring and evaluation
				Monetory	Material				
11	12	13	14	15a	15b	16	17	18	20
Nothing	Shelter by UP Bridge Corpn. (not of much use)	Death – Rs 70000/-		Rs.10000/- but not to all	—	Fair survey and relief distribution, training of local people for construction of EQ resistant houses, immediate relief and compensation	UP Bridge Corpn.	Partial	Not much
Nothing	—	—		—		Training of local people, immediate relief and compensation		No	No
Only tin sheds	Shelter by UP Bridge Corpn. And training by HUDCO for EQ resistant house construction.	—		Cash	Tin sheds and Indira Awas	Compensation distribution by advice of local representatives. Should have provided raw material for house construction	UP Bridge Corpn. And local admn.	No	Not much

Organised rehabilitation efforts by local administration and type	Any other agency which made organised intervention and how	Relief for Deceased	Relief for loss of live-stocks	Relief for Property Damaged		Expectations of people from administration	Name agencies involved in relief operation	Implementation as per assurance	Monitoring and evaluation
				Monetory	Material				
11	12	13	14	15a	15b	16	17	18	20
Nothing	Shelter by UP Bridge Corpn.	—		Delay and corruption in compensation		Should have involved local self govt. in survey and relief distribution and provided raw material for house construction.		Partial	No
Only houses under Indira Awaas Yojana	Only Admn.	—	—	Rs. 11000/- per damaged house	Tin sheds +5 houses under IAY	Fair survey and immediate action	Only local admn.	No	No
Nothing serious	College NSS,UP Bridge Corpn.	—	—	—	Tin sheds +tents	Immediate house compensation, training and raw material for house construction	NSS, UP Bridge Corpn.	Yes	Not much
Nothing	—	—	—	Rs. 5000/-	Tin sheds	Immediate house compensation, raw material and fair survey		No	No
Nothing	UP Bridge Corpn. & Admn.	—	—	Rs. 10000/- to selected	Tin sheds	Family as unit for compensation. Fairness in compn. Distribution	UP Bridge Corpn.	No	No

Organised rehabilitation efforts by local administration and type	Any other agency which made organised intervention and how	Relief for Deceased	Relief for loss of live-stocks	Relief for Property Damaged		Expectations of people from administration	Name agencies involved in relief operation	Implemen-tation as per assurance	Monitoring and evaluation
				Monetory	Material				
11	12	13	14	15a	15b	16	17	18	20
Nothing	None	—	—	Rs 2500/-	Tin sheeets	Immediate general relief, Fair survey, step to check environmental deterioration		No	No
Nothing	—	—		Rs. 10000/-	Tin sheets	Check corruption, Effective rehabilitation, Fair survey.		No	No
Under Consideration	District. Admn. Central Agencies	Rs.1,20000/-	Rs. 4000/-	Rs. 25000/-	—	Land and houses to who suffered. Check corruption and expedite the relief.		Partial	No
Nothing	Forest & Land construction Deptts.	—		Cash	Land	Rehabilitation of whole village at safer place	Only admn.	Up to an extent	Good

UP Bridge Corpn. = Uttar Pradesh Bridge Corporation, HUDCO = Housing Urban Development Corporation Limited.
IAY = Indira Awas Yojana
NSS = National Social Service.

VIEWS OF ACADEMICIAN

S. No.	Designation	Institute	Field of Study	Topic of main study	Relevance utility of the study	Suggestions for Rehabilitation	Suggestions for better disaster management
1.	Reader	Geology Department, HNB University, Srinagar, Garhwal	Himalayan Region	Landslides, avalanche, Earthquake study in Himalaya	Study categorised the region into various zones from the point of safety and stability.	Rehabilitation should be on stable zones with the availability of water and communication	Hazard Zonation Mapping, Afforestation, Coordination among Scientist, Admn. Politicians and NGOs
2.	Professor	Botany Department, HNB University, Sri Nagar, Garhwal	Garhwal, Himalaya	To find out the reasons and causes for disaster management during natural disaster	The study will help rehabilitation in safer areas.	Houses should be constructed with proper technical know-how from research institute, steeper areas should be avoided.	A need to make people aware about the unsafe areas and causes for disaster, so that they can manage disasters in a better way.
3.	Professor	Geology Department, HNB University	Himalayan Geology	Landslides, Earthquake and Flood in Himalayan Regions	Study in relevant to safety from natural disasters	Soil conservation, and other measures like Afforestation for disaster mitigation	Same as in previous columns
4.	Reader	Department of Environmental Science, HNB University	Geo-environment	Study about landslides (1998), Earthquakes (1999) and Floods (1970, 78)	Proper training and implementation of scientific suggestions certainly will help in better management of disaster.	Rehabilitation on stable areas with scientific know-how.	Trained workforce to be formed taking experts from different fields, equipped with proper equipment and tools. People should be trained on disaster management

S. No.	Designation	Institute	Field of Study	Topic of main study	Relevance utility of the study	Suggestions for Rehabilitation	Suggestions for better disaster management
5.	Reader	Department of Geology, HNB University	Landslides in Garhwal	Hazards Zonation, Mapping, Land use pattern and seismic sensitivity	Need for proper strategy and planning in such areas	Rehabilitation of people affected to safer zones and to form workforce in this regard	Scientific research to be carried out for proper rehabilitation
6.	Lecturer	Department of Geology, HNB University	Land use, Environmental degradation and causes and preventions for landslides	Proper and scientific land use and watershed management	Will help in better management of land resources along with environmental conservation.	Rehabilitation after proper scientific study and researches	Proper training, education to local people. Family planning.
7.	Professor	Indian Institute of Public Administration, New Delhi	Disaster mitigation and preparedness	Evaluation of losses due to disasters management practices	Better disaster management practices may reduce losses	Development may be linked with disaster management.	On going development schemes should be incorporated with disaster management

ANNEXURE - IX

SHOWING VIEWS OF PEOPLE'S REPRESENTATIVE FOR DISASTER MANAGEMENT

Sl. No.	Design-ation	Assistance for				Continuation of Assistance After disaster			Improvement in basic infrastructure damaged due to disaster					Major changes after disaster						Major socio-economic changes	Training programme, if any	Revival of livestocks
		Construction	Livelihood	Livestock	Food and clothing	Rehabilitation	Check dam and other soil conservation	Drinking water	Road	Water	Electricity	Health	PDS	Water	Agr.	Forest	Pasture	Communication	Bridge + road			
1	Block Head	✓			✓	Under consideration			✓	✓	✓	✓	✓	✓	✓	✓	✓			Deteriorated	HUDCO	✓
2	Village Head	✓	✓		✓		✓	✓		✓	✓									-do-	ATI	✓
3	Panchayat member	✓	✓	✓	✓				✓	✓		✓	✓	✓	✓	✓	✓			-do-	NGO	
4	-do-	✓	✓		✓		✓			✓	✓							✓	✓	-do-	Dist. Adm n.	
5	-do-	✓			✓				✓			✓	✓	✓	✓	✓	✓			-do-		
6	-do-			✓	✓				✓	✓		✓		✓				✓	✓			

ATI = Administrative Training Institute

ANNEXURE- X

SHOWING VIEWS OF ADMINISTRATION FOR DISASTER MANAGEMENT

Sl. No.	Designation	The source of information	Mode of immediate relief	Availability of Resources	Shortcomings	Beneficiaries coordination	Department involved	Works allocation	Resources from	Monitoring & evaluation	Impact of VIP visit	Rehabilitation plan/ scheme
1	DM	Local Officer	GR, Rescue, Food, Shelter	Scarce	Coordination of people	No	Almost All dept.	Supervision and coordination	Centre and State Govt. and NGOs	Partial	Good	Under Consideration
2	SDM	-do-	-do-	Scarce	Road blockage, for communication	No	-do-	-do-	-do-	Nil	Good	-do-
3	BDO	-do-	-do-	Scarce	Less Resource	No	-do-	-do-	-do-	Nil	Good	-do-
4	Technical Off.	-do-	-do-	Scarce	-do-	No	-do-	-do-	-do-	Nil	Hampered the work	-do-
5	TAHSILDAR	Self & people	-do-	Scarce	-do-	Partial	-do-	Supervision	-do-	Nil	-do-	-do-
6	VILLAGE OFFICER	-do-	-do-	Scarce	-do-	Partial	-do-	Supervision	-do-	Nil	-do-	-do-

GLOSSARY

Aftershocks : Follow-up *earthquakes* that occur after the first earthquake and are usually smaller than the first one.

Alluvial fan: A fan shaped deposit of sediment built by a stream where it emerges from an upland or a mountain range into a broad valley or plain.

Artesian pressure: Water under sufficient pressure to produce flowing wells.

Asthenosphere: The earth layer lying below *lithosphere*. It is probably soft and yielding to plastic flow.

Avalanche : An event where a mass of snow, rock, and ice falls down a mountain, Usually it refers to a snow *avalanche*. Sometimes the term snow slide is used to mean a snow avalanche.

Bio-mass: Amount of vegetation in any form in an area.

Boulder: A rock piece or fragment more than 25.6 cm. in diameter.

Blizzard : A storm that produces heavy blinding snow, near zero visibility, deep drifts and dangerous and chill.

Continental Drift : The theory that the continents have moved in relation to one another.

Controls: The need to control the activities of the enterprise. It includes identifying where targets have or have not met so that the reasons for the failure to achieve the target can be identified.

Crust: The outermost layer of the earth.

Debris flow: Rapid downward movement of rock, soil and mud.

Deciduous: A plant that sheds its leaves regularly or annually within a year of their production.

Dip: An imaginary line showing maximum slope on a dipping plane.

Dip- slip -fault: Fault in which movement of the broken parts of a rock body is in the direction of the dip of fault plane.

Disaster : An occurrence of a severity and magnitude that normally results in deaths, injuries, and property damage and that cannot be managed through the routine procedures and resources of government. It usually develops suddenly and unexpectedly and requires immediate, coordinated, and effective response by multiple government, voluntary and private sector organisations to meet human needs and speed recovery.

Disaster Management : A Collective term encompassing all aspects of planning for and responding to disasters, including both pre- and post-disaster activities. It may refer to the management of both the risks and consequences of disasters.

Discharge: Rate of flow of water.

Drainage pattern: An integrated system of tributaries which collect and funnel surface water to common water body i.e. lake, ocean etc.

Dust Storm : A strong windstorm that fills the air with thick dust. Visibility can be reduced to ½ mile or less.

Earthquake : The shaking, rolling or sudden shock of the earth's surface. *Earthquakes* happen along fault lines in the earth's crust.

Emergency : An extraordinary situation where there are serious and immediate threats to human life as a result of disaster, imminent threat of *disaster,* cumulative process of neglect, civil conflict environmental degradation and socio-economic conditions.

Epicentre: The point on earth surface, lying just above the focus (the point of origin) of the earthquake.

Erosion: Process of loosening and carrying away sediment from one place to another.

Fault: A surface along which rock body has broken and displaced.

Fault Lines : Breaks in the Earth's *crust* where pressure is created as the two sides of the rock break and rub against each other. This pressure is sometimes released in an *earthquake*.

Flash Flood : A dangerous and sudden flood that threatens lives and property and usually occurs after heavy rain. May also occur after an ice jam breaks up or after a dam breaks.

Flood Plain: Flooded, normally flat area bordering a stream.

Fold: Bend or flexure in a rock.

Fossil: Naturally preserved remains or evidences of past life giving idea about it.

Gad or Gadhera : Local term used for the small *nallah* or stream channel in hilly terrain.

Hail: Rain that has been frozen many times on the way to the ground, creating a lumpy ball of ice.

Hazard : A rare or extreme natural or human made event that threatens to adversely affect human life, property or activity to the extent of causing *disaster*.

Hazard Assessment : The process of estimating, for defined areas, the probabilities of the occurrence of potentially-damaging phenomena of given magnitudes within a specified period of time.

Hazard Mapping : The process of establishing geographically where and to what extent particular phenomena are likely to pose a threat to people, property, infrastructure, and economic activities.

Heat flow: The flow of heat from the interior of the earth.

Human-made Disaster : *Disaster* or emergency situation of which the principal, direct causes are identifiable human actions, deliberate or otherwise.

Ice sheet : A thick, extensive body of glacial ice that is not confined to valleys. Localized *ice sheets* are sometimes called *ice caps*.

Ice storm: freezing rain that creates a dangerous sheet of ice that is quarter inch thick or more.

Island arc : A chain of volcanic islands. *Island arcs* are generally convex towards the open ocean. Example: the Andaman- Nicobar Islands.

Joint : A fracture in a rock along which no appreciable displacement has occurred.

Landslide: A general term for relatively rapid types of mass movement such as debris flows, debris slides, rockslides and *slumps*.

Lava : *Magma* that reaches the Earth's surface and spreads around.

Limestone : A sedimentary rock composed mostly of calcium carbonate.

Lithosphere : The relatively rigid outer zone of the Earth, which includes the continental *crust,* the oceanic *crust,* the part of the mantle lying above the softer asthenosphere.

Lightening: A sudden visible flash of energy and light caused by electrical discharges during a thunder storm.12

Load : The total amount of sediment carried at a given time by a stream, glacier or wind.

Magma : A mobile silicate melt, which can contain suspended crystals and dissolved gases as well as liquid.

Mantle : The zone of the Earth's interior between the base of the crust and the core.

Mass movement : The transfer of rock and soil downslope by direct action of gravity without a flowing medium (such as a river or glacial ice). Synonymous with mass wasting.

Mica : A group of silicate minerals exhibiting perfect cleavage in one direction.

Mitigation : Mitigation refers to measures, which can be taken to minimize the destructive and disruptive effects of *hazards* and thus lessen the magnitude of a *disaster.*

Mountain : A general term for any landmass that stands above its surroundings. In the stricter geological sense, a mountain belt is a highly deformed part of the Earth's *crust* that has been injected with igneous intrusions and the deeper parts of which have been metamorphosed. The topography of young mountains is high, but erosion can reduce old mountains to flat lowlands.

Net Present Value (NPV): Value obtained by discounting all cash out flows and inflows of an investment opportunity by a chosen rate of return.

Peninsula : An elongate body of land extending into a body of water.

Physiography : The study of the surface features and landforms of the Earth.

Plate : A broad segment of the *lithosphere* (including the rigid upper *mantle* plus oceanic and continental *crust*) that floats on the underlying *asthenosphere* and moves independently of other plates.

Plateau : An extensive upland region.

Plate tectonics : The theory of global dynamics in which the lithosphere is believed to be broken into individual plates that move in response to convection in the upper mantle. The margins of the plates are sites of considerable geological activity.

Pore pressure: The pressure experienced by the water in the voids of a porous medium.

Post Disaster Assessment : Also called damage and needs assessment, it is the process of determining the impact of a disaster or events on a society, the needs for immediate, emergency measures to save and sustain the lives of survivors, and the possibilities for expediting recovery and development.

Preparedness : Measures to ensure the readiness and ability of a society to forecast and take precautionary measures in advance of an imminent threat, and to respond to and cope with the effects of a disaster by organizing and facilitating timely and effective rescue, relief and appropriate post-disaster assistance.

Quartz : An important rock-forming silicate mineral composed of single chains of silicon-oxygen tetrahedra joined in a three-dimensional network. It is distinguished by its hardness, glassy lustre and conchoidal fracture.

Quartzite : .A *sandstone* recrystallized by metamorphism.

Quartzite: A metamorphic rock composed mainly of silica.

Richter scale: A scale used to measure the intensity of earthquake, created by Charles F. Richter.

Risk : The expected losses (lives lost, persons injured, damage to property, and disruption of economic activity or livelihood) caused by a particular phenomenon.

Risk Assessment : Also called Risk Analysis or Evaluation, it is a process of determining the nature and scale of losses and damage due to disaster, which can be anticipated in particular areas during a specified period of time.

Risk mapping : The presentation of risk assessment on a map, showing the level of expected losses, during a particular time period, as a result of particular hazard or vulnerability.

Rockfall : The most rapid type of mass movement in which rocks ranging from large masses to small fragments are loosened from the ace of a cliff.

Runoff : Water that flows over the land surface.

Sand : Sedimentary material composed of fragments ranging in diameter form 0.0625 to 2 mm. Sand particles are larger than silt particles but smaller than pebbles. Much sand is composed of *quartz* grains, because quartz is abundant and resists chemical and mechanical disintegration. Other materials, such as shell fragments and rock fragments can also form sand.

Sandstone : A sedimentary rock composed mostly of sand-sized particles, usually cemented by calcite, silica or iron oxide.

Sea-floor spreading : The theory that the sea-floor spreads laterally away from the oceanic ridge as new lithosphere is created along the crest of the ridge by igneous activity.

Sediment : Material (such as gravel, sand, mud and lime) that is transported and deposited by wind, water, ice or gravity; material that is precipitated form solution; deposits of organic origin (such as coal and coral reefs).

Seismic : Pertaining to *earthquakes* or to waves produced by natural or artificial *earthquakes.*

Shale : A fine-grained clastic *sedimentary rock* formed by consolidation of clay and mud.

Shear: The tangential component of stress is generally called shearing *stress* or shear.

Slate : A fine-grained metamorphic rock with a characteristic type of foliation (slaty cleavage), resulting from the parallel arrangement of microscopic platy minerals, such as mica and chlorite.

Slump : A type of mass movement in which material moves along a curved surface of rupture.

Snowline : The line on a glacier separating the area where snow remains from year to year from the area where snow from the previous season melts.

Soil : The surface material of the continents, produced by disintegration of rock.

Strain: The deformation of rocks caused by stress. It may be dilation, a change in volume; distortion, a change of shape, or both.

Stress : Stress is the system of internal forces with a body which is established as a reaction to an external force tending to change the shape or volume of the body. Any stress system can be resolved into two forces acting in opposite directions on either side of a plane- the plane of maximum stress. Geologists tend to use the word stress to describe effects arising from external forces.

Strike: The bearing (the compass direction) of a horizontal line on bedding plane, a *fault* plane or some other planar structural feature.

Strike Slip Fault: *Fault* in which the movement of the broken rock bodies is in the direction of the *strike* of the fault.

Syntaxial Bands : Sudden change in the orographic trend. Himalayan mountain range is characterised by such syntaxial bands i. e. in north-west near Pir-Panjal and in south- west near Karakoram.

Tectonics : The branch of geology that deals with regional or global structures and deformational features of the Earth.

Terrain : An area of land having its distinctive landscape.

Thrust fault : A low-angle *fault* (45 degrees or less) in which the hanging wall has moved upward in relation to the footwall. Thrust faults are characterized by horizontal compression rather than by vertical displacement.

Valley buldge: Occurs where incompetent material is forced up into a valley by the weight of the hill masses on either side, which become 'turned up' at the edges in the Process.

Volcanism : The processes by which magma and gases are transferred from the Earth's interior to the surface.

Vulnerability : The extent to which an individual, community, sub-group, structure, service, or geographic area is likely to be damaged or disrupted by the impact of a particular *disaster / hazard.*

Vulnerability Analysis : The process of estimating the vulnerability to potential disaster hazards of specified elements at risk.

Weathering : The processes by which rocks are chemically altered or physically broken into fragments as a result of exposure to atmospheric agents and the pressures and temperatures at or near the Earth's surface, with little or no transportation of the loosened or altered materials.

BIBLIOGRAPHY

Abbas, N. and Subramanian, V., 1984. Erosion and sediment transport in the Ganga River Basin. *Indian Jour. Hydrol.*, 69; 173-82.

Alertnet : http:/www.alertnet.org.

Arya, A. S., 1994, Action plan for Earthquake Disaster Mitigation, In Sharma, V. K. (Ed.) *Disaster Management,* N.C.D.M., IIPA Publication, New Delhi.

Asian Development Bank, 1991. *Disaster Mitigation in Asia and the Paific.*

Bahadur, J., 1972. Role of snow and glacier melt contributions for environment regeneration in the Himalayas, *Environmental Generation in Himalayas* (Ed. J.S. Singh), Gyanodyaya Prakashan, Nainital, pp. 368-375.

Bahauguna,, V. K. and Satendra, 2002. Fire Situation in India, *International Forest Fire News*, No. 26- Jan.2002, Germany. Also at site- htp//www2.ruf.uni-freiburg.de/ fireglobe/ iffn/iffn_26/content26.htm

Bansal, R. C. and Mathur, H. N., 1976. Landslides – the nightmare of roads. *Soil Conservation Digest,* 4(1) : 36-37.

Bell, F.G., 1999. *Geological Hazards,* E&FN Spon, London.

Benfield Greig, Hazard Research Centre : ***http://www.ucl.ac.uk*** geolsci/research/ben-grei.

Bhandari, R. K., 1998. Landslides in the Himalaya and Protection facilities, *Landslides and mudflows :* Chapter 12. A joint publication of the UNESCO and UNEP, MOSCOW, Vol.2, pp.95.

Bhandani, R. K., 2000. ***An overview on Natural and Manmade Disasters and their Reduction,*** CSIR, New Delhi.

Bhatt, C.P., 1994. Impact of Natural Disasters on the Environment and Development; Examples from Himalaya and Eastern and Western Ghats, In Sharma, V.K. (Ed.) *Disaster Management,* N.C.D.M., IIPA publication, New Delhi.

Bora, R. S., 2000. Out migration : Some policy implication for Uttrakhand, In Sati, M.P. and Sati, S.C. (Ed.) *Uttrakhand*

Statehood : Dimensions of Development, Indus Publishing Company, New Delhi.

Burbank, D.W. *et. al.,* 1996. Bedrock incision, rock uplift and threshold hill slopes in the North-Western Himalaya. *Nature,* 379, 505-510.

Carter, Nick W., 1992. *Disaster Management : A Disaster Manager's Handbook,* Asian Development Bank, Manila.

Celly, R.K. and Gupta, T.N., 1999. Dimensions of Natural Disaster Management in India, In *Shelter,* Special Issue, World Disaster Reduction Day : A HUDCO, HSMI Publication, New Delhi.

Chander, R., 1989. Southern limits of major earthquakes rupture along the Himalaya between longitudes 75° and 95° E, *Tectonophysics*, 170, 115-123.

Disaster Management & Rehabilitation : A report of Himalayan Research & Development Society.

Disaster Relief : *http://www.disasterinfor.net.*

Emergency Preparedness : *http://www.floodplain.org.*

Floodplain Management : *http://www.fllodplain.org.*

Gautam, Ashutosh, 1994. *Earthquake–A Natural Disaster,* Ashish Publishing House, New Delhi.

Gaur, V.K., 1999. Earthquake Hazard in the Himalaya, *Time News Letter,* Dehradun.

Ghosh, R. C., Subba Rao, B. K. and Ramola, B.C., 1980. Interception studies in 'Sal' *(Shorea robusta)* appice forest. *Ind. Forester, 106:513-14.*

Government of India, 1991-2001. Annual Reports, Ministry of Agriculture, Government of India, New Delhi.

Government of India, Contingency Action Plan for Natural Calamities, unpublished report of Ministry of Agriculture, Department of Agriculture and Cooperation, N.D.M. Division, New Delhi.

Government of India, 1999. *Indian Rural Development Report : Regional Disparities in Development & Policy, NIRD,* Hyderabad.

Govenrment of India, 1999. *Transferring Rural India Programmes for Change,* Ministry of Rural Development, Government of India Publication, New Delhi.

Government of India, 1999. *IDNDR : India Experience and Initiatives :* Report by Ministry of Agriculture, Department of Agriculture and Cooperation, Government of India, New Delhi.

Government of India, 2000. *State of Forest Report-1999*, Forest Survey of India, Ministry of Environment and Forest, Dehradun.

Government of India, 2000. *Vulnerability Atlas of India*, Building materials and Technology Promotion Council, Ministry of Urban Development, Government of India Publication.

Government of India, 2001. Interim Report – I and II – High Powered Committee for preparation of Disaster Management (unpublished). Department of Agriculture and Cooperation, Ministry of Agriculture, Government of India.

Government of Uttar Pradesh, 1998. Memorandum for Central Assistance (1998) Relating to Landslides in Uttranchal Region, During 1998; A report submitted by Revenue Department, U.P. Government.

Government of Uttranchal, 2000. *Uttranchal At A Glance* – Data from Uttranchal Resident Commissioner Office.

Government of Uttranchal, 2000. Uttranchal State Forest Statistics (in Brief) 2000, Forest Department, Uttranchal, Nainital.

Gupta, G. P., 1975. Sediment Production, status report on data collection and utilisation, *Soil Conservation Digest*, 3, 10-12.

Gupta H. K. and Rastogi, B.K., 1975. *Dams and Earthquakes*, Elservier, Amsterdam, 229 p.

Gupta M.C. *et. al.*, 2001. Manuals on Natural Disaster Management in India, National Centre for Disaster Management, IIPA, New Delhi.

Hemmedy, A.K.R., 1996 *Earthquake*, National Book Trust of India, New Delhi.

India Disaster Response : http://www.careindia.org.

Indira Gandhi National Open University, 1999, *Course Material for Foundation Course in Disaster Management*, New Delhi.

International Federation of Red Cross and Red Crescent Societies, 1994, 1996. *World Disaster Report,* Oxford University Press.

Ives, J.D. and Messerli, B., 1984. Stability and instability of mountain systems: Lessons learned and recommendations for future, *Mountain Research and Development*, 4, 63-71.

Kharkwal, S.C., Garhwal Himalaya : A physiographic profile. In *Garhwal Himalaya : Ecology and Environment.*

Khattri. K.N., 1983. Epoch-dependent probabilistic seismic hazard map of the Himalayan region, *Geo-science*, 4(2):121-30.

Khattri. K.N. and Tyagi, A. K., 1982. Seismic pattern in the Himalayan plate boundary and identification of areas of high seismic potential. *Tectonophysics*, 96: 281-97.

Kockelman, W.J., 1986. Some techniques for reducing landslide hazards, *Bulletin Association Engineering Geologists*, 23, 29-52.

Kovach, Robert L., 1995. *Earth's Fury,* Prentice Hall, Englehood Cliffs, New Jersey.

Lawrence, R.D. and Yeats, R. 1979. *Geological Reconnaissance of Chaman Fault in Pakistan,* (*Eds*. A. Farah and K.A. Dejong), Geol. Surv. Pakistan, Quetta, pp.351-58.

Mears, J.P.B., 1970. *Essentials of Geology*, Van Nostard, New York, 420p.

Mishra, Girish K. and Mathur, G.G., 1993. *Natural Disaster Reduction,* Reliance Publishing House and Indian Institute of Public Administration, New Delhi.

Morten Ron, L., 1996. *Music of the Earth,* Plenum Press, New York and London.

Murthy, Y.K., 1981. Water-resource potential of Himalayas, *The Himalaya.* (Eds. J.C. Lall and A.D. Moddie), Oxford University Press, New Delhi, 152-174.

Nain, Huang, 1982, Engineering geological analysis method for the forecast of reservoir-induced seismicity. *Proc. 4th Intern. Egg. Geol. Congr.* Oxford & IBH, New Delhi.

Naithani, A.K. and Prasad, C., 1997 : Landslide Hazard Zonation Mapping in the Ukhimath – Kedarnath Area, Garhwal Himalaya; *Proc. Symp. Earth Sciences in Environmental*

Assessment and Management, Lucknow, Geological Survey of India Publication 48(2), pages 37-42.

Narula, P.L., Shanker, R. and Chopra, S., 2000. Rupture Mechanism of Chamoli Earthquake on 29th March, 1999 and its implication for seismotectnics of Garhwal Himalaya; *Geological Survey of India*, Vol. 55, pp. 493-503.

Natural Hazards Information Centre : http://www.colorado.edu/hazards.

Pant, B. R., 2000. Geographical personality of Uttranchal. In Sati, M.P. and Sati, S.C. (Ed.) *Uttrakhand Statehood : Dimensions of Development*, Indus Publishing Company, New Delhi.

Papola, T.S., 2000. Contradiction in Development of Uttrakahand : need for a Region Specific and Autonomous Planning Framework ; Uttranchal statehood; Dimensions of Development, In Sati, M.P. and Sati, S.C. (Ed.) *Uttrakhand Statehood : Dimensions of Development*, Indus Publishing Company, New Delhi.

Prakash Indu, 1994. *Disaster Management*, Rasthra Prahari Prakashan, New Delhi.

Prasad, C., 1991, Uttarkashi Earthquake. A Geological Analysis, Garhwal Himalaya. *Ecology and Environment*.

Rawat, A.S. and Sharma, R., 2000. *Managing floods in Eastern Uttar Pradesh (A study in community perspective)*, Centre for Development Studies, U.P. Academy of Administration, Nainital.

Rawat, J.S., 1999. Disastrous Debris flows and Rock Advanche of August, 1998, near Ookhimath, Garhwal Himalaya, Personal Communication.

Rawat, R.B.S. and Satendra, 2002. Role of forestry in Disaster Mitigation, In Nainwal, H.C. and Prasasd, C. (Eds.), *Proceedings of National Seminar on Geodynamics and Environment Management of Himalaya*, H.N.B. University, Uttranchal.

Regional Disaster : http://www.netsalud.sa.cr/crid

Risk assessment tools : http://www.geohaz.org/radius

Ross Simon, 1988. *Hazard Geography*, Longman.

Saklani, P.S. & Satendra (1986) Strain Estimation of Narender Nagar. In Saklani, P.S.(Ed.), *Current Trends in Geology,* IX Himalayan Thrust and Associated Rocks, pages 71-87.

Satendra, 1985. Geology of a part of Lesser Garhwal Himalaya : Unpublished Ph.D. thesis submitted to University of Delhi.

Satendra, 1989. *Prithvi* (The Earth); National Book Trust of India, New Delhi.

Satendra, 1999a. Forest Fire : Problem and Solution; *Kurukshetra,* vol. 47 No. 7, Government of India Publication, New Delhi.

Satendra, 1999b. Slope failure caused valley damming in Madhya Maheshwar Valley, Garhwal Himalaya; *Proc. National Workshop on Rehabilitation Problem of Ookhimath Landslide Affected Villagers,* H.N.B. University, Uttranchal.

Satendra, 2000a. The Turmoil Beneath – How the landslides of the 1998 kind in Garhwal can be prevented; *Down to Earth,* vol.8, No. 24, Centre for Science and Environment, New Delhi.

Satendra, 2000 b. *Effective Disaster Management in Garhwal Region, Uttranchal; India.* Project report submitted in partial fulfillment of the degree of Master of Business Administration, University of Hull, U.K.

Satendra, 2001c. Disaster and Development; Silver Jubilee Issue of *Employment News,* Publication Division, Ministry of Information and Broadcasting, New Delhi.

Satendra, 2001a. Management tools for Poverty Alleviation programmes; *Kurukshetra,* vol. 49 No.10, Government of India Publication, New Delhi.

Satendra, 2001b, Dealing with Disaster; *Down to Earth,* vol. 9, No. 23, Centre for Science and Environment, New Delhi.

Satendra, 2002a, Forest Fire Prevention and Control in Himayala; In Nainwal, H. C. and Prasad, C. (Eds.), *Proc. National Seminar on Geodynamics and Environment Management in Himalaya, H.N.B. Garhwal University, Uttranchal.*

Satendra, 2002 b. Forest Fire; *Employment News*, vol.-XXVII No.3, Publication Division, Ministry of Information and Broadcasting, New Delhi.

Satendra, 2002 c. Droughts; *Employment News*, 3-9 August, Publication Division, Ministry of Information and Broadcasting, New Delhi.

Sati, M.P. and Sati, S.C. (Ed.) 2000. *Uttrakhand Statehood : Dimensions of Development,* Indus Publishing Company, New Delhi.

Sharma, V.K., 1994. *Disaster Management,* Indian Institute of Public Administration, New Delhi.

Sharma, V.K., 1995. Function of Disaster Management Organisation and Methodology to cope with Disasters in India, In Sharma, V.K. (Ed.) *Disaster Management,* National Centre for Disaster Management IIPA, New Delhi.

Shastri, C., 2000. Developing Uttrakhand : Notes on Fifty teams of uphill tasks; In Sati, M.P. and Sati, S.C. (Ed.) *Uttrakhand Statehood : Dimensions of Development,* Indus Publishing Company, New Delhi.

Singh, J.S. and Saxena, A.K., 1980. Analysis of forest grazing and vegetation in parts of Kumaun Himalaya, *Ind. Jour. Range Management,* 1(1) : 13-32.

Sinha, A and Sharma, V. K., 1999. *Culture of Prevention, Natural Disaster Management : India;* National Centre for Disaster Management (IIPA) and Natural Disaster Management Division, Ministry of Agriculture, Government of India.

Suresh, V., 1999. Rehabilitation of the Housing Stock in the Earthquake Affected Areas of Chamoli and Rudra Prayag. In *Shelter,* special issue, World Disaster Reduction Day, HUDCO-HSMI Publication, New Delhi.

Swanton, D.N. and Swanson, F.J., 1978. Timber harvesting, mass erosion and sheep land forest geomorphology in the Pacific Northwest. In : Coastes, D.R. (Ed.) *Geomorphology and Engineering,* Halsted, Stroudsburg (Pennsylvania) pp. 199-221.

Tewari, P., 1999. Pre and post Disaster Management Strategies; *www.careindia.org/dmi.html.*

Tropical Storm Watch : *http://www.wsicorp.com.*

Tolia, R.S. Sharma, R. Pande, R. K. Pathak, J.K. (1999) : *http://www.ignodismgtconf.org/pathak.html.*

Turner Berry, A. and Nick, F. Pidgeon, 1977. *Man made Disasters*. Butterworth- Heineman: Oxford.

UN Department of Humanitarian Affairs : *Http://www.reliefweb.int/*

UN Global Programme : http://www.globalwatch.org/ungp/

UN IDNDR : *http://www.hoshi.cic.sfu.ca-idndr/idplandr.html*.

Unofficial Disaster Management : *http://www.rvik.ismennt.is/-gro/disaster.html*.

Uttarkashi Earthquake, 1992. GSI Special Publication No. 30.

Valdiya, K. S., 1984. *Aspects of Tectonics: Focus on South Central Asia*, Tata Mc Graw Hill, New Delhi, 319p.

Valdiya, K.S., 1987. *Environmental Geology – Indian Context;* Tata Mc-Graw Hill publishing Company Limited, New Delhi.

Validya, K.S., 1988a. *Tectonics and Evaluation of the Central Sector of the Himalaya,* Phil. Trass. R.Soc. London, No. 4326, Pages 151-175.

Valdiya, K. S., 1998c. *Dynamic Himalaya*, Universities Press (India) Ltd., Hydrabad.

Valdiya, K.S., 1998b. Catastrophic landslides in Uttranchal, Central Himalaya; *Journal Geological Society India,* Vol. 52.

Virtual Emergency Management : *http://www.hoshi.cic.sfu.ca/epix/vemis*

Volunteers in Technical assistance : http://www.vita.org.

World Meteorological Organisation : *http://www.wmo.ch/index.html*.

INDEX